Andrew G. Marshall is a marital therapist and author. His books include the bestselling title *I Love You But I'm Not In Love With You,* which has been translated into over fifteen different languages. He writes for publications including the *Mail on Sunday, Daily Mail, Guardian, Psychologies* and women's magazines all over the world.

Andrew trained with Relate (the UK's leading couples-counselling charity) and has a private practice in London and Sussex offering therapy, workshops and inspirational talks. More information about Andrew and the Marshall Method can be found at:

www.andrewgmarshall.com

Also by Andrew G. Marshall

I Love You But I'm Not In Love With You
The Single Trap
How Can I Ever Trust You Again?
Are You Right For Me?
Build a Life-long Love Affair
Heal and Move On
Help Your Partner Say Yes
Learn to Love Yourself Enough
Resolve Your Differences
Make Love Like a Prairie Vole
My Wife Doesn't Love Me Any More

I
LOVE
YOU
BUT
YOU
ALWAYS
PUT ME
LAST

Andrew G. Marshall

MACMILLAN

First published 2013 by Macmillan
an imprint of Pan Macmillan, a division of Macmillan Publishers Limited
Pan Macmillan, 20 New Wharf Road, London N1 9RR
Basingstoke and Oxford
Associated companies throughout the world
www.panmacmillan.com

ISBN 978-0-230-77035-5

1 3 5 7 9 8 6 4 2

A CIP catalogue record for this book is available from the British Library.

Printed by CPI Group (UK) Ltd, Croydon CR0 4YY

Visit **www.panmacmillan.com** to read more about all our books
and to buy them. You will also find features, author interviews and
news of any author events, and you can sign up for e-newsletters
so that you're always first to hear about our new releases.

To Tony Marshall
(who always claimed that he
came after the guinea pigs)

Contents

I LOVE YOU
BUT YOU ALWAYS
PUT ME LAST

Introduction

I've spent almost thirty years helping couples resolve their arguments, turn round their relationship and fall back in love again. I've written eleven books, answered countless letters to my website, given talks and appeared on numerous radio and TV shows. However, in all that time, I've never really addressed one of the most fundamental issues that is driving so much of the misery I encounter: how to stop your children from ruining your marriage. My silence is not because I've got nothing to say – as you'll discover I've a whole book – but because I know from experience that most parents don't want to hear my message. Unfortunately, it goes against much of our contemporary culture and all the received wisdom. I scout round the edges, approach the problems from another angle and deal with the fallout. So what has made me finally decide to speak out?

Every hour at my practice in London, the buzzer goes and a couple (or individual) sit opposite me and pour out their feelings. On one occasion, I had a thirty-one-year-old woman sobbing about her parents' divorce over twenty years previously and asking me why she couldn't find a lasting relationship. Despite being a top-flight government adviser, it felt like I had a small child in the room as she looked up from her pile of crumpled tissues and asked: 'Why did nobody think about me?'

My next clients were a deeply unhappy couple – on the point of divorcing – who were fighting about weekend access visits. He thought she was turning their three children against him. She was angry that he was bailing out of their marriage – he had found another woman – without even trying to sort out their differences. Suddenly, I had this mental flash-forward twenty years and saw one of this couple's daughters sitting in the seat opposite me. Despite my clients doing everything in their power for their children to be happy, confident and successful (the best schools, extensive extracurricular activities and all the latest gadgets), they had exhausted first their marriage and then themselves – so running away and starting again seemed the only way for the husband to reclaim his identity. What made this story doubly tragic is that they used to have such a happy relationship.

When we unpicked what went wrong, the problems could be traced back to choices made when their children were small. I knew from my work with my single client that her fear that she was 'too much for anyone to handle' were down to decisions made by her parents during this key window too. On the train home that night, I decided to break my silence and write this book so that I could help people protect their marriages and avoid turning their children into my future clients.

There's another reason why I haven't written about parenting before. I've never had children, so what right do I have to give advice? I've had no first-hand experience of arguing about whose turn it is to get up for the baby, what time small children should go to bed or how to stop teenagers smoking. However, I am an expert on relationships. I know how easy it is to lose sight of being husband and wife when you become Mummy and Daddy, and how that breeds not only unhappy parents but fractious and desperate kids. Time and again, the first sign that my clients have turned the corner is when they report that their children are much happier – because kids thrive when their parents are in harmony and tackle problems as a team. In addition, after thousands of hours listening to adults talk about their childhood, I also have a clear idea of what can go wrong and how to help your children grow up to be happy, balanced and resilient.

If you've recently had a baby, this book will give you a sense of the road ahead and how to avoid the pitfalls. I also cover the impact on your family of the second and subsequent children. If your family is complete and your children older, my argument is just as relevant if they are eighteen months or eighteen years old. Please don't skip the early chapters, though, as they will help you diagnose where any problems might have started and target your energy towards where it will be most effective.

Ultimately, this is a positive book. Having children is a great opportunity to grow and change. It can help put pain from your own childhood behind you and bring you closer to your own parents. It can also deepen the bond with your partner, because there's nothing more awesome than creating a new life together. However, you do need good relationship skills and to know how to communicate effectively – even when you're tired and stressed. In fact, especially then! But don't worry, I've lots of practical advice and tips that will help you talk, listen to each other and find a solution that's acceptable to both of you. There's also information on how to foster a great relationship with your children and therefore provide good emotional support. At the end of each chapter, there is specific advice on how to strengthen your relationship with your partner; and because I know you are busy and juggling lots of different tasks, I've boiled everything down to ten golden rules (which are summarized at the back of the book).

Although I've used the word 'marriage' in the subtitle for this book, I don't think you have to be married to have a secure relationship or raise happy children. It's just that 'marriage' makes it clear what kind of relationships I'm discussing. I also want to stress that this book is just as much for fathers as for mothers – both women and men can feel that their partners put them last. Unfortunately, there's a tendency in our society – and I'm thinking particularly of politicians – to lay the blame for everything at the door of mothers. No wonder mothers can feel under attack and sometimes hear criticism when none is intended. So let me be clear: I believe in *equal* parenting responsibilities, and when relationships hit a problem it is generally six of one and half a dozen of the other.

The case histories come from my practice as a marital therapist as well as interviews with mothers and fathers not in counselling. I have changed details and sometimes merged two or three cases, so nobody can be recognized. Finally, I would like to thank my clients for their generosity in allowing me to share what we have learnt together.

Andrew G. Marshall
www.andrewgmarshall.com

Getting Your
Priorities Right

Although bringing up the next generation is possibly the most fulfilling and life-affirming thing anyone can do, babies and small children do seem to have a mission to destroy everything they come into contact with, from your clothes and furniture to your nerves, sex life and sometimes even your marriage. Even when they're older, children have so many needs and make such demands on your time, it is easy to lose sight of your partner. Fortunately, it does not have to be like this. Over almost thirty years as a marital therapist, I've seen many couples whose relationships have been beaten into submission by the child-rearing years, but I've helped many more turn their sons and daughters into the glue that binds them together. So what makes the difference? In a nutshell, it's down to getting your priorities right and balancing three key elements: your marriage, your children's welfare and your own needs.

When you first fell in love, you only had eyes for your beloved. He or she was the centre of your universe, the light of your life and the reason why you got up in the morning. When you walked down the aisle or joined hands in a register office, it was impossible to believe that anything would come between you. OK, you'd discussed at some point that you wanted children, but in this abstract form they would bring you together, be a living, breathing proof of your devotion, and there would be more than enough love to go round. So it comes as a complete surprise when, in the hurly-burly of bring-ing up a family, earning enough to provide food, shelter and clothes, you drop down each other's list of priorities until one or other of you complains: 'You always put me last.'

Men find that they come after the children, housework (especially when their wife won't come to bed, and potentially have sex, because she's wiping down the kitchen worktops), her job and maybe even the dog. Women discover that they come after their husband's work, the children (because he's happy to play with them when he comes home, which is fine because she wants him to be a good father, but she can't help feeling ignored), and sometimes rank lower than his football team.

After the seductive promise of romantic love, the everyday grind of babies and small children comes as a nasty shock. In an ideal world, couples would talk about their disappointments, regrets and losses, have a cuddle and support each other through the adjustment from lovers to parents – without losing sight of either role. Unfortunately, many couples get into a downward spiral where he feels excluded at home, so buries himself in his work (after all, it pays the bills and keeps the show on the road) and she hardly ever sees her husband – because he's working late, upstairs catching up on his emails or off at a confer-ence – so buries herself in the minutiae of her children's lives (because what is more important than raising the next generation?). Perhaps the problems start because she's always felt she played second fiddle to his work. So the arrival of a baby – for whom she is definitely number one – bolsters her self-confidence and she throws herself further into this demanding but rewarding new role. Whichever way round everything starts, couples can withdraw further and further into the stereotypes of what it means to be a man, a woman, a father or a mother and find it harder to reach out to each other and be a team.

With so much unspoken resentment, it is not surprising that people prioritize family time over couple time. Not only is there less chance of a row with the children around, but it is easy to hide behind the comfortable intimacy of being Mum and Dad together and forget the problems of being husband and wife.

Fortunately, it doesn't have to be like this . . .

Revolutionary ideas

At the centre of this book is a radical idea, so radical I will be surprised if you buy it. So please feel free to say, 'Yes, but . . .', or complain that I don't understand, or maybe even think that I'm mad, bad and dangerous. However, I hope that you'll suspend your judgement for a while and mull over my suggestions rather than dismissing them out of hand. So what is this idea?

You should put your children second.

Of course, there will be times when the children need you – perhaps they are ill or it's their first day at school. What I'm talking about is that on an everyday basis your husband or your wife should be your number one priority. I know this is a tough idea to swallow – particularly when you have a small, helpless baby on your lap – but children are just passing through, while marriage should be for ever. (I know this stands on its head today's perceived wisdom that marriages come and go but being parents together endures.) Before you throw the book or the e-reader across the room, I'm not just saying that you should prioritize your partner because it will be good for your marriage, but because it's good for your children too. In a nutshell, a happy marriage means happy children. If you put your children first – as a matter of course, day in and day out – you will exhaust your marriage. Children sense the unhappiness, they try to build bridges for their parents and get drawn into things they are too young to understand, or, worse still, think the problem is down to them in some way. Time and again, I know the couples that I'm counselling have turned a corner because they report that the children are happier.

So what happens if you *do* put your child or children first? Amanda is forty-one and married with a three-year-old daughter: 'We do a lot of things at the weekend that are very child-orientated and focused on her. I'll make arrangements with people we're not particularly friendly with – or have much in common with – but who have children of the same age, because I believe that being an only child is unfair on our daughter. For example, last night, I had six children round for her to play with and set up craft activities on the kitchen table – like decorating a card or cooking.' Amanda's determination to provide plenty of opportunities for her daughter to mix with other children came at a cost. 'If we were going out for dinner or I've made arrangements for my husband and I to meet friends without our daughter, and I got a phone call for a play date, I would cancel the adult event – without a second's thought.' Obviously, I was interested in the impact on her husband. 'Regardless of whether he will be stuck having a conversation with a guy he's only just met, I never say no. Sometimes he says: "Can't just the three of us do something?"' Amanda explained.

Although I can easily imagine the look on her husband's face when he comes home after a long day to find six strange children in the kitchen, it is Amanda's last sentence that really worries me. Not only is her husband very aware of how low he comes on his wife's list of priorities, but he can't even ask: 'Can't we do something just the *two* of us?'

When I explain about putting each other first, clients often look at me blankly – almost as if they can hear my words but can't quite process them. Of course, they don't want to neglect their marriage, but they want to give their children every opportunity in life and, although they don't necessarily use this word, to be 'perfect' parents. So if that involves putting your relationship on to autopilot during your child's crucial formative years, isn't it worth it?

At this point, I should introduce the accompanying idea that sits alongside *Put your children second*, and that is *Be a* good enough *parent*. Unfortunately, 'good enough' is not a popular idea either. We want the very *best* for our children. So perhaps I should explain what I mean by 'good enough'. Donald Winnicott (1896–1971) was one of Britain's most influential paediatricians and child psychiatrists. He believed that if, by some miracle, we could fulfil all our children's needs on the spot, they would have the illusion that the world revolved around them. Worse still, they would never need to overcome any obstacles – because we'd have carried them over or given them a leg-up – and therefore not have the opportunity to test things out for themselves, make mistakes, grow and become independent. Obviously, neglecting a child is equally dangerous, so he proposed a middle way: being 'good enough'. In other words, you look out for your children but do not micromanage them.

There are two advantages to taking this concept on board. First, it will help keep your sanity, as it accepts that every parent makes mistakes and it's not necessarily the end of the world. 'I'd forgotten that our son needed a costume for World Book Day at his playgroup on Monday morning and all the shops were shut,' explained Muriel, thirty-two. 'In my mind, I could see him upset about being the only one who hadn't dressed up or, worse still, bullied because he had a third-rate costume. So I went online and fortunately found a Thomas the Tank Engine outfit on eBay.' Unfortunately, collecting it involved driving halfway across London and out to one of the towns that circle the city, a round trip of at least three hours. 'Aiming to be a "perfect" mother, I packed my husband, my son and my one-year-old daughter into the car and set off. Nobody was in a good mood and the tension in the car started to grow and grow.' Fortunately, we had already covered 'good enough' in counselling and instead of rowing, Muriel and her husband, Neil, stopped the car and started talking.

'I wondered if going to Chelmsford was the best way to spend our Sunday,' said Neil.

'And I began to question if the journey was really necessary,' added Muriel. 'I could try and make the costume. Did it matter if he went in something home-made? So we turned round and went out for something to eat instead.'

In the end, Muriel made a 'good enough' costume and her son enjoyed helping her to turn a hat into a funnel. Over the next couple of weeks, Muriel became less and less anxious about being perfect and allowed herself time off – for example, to have a nap – rather than pushing herself to be 'ever present' and always 'on top of my game'.

Second, and equally importantly, good enough stops you from competing with other parents. Rachel, who had given up her career to focus on her child, found that she transferred her natural competitiveness from her work on to her son: 'It was like the mothers at playgroup were all engaged in some kind of arms race. It wasn't just whose child reached all the landmark events first, but if one of us started something like baby yoga, it suddenly became necessary for everyone else to go or in some way we'd be "neglecting" our baby. When I opted out and start laughing at how they wound each other up, I not only relaxed and started really enjoying my daughter, but I had funny anecdotes to share with my husband, David.'

Returning to Amanda, what had been the impact on her daughter of aiming to be the 'perfect' mother (and compensating for the lack of siblings) rather than 'good enough'? 'Yesterday, when we had the other children over to play, my daughter was bossing everybody around, even though she's only three and one of her playmates was nine years old. If they weren't doing what she wanted, she'd send them to the "thinking corner" – which is where I send her if she misbehaves,' Amanda explained, and a worried tone entered her voice. 'I'm also at risk of turning our daughter into a very unpleasant person because she'll expect to always be the centre of attention.'

In other words, pulling together both of my revolutionary ideas is best for your marriage *and* your children. I know this takes a bit of getting used to, so don't worry. I will be returning to my two central themes – 'Put your partner first' and 'Be a good enough parent' – and exploring them in each chapter.

There is one final idea that runs through this book, but I wouldn't describe it as revolutionary. In fact, most people would accept it, but some parents lose sight of it during the first five years of their child's life. So what is this idea?

You have needs too.

Unfortunately, in the rush to be perfect parents, the easiest person to neglect is yourself. If you do stop and think, What about me?, it's hard not to feel guilty or even a 'bad' parent, because there is a small, trusting, beautiful baby whose immediate need for food, nurturing and protection must trump your selfish needs. Hopefully, by the end of the book, I will have helped you to stop thinking in such black and white terms and to realize that completely burying your needs brings long-term problems – not only for your personal welfare but, crucially, for your marriage too.

■ ■ ■ ■ ■ ■

What Are Your Priorities?

This exercise is about taking stock of your priorities and under-standing where, on an everyday basis, you rank each of your responsibilities. It works best done as a couple but can be completed alone.

1. Look at the list below of different priorities – which I use with clients – and check there's nothing important in your life that's missing. If there is, please add it in.

Self	Partner	Children
Work	Friends	Parents
Siblings	Hobbies	Fitness/Health
Fun	Home	Pets
Status	Personal development	
Sex	Intellectual nourishment	

2. Make up a series of cards, one for your partner and one for yourself. Write the elements of your list on the cards.

3. Independently of each other, put them in order from most important to least important. Let me stress, there are no right or wrong answers. It is a matter of opinion and personal choice.

4. When you've finished ranking your everyday priorities, explain the reasoning behind your choices to your partner.

5. Listen while your partner takes you through his or her priorities.

6. Finally, discuss each other's rankings and whether they were a surprise or as you expected.

What happens if you do put the children first?

At this point, I don't expect you to have bought into my idea that children come second – especially as I've yet to explain how this translates into everyday life. So don't worry if you've made the children your number one priority. Most marriages will survive this choice, especially if both partners agree and find ways to mitigate the impact on their relationship. Hopefully, the previous exercise will have started this discussion. Unfortunately, most couples never talk about their priorities and blindly fall into one or more of the following five common traps.

TAKING EACH OTHER FOR GRANTED

Christine and Mark had been married for fifteen years and had three children. Although they both worked in London, they'd moved to the countryside as they felt it was best for their children. 'In our previous house, they would run out of the back door and hit the garden wall in about five steps,' explained Christine. 'We wanted space for them to play and have a carefree time, climb trees and be able to ride their bikes without the risk of being mown down by the traffic.' Unfortunately, it meant a two-hour-plus commute in the morning and the evening for Mark, and only a marginally shorter one three days a week for Christine. Worse still, the logistics of getting the children anywhere meant that Christine had to hold huge amounts of information in her head at any one time.

'Our youngest will be going swimming – which is twenty-five minutes away – and the middle one will need new shoes and the eldest will have a piano lesson,' she explained. 'I don't think Mark understands just how tough it can be running a family. It only takes for him to be half an hour late coming back home or for the dog to be sick and have to go to the vet, and all the complicated arrangements come tumbling down.'

'And I don't think Christine understands the pressure of getting up each morning at six, entertaining clients and getting the last train home. Sometimes, I don't get into bed until two in the morning,' Mark retorted.

In their own way, each of them felt exhausted and taken for granted. I had a picture of them living life on 98 per cent capacity, so that even the smallest problem could send them into a spiral of resentment. When I did the 'What Are Your Priorities?' exercise with them, Christine put 'Children' first and then 'Work' and 'Home'. She put Mark fourth, 'Fun' fifth and 'Self' down at ten. When Mark looked at her priorities, he thought he would have come a lot lower down.

'I do consider you, but maybe you don't notice it. If there are two shitty jobs to be done, I always take the worst one myself – like going to the supermarket for the weekly shop – while you stay home and look after the kids,' Christine explained.

I could understand how Mark might not have noticed this type of consideration or felt particularly cherished.

Meanwhile, Mark had made 'Work' his number one priority, followed by 'Home', 'Children', 'Partner' and 'Status', with 'Self' at sixth. When Christine looked at the rankings, she had imagined that 'Self' would have been much higher.

'I don't really get much pleasure out of my work,' Mark explained. 'It pays the bills and of course I went after promotion because I thought it would give the children a better future – certainly if we're going to send them to the best schools – but it doesn't feed me. It's not me. I do it for you and the children.'

Once again, I could understand Mark's sacrifice, the long commute, going for extra responsibility and stress – more for the money than because he was passionately interested in his work. It must have been tough spending so many hours doing something that did not inspire him. However, I could equally understand how this kind of caring did not make Christine feel particularly cherished either.

Over the next few months, I worked on their communication skills and helped them find more visible ways of showing that they cared. For example, Mark offered to stay home and plug a particularly difficult childcare problem during the school holidays, and Christine organized a weekend away – just the two of them – in Paris. When I repeated the priorities exercise, the situation had begun to change. Christine put 'Self' at third and 'Personal development' at fourth. Mark put 'Children' first, 'Partner' second, then 'Work'; meanwhile 'Self' and 'Status' had dropped dramatically.

FUSING PERSONAL INTERESTS
WITH CHILDREN'S INTERESTS

There is no right or wrong place to put 'Self' on your list of priorities – although I'm concerned if someone puts themselves at fifth or lower. At this point, there is normally a subtle but deadly phenomenon that kicks in. If you consider yourself a low priority, you will find it hard to ask for what you need – whether it is something practical ('Please sort out my computer because it seems to have a bug in it') or something emotional ('I really need a hug and a back rub'). However, it is very difficult to live without care, consideration and feeling appreciated.

So what do people do? This happens entirely unconsciously, but they ally themselves closely with something that does come higher up their partner's priorities. You've guessed it: the children. So instead of asking for something for themselves – which they expect to be refused – they ask for something for the children that fulfils some of their needs. For example, Amanda's husband requested time as a family (without other people's children) rather than couple time (what he really wanted). Christine was pleased with Mark offering to help with childcare (because it made her life easier) but what she needed was a spontaneous gesture that would make her feel special (for example, Mark turning up at her workplace and taking her out for lunch).

Not only does someone who fuses their interests with the children only get some of their needs met, they also risk their partner misunderstanding their request and rejecting it. For example, Amanda could easily respond to her husband by saying: 'It's important for our daughter's development to mix more with children her own age.' He would have been more likely to succeed if he'd been upfront: 'I think it's really important for our marriage to have a night out just the two of us.'

Ciara and Thierry, in their late thirties, had two children under five and came into counselling because of arguments that were never sorted. Ciara felt particularly resentful because Thierry had gone away on a work contract – he was freelance – just two months after their youngest was born.

'But you didn't tell me not to go,' said Thierry angrily.

'I shouldn't have to tell you,' Ciara rounded on him.

I had a very clear idea of how their rows escalated at home.

'How would Thierry know that you wanted him to stay?' I asked.

'I explained how our eldest needed his dad because he was unsettled by the new arrival, and I explained how difficult it is to breastfeed a baby while a toddler is trying to get your attention.'

'But you had your mother staying, she could help. It was not like you were all alone.'

'You know how she bosses, how she takes over. I'll turn round and she's going through the cupboards throwing away everything that's past its sell-by date.'

'What would happen if you'd just said, "I'm lonely, frightened, worried whether I can cope and I need your support and love"?' I asked.

At this point, Ciara burst into tears. When she stopped crying, she explained that she didn't dare risk being rejected and that she secretly feared that he didn't truly love her. Thierry was able to reassure her and the counselling turned a corner.

However, until we could uncouple her interests and the children's interests it was difficult to have an honest and open discussion.

MID-LIFE CRISIS

The next trap for couples who put their children first is closely related to the previous one. If you fuse your interests with your children's, you are also likely to encourage or expect your partner to do the same. And here is the dangerous twist: you can use that love for the kids to control him or her and get your own way – but without having any blood on your hands. So how does it work? A wife will say, 'You don't want to play golf now you're a father' or 'You've got to stop going out with the lads as you've got responsibilities.' Of course, she is half right. He does want to be with his kids. She does need extra help. However, instead of putting all the issues up front – 'I don't like your mates' or 'Four hours is a long chunk of the weekend' – where they can be debated, negotiated and a compromise found, the conversation is closed down by implying that anything else would mean 'You don't love me and the kids' or 'You're a part-time dad.' Obviously, it's not a game that just women play; men are equally adept. For example, 'Do you really want to retrain, because all that extra studying will mean you've got less time for the kids' or 'Our youngest is having a bad time at school, so I don't think now is a good time for you to go away for the weekend.' And how do you challenge such a reasonable approach – especially if you're putting your children first and your own interests sixth or seventh? Nobody wants to feel a 'bad' mother or father, so they are easily manipulated into burying their needs.

Perhaps you're thinking, What's wrong with being altruistic and thinking of others? My answer is: Nothing, if that's your choice – by all means put the children first – but I would question whether you have the right to make that choice for your partner. Whatever the rights and wrongs, in the short term there isn't a major problem – especially when the children are small and really do need a lot of care. However, it can quite easily become a habit and before you know it, five, ten or fifteen years have passed.

One morning you wake up and think, There's got to be more to life than this. Perhaps your partner's father dies and, sitting by his bedside, he or she is reminded that we have only a fixed time on this planet. Maybe both of you have reached forty; your life is half over and you're thinking about what comes next. Obviously, these are per-fectly natural feelings. It can be really healthy to take stock from time to time, but if you've buried your needs, if even questioning the

17

supremacy of your children is forbidden, what should be a mid-life adjustment quickly turns into a mid-life crisis.

'We got together when my husband was seventeen, I was twenty-two. After five years, we moved in together and shortly afterwards got married and had two boys who are now aged six and five,' Vicky wrote to my website. 'He said that he felt like in the blink of an eye it was seventeen years later and he didn't know what he'd done with his life. It sounded like a typical mid-life crisis to me – his life had become humdrum, work had turned particularly pressured (and in a way made him powerless) and he seemed to blame me for his lot in life. He thinks that he made all these sacrifices for me, but I gave up a lot for him too – I just wasn't as audible about it, nor was I keeping score. I gave up on the notion of pursuing the career I had always wanted – for him, mainly because it would have meant that I had to give up my role as breadwinner, and go to university. The things he "gave up" for me were things like only going to meat-only restaurants without good vegetarian options for me. It's not like he still doesn't get to eat meat.'

In the next part of the letter, Vicky's husband prioritizes communicating with the children over talking to her.

'Just before he moved out, he started to really mess me about – even on the day we'd agreed was his moving-out day, he decided to move it back a week, saying that he'd told the boys that he'd stay for the week – but hadn't told me! I know that he is in turmoil but he's turned into someone else who I don't recognize.'

I can quite believe that Vicky's husband seemed like a stranger, but after years of putting the children first and downgrading his needs, he exploded and started an affair. I have met many men, and plenty of women too, who after years of 'thinking of others' felt 'entitled' to 'put myself first for once'. So although it seems admirable to put your children first, it can rebound with the most extraordinary acts of selfishness.

LACK OF SEXUAL INTIMACY

Jack and Layla, both in their early forties, were agreed on one thing: 'The children are the centre of our lives.' After one session, Jack insisted on showing me a photo on his phone of his two sons climbing all over him. It was the first time in almost thirty years' counselling where I'd seen a picture of a client's children. Although only a snapshot – probably taken on holiday after a dip in the pool – it could have been an advert for fatherhood from a magazine. Everybody was laughing and jostling for position and I could picture Layla taking the shot and smiling too. There was just one problem with this happy family. Jack and Layla had only had sex on a handful of occasions since their youngest son had been born – six years ago.

'I had a difficult birth and complications. I was breastfeeding and not getting enough sleep, and when I look back I probably had post-natal depression too,' explained Layla.

'I told you as much at the time,' Jack interjected.

'So starting sex was the last thing on my mind, I suppose,' said Layla.

Although I could understand the initial problems, we were talking about six years later!

'I had two small children hanging off me, I didn't want Jack mauling me too,' Layla continued.

'Motherhood is very physical – feeding babies, washing them, changing their nappies – with lots of skin-to-skin contact,' I reflected. 'You can get almost all your needs for intimacy met.'

Obviously, there's nothing wrong with enjoying cuddles with your kids, but it can become a way of compensating or feeling less alone when the central relationship between husband and wife is not being fed. Unfortunately, instead of talking about their lack of sexual intimacy – and getting help earlier – Jack and Layla had been able to hide behind being 'great parents' and 'doing what's best for the kids' and months and then years had gone by.

By the time I met them Jack had said, 'I love you but I'm not in love with you' and Layla was furious because she suspected that Jack was having affairs while off on business trips – something that he strenuously denied.

They reminded me of another client, Lucy, a thirty-something single woman whose parents split when she was six years old: 'Years later when I had a long chat with my father,' she told me, 'he admitted, "I fell out of love with my wife and in love with my daughter."' Is this what had happened to Jack and Layla?

VULNERABILITY TO AN AFFAIR

Martin and Sarah, both forty-three with three children under twelve, came into counselling after Martin discovered some intimate texts on Sarah's phone from a contractor who had been helping them remodel their house. Although the affair had not gone further than kissing and cuddling, Sarah had fallen deeply in love with the other man. She wanted to save her marriage but was not certain if she could get her feelings back for Martin. 'I'd felt lonely and undervalued for a long time and this man listened, he seemed genuinely interested in what I had to say. It wasn't just that we talked but shared similar values and a friendship together,' Sarah explained. Over the next few weeks, I helped Martin deal with his panic, to stop pressurizing Sarah for reassurance and tackle the everyday issues between them, rather than sweeping them under the carpet.

When I did the 'What Are Your Priorities?' exercise, Martin placed 'Self' first, 'Status' second, 'Children' third and 'Partner' fourth. In contrast, Sarah had put 'Children' first and 'Partner' second but 'Self' only seventh in her priorities and 'Fun' only eleventh. It was perhaps not surprising that she had felt so unhappy.

'I was like an alcoholic desperate for a drink – or in my case love, affection and a little attention – but fearful if I had even a drop, I

GETTING YOUR PRIORITIES RIGHT

would never be able to quench my thirst,' she explained.

'And if I was brutally honest with myself, I was aware that Sarah was miserable but I thought there was nothing I could do about it and told myself, selfishly, "Get on with it because I'm not going to let you drag me down with you", and I got on with my life,' Martin added.

Very few people go out looking for affairs, but if someone feels unappreciated and not valued at home – or, like Sarah, has completely neglected their own needs – they become vulnerable to the attention of other people. 'It was almost like this man finding me special allowed me to accept that I might be someone more than a wife and a mother. I had needs and that was OK,' explained Sarah.

In most cases, affairs start innocently enough: a simple working relationship or going on to the Internet to switch off and forget everyday troubles. If someone feels cherished and a priority at home, it is easy to back off before any harm is done. However, if you feel that your partner routinely puts you last, it is not surprising that a 'special' friendship becomes so important so quickly and causes so much pain.

■ ■ ■ ■ ■ ■

How Strong Is Your Marriage Right Now?

It is difficult to balance being parent and a partner – especially if you're dealing with a multitude of other pressures. To get a sense of how resilient your marriage might be and how well you deal with conflict, I've devised a test and some tailor-made advice for your situation.

1. Which of the following statements describes your relationship? Tick as many as apply.

a) We were childhood sweethearts and have had no other serious relationships.
b) One of our parents died in the last twelve months.
c) One of us is dreading or recently dreaded their fortieth birthday.
d) One of us travels a lot for work involving overnight stays.
e) One of us has a lot of extra stress at the moment.
f) We're moving house at the moment (or about to move).
g) There's an elderly relative who requires help.
h) We have two children under five.

2. Which of the following statements are true? Tick as many as apply.
a) I can name at least five of my partner's friends.
b) I can name five or more people at my partner's place of work (or, if less than five co-workers, all of them).
c) I can explain my partner's life philosophy.
d) We have talked in the last twelve months about our dreams for the future.
e) I can name someone who has irritated my partner recently (beyond me!).
f) I can name three of my partner's favourite TV shows.
g) We both know the names of each of our children's current best friends.
h) My partner knows what's been worrying me lately.

3. If you already have children, which of the following best describes your attitude to free time? (If you're expecting and don't have children yet, please skip this question.)
a) We make certain that we have nights out as partners and weekends away on our own.
b) We might aim to go out without the kids but it's not often practical or affordable.

c) We'd rather go out as a family and it feels strange on the rare occasions it's just the two of us.

d) We both work and alternate childcare. Generally, we're too tired to do anything beyond order a takeaway and watch a movie.

4. **At a party, an attractive stranger shows a lot of interest – nothing happens beyond sharing a laugh and a joke but you have a really good time. On the way home, your partner asks about it. How do you reply?**

a) Tell the truth: 'I enjoyed the attention because it made me feel special.'

b) Make a barbed comment: 'It's been a long time since you've noticed me like that.'

c) Deny everything: 'Don't be so stupid. You're imagining it.'

d) Go on the attack: 'That was nothing in comparison with how you leer at everybody.'

5. **How often does your partner let you know how much he or she appreciates you by saying 'Thank you' or 'I love you' or giving a compliment?**

a) I'm sure he or she means to do it but it gets lost in the hurly-burly of day-to-day living.

b) All the time.

c) Only when he or she is after something or trying to sweet-talk me after a row.

d) On special occasions when I've make a special effort, or when I've dropped pointed hints.

6. **When there is a major dispute between the two of you, how is it most likely to be resolved?**

a) I will back down and keep the peace.

b) My partner will huff and puff but generally accepts when I have the stronger case.

c) We talk it through and although it takes time we'll find a compromise.
d) It doesn't generally get sorted and we have several such 'no-go' subjects.

7. When your partner does something irritating, like forgetting to pick up something on his or her way home or make an important phone call, what do you think?
a) For goodness' sake, get your act together.
b) Why did I trust him or her? I should have done it myself.
c) If he or she really loved me, I wouldn't be such a low priority.
d) My partner is really busy and has a lot on his or her mind.

8. If your partner was being honest, which of the following statements would best describe how he or she often feels?
a) Sometimes I just can't win.
b) Deep down, I know I'm appreciated but it would nice to hear it more often.
c) I feel supported, loved and cherished.
d) I sometimes feel sex is rationed out and used as a reward for 'good behaviour'.

9. Which of the following statements best describes how you would rate the levels of intimacy in your relationship?
a) To be honest, nothing much would happen if one of us didn't take the initiative.
b) There's something in bed that I'd really like to do but my partner is not interested.
c) Although everybody would like more intimacy, I feel cherished and loved the majority of the time.
d) We should do more casual touching outside the bedroom, a cuddle on the sofa or hand-holding.

10. What happens when there is an important decision to be made about the children's welfare – for example, schooling or disciplining?

a) One of us does the necessary research but consults the other before making a decision.

b) We're a team and everything is done jointly.

c) The parent who's on the spot, or knows most about the topic, makes the call.

d) There's a lot of arguments and resentment.

11. When your partner is stressed out, how does he or she deal with it?

a) Offloads on to friends or family.

b) Bottles everything up.

c) Talks it over with me.

d) Forgets by having a drink, going for a run, playing computer games, opening up the fridge or some other distraction.

12. How has your relationship been over the past six months?

a) We've been really close.

b) The usual ups and downs.

c) Incredibly busy: we've barely had time to talk beyond functional conversations about running the house or what time to pick up the kids.

d) Difficult. My partner or I have been prickly, dismissive or out more than usual.

SCORE YOUR RESULTS

1. Score 2 points for each description that you ticked. If b), c), d) or e) applied to you and your partner, please score 4 points. (If none of the descriptions fits your relationship, score 0.)

2. Take off 1 point for every statement that you agree with. (If none of them is applicable add 2 points.)

3. a) 1   b) 2   c) 4   d) 3
4. a) 1   b) 2   c) 3   d) 4
5. a) 2   b) 1   c) 4   d) 3
6. a) 3   b) 2   c) 1   d) 4
7. a) 3   b) 2   c) 4   d) 1
8. a) 4   b) 2   c) 1   d) 3
9. a) 3   b) 2   c) 1   d) 3
10. a) 2   b) 1   c) 3   d) 4
11. a) 2   b) 3   c) 1   d) 4
12. a) 1   b) 2   c) 3   d) 4

Add up your points to discover the state of your relationship, but read all the categories to put your relationship in context.

UP TO 15: HIGH RESILIENCE

Congratulations, your relationship is in great shape! Although you've your fair share of stress and the problems that life throws, you're involved in each other's lives, understand each other's problems and work as a team. Be aware that certain circumstances – like two children under five or approaching forty and wondering about the paths not taken – can put a marriage under extra strain. If that's the case, it is important to communicate clearly and effectively. Fortunately, this book will provide an opportunity to brush up your skills and add new ones to your repertoire.

16 to 28: GOOD RESILIENCE

This score is like going to the doctor and being told everything is fine. However, there's 'Fine, fine' ('Go away and don't darken my door again') and 'You're fine but take care of your health' ('So let's keep an eye on things to be on the safe side'). Your relationship falls into this second category. You've got good communication skills but they might need brushing up.

It is particularly important to ask rather than assume – especially if you have lived with your partner for a long time or were childhood sweethearts. Under these circumstances, it is easy to imagine that you *know* what he or she is thinking or why he or she has done something. That's fine when you're relaxed and in a good mood, because those interpretations are largely positive. For example, 'He or she didn't mean to upset me.' However, when you're stressed and fed up, they can easily become negative. For example, 'He or she did that on purpose to wind me up.' Before you leap to conclusions, ask your partner: 'Why did you . . .?' or check it out: 'Are you angry with me?' It could be he or she is just annoyed or maybe preoccupied about something else.

29 to 39: OK RESILIENCE

I'm pleased that you've bought this book because I hope it is going to make a big impact on your relationship. When you have children – and more demands on your time and energy – it's important to have good communication skills in order to deal with the ups and downs. However, you probably believe that connection, chemistry and really loving each other are the guarantees of a happy rela- tionship and, with those elements in the bag, you can coast along and concentrate on more immediate concerns like getting the youngest off to sleep, arranging a play date for your eldest and checking on supper.

However, a relationship is a living thing and needs tending. Think of a pot plant. It's fine if you don't water it for a while, but pretty soon it will begin to wilt. If you don't keep an eye out, it can develop a nasty fungal infection. Fortunately, I've lots of ideas for tending your relationship. Unfortunately, you're also likely to be resistant to my ideas – especially 'children come second' – because you think, If my partner loves me, he or she *should* understand.

It's words like 'should' and 'must' that really drive anger – and turn a minor spat into a full-blown row. Who says, for example, a man *should* fix things round the house or a woman *should* have the house tidy for when her husband comes home? The government? The Pope? All right-thinking people? What you mean is 'I think. . .' or 'My parents always did . . . and therefore I believe . . .' (fill in the gaps with your particular 'should's). If you put something as 'I think . . .', you and your partner can discuss the pros and cons (and probably find an amicable solution). In sharp contrast, 'should' makes you right and your partner wrong (and both of you mad at each other).

40+: IN DANGER OF FEELING OVERWHELMED

Your relationship is suffering from one or more of these toxic problems: inability to communicate, general dissatisfaction with each other, putting your heads in the sand. You might hope for the best and tell yourself 'It'll get better when . . .', but your partner could easily be slipping into depression or inappropriate coping strategies – or perhaps it's you who's at the end of your tether.

If a problem seems insoluble, most people come up with only two ways forward: to walk away (which seems drastic) or to put their head down and soldier on (which keeps the peace but resolves nothing). If you, your partner or both of you have chosen the second option, the only way to cope with the daily stress of work, the demands of a small baby, financial worries and feeling unloved is to switch off (and risk becoming clinically depressed) or blank out your feelings – what I call self-medicating – with alcohol, fattening food, pornography, or maybe the attention of someone else.

I know the situation looks bleak but let's focus on the positives. You have recognized that your relationship isn't working and buying this book is proof that you want to do something about it. That's not only brilliant but the first step towards change. So what should you do next?

If it's you who is feeling overwhelmed, anxious or depressed, please speak to your health visitor or doctor. My guess is that you're a perfectionist and asking for help is hard – because it means admitting that you're not a 'perfect parent'. Hopefully, you have begun to consider the idea of 'good enough' and imagine what it might mean for you.

If it's your partner who is self-medicating or you suspect him or her of an inappropriate relationship, it is important to tackle him or her calmly – rather than in an accusing manner. Talk about what has been going wrong in your relationship, what you'd like to change, and then bring up your concerns about his or her behaviour. Finally, discuss together how to make things better – rather than laying down the law or issuing ultimatums, which will get your partner's back up. (There is more specific advice about infidelity in my book *How Can I Ever Trust You Again?*.)

■　■　■　■　■

How to put your partner first

At the end of each chapter, I will be giving practical ways of showing your partner he or she is a priority in your life and strengthening your relationship. I call this first tip 'Guarding comings and goings'.

Returning to Christine and Mark, who had taken each other for granted, towards the end of our counselling I repeated the priorities exercise and they both put 'Partner' first, 'Children' second, 'Fun' third and 'Self' fourth. Next we had to change these from aspirations into day-to-day behaviour.

'Who do you speak to first when you get home? Christine or the kids?' I asked Mark.

'The children are normally in bed but if they're not my eldest daughter opens the door because Christine is bathing the younger ones.'

'I know it's tough because she probably wants you to "just look at this", but what would happen if you said, "In a minute, I've just got to say hello to Mum," and went to find Christine, say hello, give her a kiss and then attend to your daughter?'

'It would make a powerful statement,' replied Mark.

'We already don't let them interrupt us when we're chatting; I'll say, "Hang on a second, I'm talking to Dad,"' Christine added. (I thought this was a brilliant idea, so pass it on to you.)

So how does 'Guarding comings and goings' work in practice? If your partner is already home when you return, go immediately to where he or she is and give him or her a kiss (rather than settling down for a drink in front of the TV or sorting out something for your son or daughter). If your partner is with the children, it is doubly important to greet him or her first. I know your children will be excited to see you (that's why you love them) and your partner is busy doing stuff (and preoccupied) but getting off to a good start sets up an evening of cooperation and pleasure in each other's company – rather than your partner feeling like part of the furniture. 'Guarding comings and goings' is particularly important when you have a baby. It is very easy to greet or tickle your son or daughter under the chin – because babies are designed to bring out our protective streak and encourage us to pick them up – and thereby completely ignore the person holding him or her! For the first few days, it takes a bit of willpower to greet your partner first and then cuddle the baby, but soon it'll become second nature.

If you're the person already at home, I'm not asking you to drop everything and go to the door – although that would be nice. (I know it's not always practical because you're busy cooking, feeding the children or supervising something potentially dangerous.) However, you can stop what you're doing for a second to give your partner a kiss and maybe a quick cuddle. You might also like to exchange the top line of your news about what has happened today.

Guarding your goings is equally important. When you leave the house, give your partner a kiss and, if it's not obvious, tell him or her where you're going and when you'll get back. You might like to throw in a compliment like 'I love you' or 'Can't wait to get back' or 'You smell nice.' If you just disappear – even if it is for ten minutes – without saying goodbye, it gives the message that your partner is not important or that you don't see the two of you as a team. After all, if you're just going up the shops, you could pick up something your partner or the family needs too.

My next tip takes the concept of guarding one stage further: 'Put a lock on your bedroom door'. This is seldom a popular idea. Somehow parents think they have to be 100 per cent available, all the time, whatever the circumstances.

'What if the children need us?' they ask.

'If there is an emergency your children can knock, or shout "FIRE",' I always reply.

A locked door sends an important message. It will make your children think twice before demanding attention and help them realize that even parents need a private space. As my clients who have teenagers admit, they would never dream of entering their son's or daughter's room without knocking, but they allow their children to just wander into their bedroom whenever they wish.

If you've done the first exercise in this chapter, you have already started on my third tip for putting your partner first: 'Discuss your priorities'. Nobody minds dropping down the list if they understand the emergency – for example, your mother is in hospital and needs extra support – but your partner needs reassurance that it is not for ever and to feel able to discuss the day-to-day implications. And, most important of all, not to fear that he or she will get their head bitten off if they say: 'What about me?' So set aside a regular time to talk to each other – for example, over your evening meal, or switch off the TV/computer for fifteen minutes after the children have gone to bed – and explain the current demands on your time. Once again, I'd like you to guard this time to unwind together and not let it get trumped by work demands or a pressing need to empty the dryer. Time together says 'You're important to me; I'm interested in what's happening in your life and I want to share what's going on in mine.'

Summing Up

When you first said, 'I love you' to your partner, you never imagined that it could be followed by 'but'. When you walked up the aisle, you never thought you would let your relationship drift. Of course, children are wonderful and give your life shape and meaning. Unfortunately, it is easy to get carried away, put your children first and run yourself ragged trying to be perfect parents. Fortunately, you don't need to be perfect – just good enough. And the good news is that's better for your children and your marriage.

I know it is tough being a parent, how you feel torn in two and how little time you have. That's why I have boiled my advice down into ten golden rules (recapped at the end of the book) and designed some simple exercises to help. However, it is important that you stop taking each other for granted and start nurturing your love for each other again. Your children's, your partner's and your own happiness are all at stake.

How Did We Get Here?

'Having our daughters has been one of the best experiences of my life. I'd never known unconditional love before,' said Blake, thirty-seven, whose youngest was just three months old when he started couples counselling with his wife Emily. 'If anybody asked, I'd definitely recommend starting a family, but I'd warn them that they'd better have a rock-solid relationship first.' It is great advice and in an ideal world everybody would be sure of their partner, their relationship and themselves. Unfortunately, we don't live in an ideal world and most people go into parenthood hoping for the best, worried about what sort of parent their partner will be or secretly frightened they won't measure up themselves.

So what do you need for a rock-solid relationship? Most people think the answer is love: if you *truly* love each other, you can withstand any pressures from outside or within. I would certainly agree, but only up to a point. What makes the difference between growing closer and being split apart during the children years is *good communication*. That's why I have devoted this chapter to understanding how, despite the best intentions, things can go wrong, and I will return to this theme throughout the book.

When is the right time to have children?

The debate in the media and parenting forums is normally about whether it is best to have your children younger (when you have more energy and are more flexible) or to leave it until you are older (when you have more self-knowledge and are better established). However, I think this overlooks the most important element: how long have you and your partner been together? Love changes over time and goes through six distinct stages – each with its own particular joys and challenges. These stages will help you understand how minor problems can escalate into major ones and why you might have stopped prioritizing your partner.

BLENDING: FIRST SIX TO EIGHTEEN MONTHS

Falling in love is a magical experience. It is almost like walking on air, and you spend half your time sighing or thinking about your beloved. I call this stage 'Blending' because you want nothing more than to be together or, when that's not possible, to talk about your beloved (until your friends want to throw things) or to imagine what he or she would make, for example, of the TV programme that you're watching. The intense feelings are so different from the everyday love of couples who've been together longer – who can't afford to spend every waking thought thinking about each other – that psychologists have coined a specific word for it: limerence. What is particularly significant about the influence of limerence is that it emphasizes what is truly admirable about the other person ('He really wants to help me reach my potential' or 'She wants to make me happy') and downgrades what might be a problem. For example, it doesn't matter if he slurps his tea ('because it's really cute') and it doesn't matter that she is not very confident ('because I can boost her self-esteem'). By contrast, in a settled relationship, one partner making noises as he or she drinks is irritating or disgusting and it can be exhausting to be forever giving compliments and terrified of saying anything negative in case it is heard as criticism.

During the Blending stage, couples accentuate their similarities and minimize their differences – so that two individuals merge into one couple. It is a heady time as sex is easy and plentiful and each partner feels completely understood. No wonder songwriters and poets talk about the blindness, madness and ecstasy of falling in love: 'I only have eyes for you', 'Can't take my eyes off you', 'All you need is love'. Unfortunately, limerence does not last for ever. In my experience, it is somewhere between six months (perhaps when the love is not returned) and eighteen months (for most relationships), and thereafter it reduces gradually until three years have passed (at the top end). Interestingly, neuroscientists have tracked the chemicals associated with bonding – dopamine, oxytocin and phenylethylamine – and found they are at their height for somewhere between eighteen months and three years (the average span for limerence).

Problems: When Natasha, thirty-eight, arrived in my counselling room, she was almost seven months pregnant and extremely angry. Her partner, Josh, thirty-two, was sheepish and looked like he would head out the door at any moment.

'I'm just not getting any support from Josh. I know he has to work hard and it is difficult to coordinate when we can talk,' she complained.

'I'm working shifts in India and when I finish it's the middle of the night in the UK,' Josh explained. 'So I go out for a couple of drinks to unwind with my friends but by the time Natasha rings I'm merry and she either gets angry or I'm tired and don't want to hear her moan.'

'It's hard being apart. I get tearful. My back hurts. I feel very alone.'

They had been a couple for eighteen intense and exciting months, flying backwards and forwards between Europe and Asia. Under the influence of limerence, overcoming the obstacles of different continents and time zones had been part of the attraction. However, as the peak of the passion had begun to wear off, everyday realities were becoming more and more of a problem.

In addition, I wondered how much the baby had been planned.

'We both wanted this baby,' said Natasha firmly.

'Sure.' Josh shifted in his seat.

'We had talked about having children,' Natasha cut in before Josh could say anything more.

Once again, under the influence of limerence, people say what their partner wants to hear – 'Of course I want children' – when what they mean is 'I'd like to have children *someday*.' It doesn't necessarily mean that day has arrived yet.

Indeed, Natasha and Josh had 'talked', but in very much the same way they'd covered living in the same country, going backpacking in the Andes and renovating a villa in Tuscany. In the heady days of Blending, everything is possible, reality has not yet intruded to spoil the fantasy, and they wanted to please each other. So Natasha did not spell out that she was about to turn forty and needed to get pregnant sooner rather than later. Josh did not explain that forging a career was his number one priority and that he would need to be based abroad – at least for the next three years.

There is a third way that limerence and the Blending stage can store up problems for the future. At the very beginning of a relationship, a row feels like the end of the world – because new couples have no experience of falling out and making up. So they tend to bury their issues and leap into bed instead. Not only was this option not available to Natasha and Josh – because they spent so much time apart – but their differences were too great to overcome by a kiss and a cuddle (however passionate).

Turn it around: I don't want to knock limerence because it helps us overcome our fears of getting hurt and allows us to throw our lot in with someone who is, after all, a complete stranger. Our desire to be with our partner can make us try out new hobbies or experiences and find enduring interests. Love can also help surmount what seem like impossible odds. However, you should take promises made during this heady phase with a pinch of salt – much as you would check out whether someone really meant something said under the influence of alcohol. So if you have a contentious topic where your understanding of your partner's views is based on conversations during Blending, it is best to revisit it. Of course, it is hard to hear the caveats that might have been added, but better to have issues out in the open. Later in the chapter, I will explain how to resolve any differences.

NESTING: SECOND AND THIRD YEARS

Couples decide to move in together and their home becomes an expression of their love for each other. While Blending capitalized on the attraction and minimized the differences, living together full-time can bring issues to the surface and couples will begin to risk arguing over small and manageable questions – like what colour to paint the bedroom or the best way to grout tiles. Desire is reduced to a more manageable level, rather than making love twice or three times a day. However, limerence has not disappeared completely and can help smooth over the transition out of Blending – especially as friends and family become more important again and familiarity can breed annoyance. Interestingly, long-term tracking by the University of Texas suggest eighteen months' to three years' courtship as the optimum period for a happy marriage.

Problems: 'It seemed the most natural next step to move in together,' explained Justine, thirty-six. 'I spent most weekends and several nights during the week at Murray's flat and it was much more convenient for work than mine. So it would have happened anyway but me getting pregnant just brought it forward.'

However, they had only been going out together for eleven months when they 'officially' started to live together and almost immediately a few cracks began to show in their relationship.

'I found that Justine did not respect my standards,' said Murray, forty-one. 'I know I'm set in my ways and it's not like Justine is particularly untidy, it's just everything has its place and I like structure and order. I can't relax otherwise.'

'And I respected that when we were just seeing each other,' said Justine – which is typical of Blending, because couples try to appear as similar as possible. 'However, it's my home now and I need to relax. I can't if you're hovering, about to take my coffee cup away before I've finished.'

After the initial excitement of the birth of their daughter had worn off, the cracks began to turn into chasms.

'Sometimes I worry that Murray doesn't want me and Chloe there.' Justine had tears in her eyes. 'I feel that we've upturned his nice ordered bachelor lifestyle.'

'I gave up my study so we could turn it into a nursery but that's not enough. I come home and find Chloe's stuff all over the house.'

Unfortunately, the usual territorial issues – especially when one partner moves into the other's home – had been exacerbated by having a baby, the stakes had been raised and they still had not yet learnt to disagree, find a compromise and move on. Instead, Justine would back down or Murray would be resentful and, the next time they rowed, all the old unresolved issues came back up again.

Turn it around: Arguing is one of the most intimate things that you can do with your partner. This is going to sound a little strange, but arguing shows that you care, as opposed to just sweeping it under the carpet. There's another bonus: sorting everything out and overcoming a small but manageable amount of adversity can bring back a momentary flutter of limerence. For example, she smiles after an argument and it feels like the sun has come out again, or he admits that he overreacted and it seems he does understand after all. In many cases, all it takes to resolve a problem is to keep arguing a bit longer and resist the temptation to throw in cold cases – even if they seem like part of a pattern – as this will make your partner more defensive and less likely to budge.

SELF-AFFIRMING: THIRD OR FOURTH YEAR

By this stage, couples realize that they don't have to do everything together. After all, it doesn't take two people to go to the DIY store and buy a pack of nails. While previously the stress was always on 'we', each partner begins to remember that there is a 'me' too. So one partner will go off fishing for the day and the other doesn't feel compelled to try it out or take a book to read by the lake. On another weekend, the other partner will sign up for a course – even though it will eat up precious time they might otherwise have spent together. Not only is it natural for habits, traits and characteristics to re-emerge, but relationships need each partner's individuality to grow and develop. Otherwise, a couple will have only shared interests – like eating out or going to the cinema – which both enjoy but do not necessarily feel passionate about. If there is no room for private space or interests, one partner can end up feeling stifled or, worse still, controlled.

Problems: This is the most tricky of all the stages of love. After being 'everything' to each other, it is easy to worry that you are falling out of love. (Indeed, one of the most common times that people complain 'I love you but I'm not in love with you' is at three years, when limerence is definitely on the wane.) Lots of couples find it hard to balance the needs of the relationship and their own needs. If you have low self-esteem, it is easy to see your partner's natural desire for personal time as a reflection on you (and become clinging or anxious) or a threat to your relationship (and bury your personal needs or pretend they don't matter but end up secretly resenting your partner). It is not uncommon for couples to have power struggles, some really quite nasty rows and lots of long talks into the night to sort out a solution that works for them.

It goes without saying that this is probably the worst moment to have a baby. Unfortunately, we are settling down later and later and that means lots of thirty-five-plus couples need to try for a baby almost straight away and find themselves struggling with Self-affirming *and* baby issues at the same time.

'I really resented Matt doing anything out of the house,' said Alice, thirty-seven. 'I knew he had to go to work, but surely if he loved us, he'd not want to miss a moment more.' Everything came to a head when Matt's parents came to visit one Sunday and, after cooing over his grandchild, Matt's father suggested he should take his son down the pub. 'Matt just got his coat, as if it was the most natural thing in the world to have a pint while his wife and his mother cooked lunch. I wanted to scream, and I did when they had gone. How dare he!'

'It was just forty minutes. My dad and I haven't talked for ages. And if you cared so much about going for a drink, I would have looked after the baby while you and my mum went to the pub,' Matt replied.

'I thought we were going to do this as a team, equal partners.'

It is not uncommon for issues about men's and women's roles to come to the forefront during Self-affirming, but these are particularly difficult if a couple have not yet begun to balance reasonable personal needs (like talking to your father without distractions) and couple needs (like your wife wanting support and to know that she is loved and cherished).

Turn it around: In many ways, just knowing about Self-affirming – and that it is a natural phase rather than something wrong with your relationship – can be immensely reassuring. It might be disappointing after the magic of limerence to realize that you are two different people with different strengths and interests. Fortunately, you need complementary skills for bringing up children, rather than just being carbon copies of each other.

COLLABORATING: FIFTH TO FOURTEENTH YEAR

After the worry of Blending (will your love be returned or will an argument prove fatal?), the shock of Nesting (when you have to accept that your partner is not perfect) and the stormy waters of Self-affirming (and reasserting your individuality), you have really got to know each other. Couples can use the greater security within the relationship and a stronger sense of themselves to launch successful projects. It could be something outside the relationship – like a new job or further education – but each partner brings the excitement, freshness and new friends back home. More likely, couples start a new project together – like a business, renovating a house or travelling together. The most common choice at the Collaborating stage, of course, is having a baby. Whatever the choice, it will help to revitalize your relationship.

Problems: This is the best time to have a child. However, I sometimes see couples who have been together for five-plus years but have got stuck in Self-affirming rather than truly moving on to the Collaborating stage. Although they should have been ready for parenting, they were still struggling with getting the right balance between being an individual and being half of a couple. Blake and Emily from the beginning of this chapter had lived together for nine years before starting their family. Blake was an artist and although he had had some success, he was still struggling to get properly established. 'My painting is not just something important to me but how I see the world. Sometimes, I struggle with being a father and a husband because it takes up so much of my time, energy and thinking

41

space that I should be channelling into my art,' he explained. 'Don't get me wrong, because I love my daughters to bits, but I have to be honest: I need to focus on my career.'

Meanwhile, Emily came from a family where her parents were always arguing and caught up in their own problems. 'I was constantly trying to please my mother and father and keep the peace between them. When that didn't work, I started shoplifting to get some attention. I truly believed that they must have adopted me, because I felt they didn't love me.' For Emily, the closeness of Blending and subsuming her identity into being a couple had been completely intoxicating. However, she found it hard to express her needs during Self-affirming. 'I've never really stopped and thought about what I want, just what would make Blake happy.'

My job was to help them find a balance, so that Emily could ask for what she needed and Blake could stop focusing only on the painting currently on his easel and see the bigger picture. In this way, they would truly start collaborating.

Turn it around: Although it might be sad to give up some of your old pre-children ways, a relationship needs to grow and change or it will stagnate and become boring. By this stage, you can think you know each other so well that communication has been boiled down to a shorthand. However, this can easily slip into assuming you know what your partner is thinking. So instead of taking something for granted, try asking instead.

ADAPTING: FIFTEENTH TO TWENTY-FOURTH YEAR

These couples are busy adapting to the changes thrown at them, rather than dealing with internal changes within the relationship. Demands from outside could be parents getting older and needing more support, the upheaval of having a teenager in the house, or the youngest son or daughter about to leave home for university. Each partner has given up the fantasy of changing their partner and thinks, They will always be like this, or Actually it's quite sweet. Perversely, when someone accepts who we are, we are more likely to bend and change.

Problems: The empty-nest syndrome can be particularly difficult for parents who have prioritized the children, exhausted their relationship and find it hard to relate to each other as partners rather than co-parents.

Tracey and Gregory had been married for twenty years and had three children. The oldest had gone off to university and Tracey could see the day coming when she would be needed less by the others. 'I don't have a role any more. I've spent years being a mum and I don't resent that, but I'm beginning to wonder who I am,' she explained. 'Sometimes, I feel I don't get any support from Gregory, who is either at work, dealing with work-related problems or too tired to do anything. I hate to think what it will be like when it's just the two of us because all the conversations are either about the children or the business.'

The problem had come to a head because Gregory also felt unsupported. 'My mother died last year, after a long illness, and I spent much of the past year travelling up and down the motorway. My father is eighty and he's finding it hard to manage on his own. He doesn't really cook and the slightest problem, he's on the phone to me.'

'I did all the catering for your mother's funeral. I ran myself ragged,' countered Tracey.

'I know, and I'm grateful, but there were times when I really needed you – particularly towards the end. It was really tough sitting by my mother's deathbed. My father was in pieces.'

'But it was our daughter's school play.'

Gregory sat there glumly staring into space.

Turn it around: When your partner is struggling to cope with a crisis, it is vital that you are 100 per cent behind him or her – particularly if you routinely put the children first. Otherwise, you are likely to prioritize the run-of-the-mill needs of your children over the extraordinary ones of your partner. In particular, do not underestimate the trauma of losing a parent – however expected – as your partner will definitely need extra support.

RENEWING: TWENTY-FIVE YEARS-PLUS

Many people look back to the beginning of their relationship as the best of times, but what most don't realize is that twenty-five years together can be just as good – if not better. In many ways, the final stage of love is an echo of the first one. During Blending, the bond is heightened by the promise of a future together, while Renewing is all about the reality of that shared life. After the battles of earning a living and raising a family, all the attention is focused back on to the relationship – like the early days of courting – and couples become everything to each other again. In addition, they can look back with a real sense of achievement for weathering the storms, and enjoy shared memories or private jokes.

Problems: It is not surprising that I see only a few couples who have been together twenty-five-plus years. There are occasionally health problems that cast a shadow, or unresolved issues from the Adapting stage, but generally this is the best of times. More recently, I have started seeing parents in their sixties struggling with their grown-up sons' and daughters' emotional crises (which in some cases have brought them back home again).

'It's clear that our son is having problems with his wife,' explained Martha, sixty-two. 'He visited us with the grandchildren on his own last weekend. I gave him the chance to open up and talk to me but I don't think we've been that kind of family.'

'We've been talking about whether we could afford to support him more financially – without adversely affecting our retirement plans,' added her husband Tony, sixty-three.

'I can't help wondering if we let our children down because we were too wrapped up in our own problems,' said Martha. (Tony had travelled constantly for work and had been unfaithful on several occasions.)

'I have lots of regrets and I wish we'd been able to communicate better with each other and as a family,' Tony told her.

Although there was sadness in my counselling room, there was none of the bitterness of similar arguments from younger couples – who have not been together so long and can't fall back on the evidence that their love has overcome plenty of obstacles before. Fortunately, Martha and Tony were tackling their son's problems as a team rather than tearing into each other.

Turn it around: When you are stuck in the trenches of child-rearing, it is easy to think the good times are behind you. However, I ask clients to think of their marriage as being U-shaped. There is a high when we first get together, but older couples are often the most romantic. It's the bit in the middle – rubbing the rough edges off each other and bringing up children – that's hard-going. If you're currently immersed in a tough patch, talk about it, remind each other about the bright times ahead (for example, a holiday together) so you don't feel that you will be in this place for ever. If you're struggling with your grown-up son or daughter's problems, don't forget that they are indeed an adult. Of course, you should be supportive, but don't feel responsible for sorting it out.

■ ■ ■ ■ ■ ■

Communicating Better

If circumstances meant that you did not start your family during Collaborating, don't worry. There is no reason why you can't still have a great marriage and raise happy and contented children. The secret is to be able to communicate well. In this way, problems are sorted rather than ignored or allowed to come up time and time again. The following exercise will help with one of the most important components: listening.

1. *Know your weakness*. It's easy to think you're good at listening, but do you fall into one of the following traps? *Interrupting:* before your partner has even finished his or her case, you're chipping in to rebut something. *Preparing your case:* you're silent but not really listening because you're marshalling your evidence. *Putting brackets round something your partner says and discounting it:* for example, you meant to collect the milk on the way home and therefore you consider your partner's fury not to be unjustified. Alternatively, when your partner brings up something from the past, you think, That happened years ago so doesn't count. *'Yes, but . . .':* not really acknowledging your partner's anger before launching your defence. *Second-guessing:* you think he or she is angry about one thing but actually the row is about something else.

2. *Flip a coin to decide who goes first*. The winner has as long as he or she likes to put their case about something contentious – without interruption. You might fear your partner will talk for ever, but I've yet to meet someone who talks for over five minutes. Most people need only thirty seconds.

3. *Summarize*. The person who has been listening proves that he or she has been paying attention by simply summarizing the main points, and only the main points. (They will have a chance to respond soon.)

4. *Feedback*. The talker gives feedback about the summary. How accurate was it? What was missed out? Has anything been exaggerated?

5. *Swap over*. The listener becomes the talker and finally has the chance to refute their partner's case and make any fresh points. Afterwards, the listener summarizes (but does not respond) and the talker offers feedback about the accuracy.

6. *Repeat as many times as necessary.* Keep going until each of you feels truly heard. With a better understanding of each other's position, you are ready to start discussing possible solutions. If the negotiations turn nasty, flip a coin and start the whole process again.

■ ■ ■ ■ ■ ■

How disagreements pile up

Every relationship has sensitive topics: maybe she earns more than he does, or he really dislikes her mother. However, most couples avoid talking about them because they cause lots of upset and in normal everyday life they are easy to circumnavigate. For example, she will ask his permission before spending 'her money' and he will go fishing when her mother comes round. I call these topics 'buried bodies' because we know where the problems are but through an unspoken agreement choose not to disturb them. Unfortunately, becoming parents will often bring these buried bodies up to the surface. For example, can the couple cope on just the husband's salary? If child-care issues mean that one partner should work part-time, who should speak to their boss first? These are hard enough topics even without years of unspoken resentment. In addition, babies bring families centre stage. So while the husband could use his love of fishing to avoid his mother-in-law in the past, if she's coming round three times a week this is no longer practical.

So how do you tackle these underlying problems? The answer, of course, is good communication. If you're new parents of course you need to focus on your baby's needs first, but be aware of any relationship issues and make a note of discussing them after the all-consuming first few weeks. If you're already a parent, it's never too late to exhume your buried bodies and put them properly to rest.

Simon, twenty-seven, had met Belinda, thirty-five, when he was twenty and they had got married shortly afterwards. She already had two children from a previous marriage.

'They call me Dad because they don't see their father and I'm all they've ever known,' explained Simon.

The couple had finally decided to start a family themselves and Belinda was five months pregnant.

'He really gets on my nerves, following me round the house like a sick puppy,' said Belinda. They had been having a lot of rows recently. 'It's like he's begging me to stop being angry and make up.'

'You've had a really difficult pregnancy, there was that scare and you had to spend time in hospital,' said Simon, trying to appease her.

'You keep on messing up my systems and putting your oar in where it's not wanted. It's beginning to affect the kids too: they don't know whether they're coming or going.'

It didn't take long to discover the buried body in Belinda and Simon's relationship. He had moved into her house, with her children and her rules.

'I was young and inexperienced, so I accepted that she knew best. Obviously, I left the discipline up to her,' explained Simon. 'But I want a greater say with *my* child and although Belinda's a great mum and the kids are a credit to her, I want to be more hands-on.'

'But I'll be negotiating with our eldest about what time she has to be back – she goes up the shops with her mates – and you'll keep sticking your oar in.'

'I'm trying to back you up.'

'But you're just parroting back what I'm saying,' Belinda snapped.

In effect, they were dealing with not only the buried body of how best to bring up their unborn child, but years of swallowing their differences, brushing stuff under the carpet and the occasional explosion when everything got too much. At first glance, the problems seemed almost overwhelming but if I could help them communicate better, they could begin to sort their everyday niggles before they became so destructive.

However, we are not taught how to resolve our differences at school and if your parents divorced (like Belinda's), avoided issues (Simon's mother smoothed over his father's nasty temper) or fought like cat and dog, you won't have learnt at home either. Most couples are left hoping that love will save the day or looking for a mythical soulmate who 'gets' them on such a profound level or is so alike that all differences melt away. Unfortunately, it's impossible for two people to live together without having disagreements – however much they love each other. The only answer is to roll up our sleeves and start talking. Except, not only is it hard to ask for what we want, but we don't know how to deal with the conflict when our needs and beliefs don't match our partner's. The result is that most people muddle along using one of three unhelpful strategies.

BEING PASSIVE

When there are conflicting desires, your needs, wants and beliefs are of *less* importance than those of your partner. It could be that you're a people pleaser and hope that if you meet other people's needs then they will meet yours. Alternatively, you could hate conflict so much that you will do anything to avoid it, or feel uncomfortable if you stick up for yourself (and therefore prefer to fold). Finally, you might be incredibly generous and get your pleasure from making other people happy. Whatever the combination of motives, *your* needs are of secondary importance.

Simon hadn't stood up for his rights as a parent to his stepchildren – even though he was paying for the food on the table and the roof over their head – because he thought his wife was the expert on child-rearing (and therefore his opinions were of no consequence), he hated conflict (because he had often suffered from his father's sharp tongue) and he generally thought that Belinda was wonderful: 'She's a great mother and I will do anything to please her.'

The problem of being passive is that not only do you seldom get your needs met (which leads to resentment in the long term) but if nobody asks what you want (not even yourself) you can easily lose touch with what makes you happy. All too often, passive people are boiling over with unexpressed anger that slips out through sighs, pointed comments and outright sarcasm.

BEING DOMINEERING

In sharp contrast to someone who is passive, you believe that your needs, wants and beliefs are of supreme importance. It could be that you're always right (like Belinda) and your partner is wrong (so his or her needs can be downgraded and ignored). Perhaps you've never given much thought to your partner's needs, wants and beliefs – maybe he or she is passive and therefore never told you about them, or your parents brought you up to believe your needs were of paramount importance and trumped everybody else's. Being domineering does not necessarily mean being aggressive and demanding: getting your own way can just as easily be achieved with charm, sweet-talking or bribery (men sometimes buy off their wives with expensive baubles, and women will offer sex to get their way).

Belinda liked to be in control. She had her way of doing the dishes and knew how the sink should be left afterwards – which way round the washing-up bowl should go and where the cloth to wipe down the surfaces should be left to dry. She would lose her temper if Simon did not follow her rules to the letter. She simply could not accept that there might be another way.

On the surface, being domineering seems a better option than passivity – at least you get your needs met. Unfortunately, you can also lose respect for your partner because most people want an equal relationship (rather than someone who trots a couple of places behind saying, 'Yes, dear').

ALTERNATING BETWEEN BEING PASSIVE AND BEING DOMINEERING

When it comes to who's in charge, most couples divide up the responsibilities, so one partner takes charge in one area (being domineering) but lets the other be in charge in another (being passive). For example, Simon would make decisions about what car to buy, where to service it and who their insurance provider should be. Belinda would control their social life and decide who to invite, and when and how often to see family. Whichever way responsibilities are divided in your home, be aware that having a baby can upset these cosy arrangements. Unlike smaller domains (washing, gardening, shopping, recycling, present-buying etc.), the care and well-being of a child is such a huge responsibility and demands so much time that it does not easily fit into 'him' or 'her' being in charge.

Another common way of alternating between being passive and domineering is to put up with something for years and years without saying anything (and thereby downgrading your needs, wants and opinions) until suddenly you explode and demand a change (overnight your needs, wants and opinions become of supreme importance). For example, Simon had been in charge of the couple's finances but during a row Belinda exploded.

'You're really cavalier with our money. You never shop around for an alternative quote for anything, just accept the first figure. That's just plain lazy. You could probably save seventy or eighty pounds – that's a supermarket shop for me.' She had always been worried about money as it had been tight when she was growing up and there was never enough to go round.

She was also angry about the amount of time Simon spent at work, how he let them take advantage of him and that he could have been earning more elsewhere. However, until this argument, she had not said anything.

'I can't manage any more. You're going to have to get another job,' Belinda demanded.

The third common pattern involves being both passive and domineering at the same time. For example, Simon seemed to go along with Belinda's rules on bedtimes for their elder children but when she was out he allowed them to go to bed when they chose, but to 'keep this our little secret'. This is called being passive-aggressive. On the surface, you might give the impression that your opinions don't matter (being passive) and readily agree to complete a task, but then go your own sweet way because you do feel your opinions count (being aggressive) but are not able to debate your case openly.

Another combination of passive and aggressive is playing the martyr – 'Don't worry about me, I'll just sit here in the dark' – where on the surface it seems someone's needs are of no importance but they are demanding in a passive way. Alternatively, people can be manipulative by using behaviour that might seem passive but is actually quite controlling: 'My husband thinks he's in charge because he's come up with a great plan, but I've *let* him think it's his plan.'

Being assertive

Fortunately, there is a middle way to deal with conflicts of interest. It is called being assertive. Let me explain exactly what I mean, because some people mix up being demanding and being assertive. With assertiveness, your needs, wants and beliefs and those of your partner are *equally* important. You both have the right to ask for what you want but there is a second half to the equation that is equally important: you both have the right to say no. (In this way it is a request, not a demand.) But what happens when, inevitably, your needs, wants and beliefs clash?

- *Compromise*: You listen to each other's cases and find a middle way. For example, you want to see one film at the cinema and your partner wants to see another. Instead of one of you sitting through a film that he or she would not enjoy, you choose a third film that is acceptable to both of you.
- *Negotiate*: You listen to both cases and do a deal where each of you gets something you want. For example, this can be a trade ('If we watch your film, can we go to my favourite restaurant afterwards?') or taking it in turns to decide ('I'll watch your superhero movie this time but next week we'll see my romantic comedy').
- *Back down*: Once again, you both listen to each other's needs, wants and opinions but one partner has a compelling case and, it turns out, the other partner does not care that much. However, this is different from one partner simply demanding or deciding and the other person automatically agreeing. Returning to our couple at the cinema, one movie is based on a book that is being discussed at her book club and she'd like to be able to compare and contrast. The man might find, with a closer look at the poster, that there's one of his favourite actresses in a supporting role, or, hearing his partner talk more about the story, decide it sounds interesting after all.
- *Agree to differ*: After a long discussion, it might be that you still have different views but actually it doesn't matter. For example, you might decide it is more important for each of you to see your preferred choice of film than be sitting side by side in the dark for an hour and a half – after all, you're going out for supper together afterwards. This option can only work if both parties feel they have made their case, their partner has acknowledged their feelings and their opinions have merit.

After I explained being assertive to Simon and Belinda, they returned the next week with this example. Simon needed to send a letter by recorded delivery and the post office was opposite their son's school.

'I asked if I could take him to school, so we could spend some time together.'

'The school run is one of the highlights of my day. I see other mothers and catch up on the gossip.'

Simon had exercised his right to ask and Belinda had exercised hers to say no. At this point, lots of people fold. Fortunately, Simon had used other assertive skills, i.e. *Explaining your request better*: 'I'm not asking to do this on a regular basis, it's just that I need to go to the post office tomorrow.'

Belinda stood firm. 'That's all very well, but I promised to give one of the other mothers something.'

So Simon used another assertive skill: *Changing your request*. 'Could you take the letter to the post for me?'

Belinda readily agreed, and although Simon did not get everything he wanted, he did get something. Previously he would have backed down immediately (because his needs, wants and opinions didn't count) and felt resentful when he had to stop opposite the school and register the letter. There was another positive that came out of this discussion. In the evening, Belinda used another assertive skill: *Offering something different*.

'I told him if he really does want to be more involved, it would be really helpful if he could take our daughter to swimming on Saturday as it is a real rush for me to fit everything in.'

Simon had readily agreed and both parties were happy.

ASSERTIVENESS RIGHTS

Assertiveness training has got a bad name because many people associate it with being aggressive. However, good courses stress the importance of both parties having rights and responsibilities.

My Rights	*My Partner's Rights*
To ask for what I need want.	To refuse my request.
To be listened to and taken seriously.	To be listened to and taken seriously.
To be myself and have space/time to fulfil my needs, wants and interests.	To rely on me for love, support and consideration.

My Responsibilities	*My Partner's Responsibilities*
To judge my own behaviour, thoughts and emotions.	To judge their own behaviour, thoughts and emotions.
To ask: Is my request reasonable?	To ask: Is it reasonable to say no?
To be responsible for the consequences.	To be responsible for the consequences.

How to put your partner first

The best way to show your partner that you truly value him or her is to give his or her concerns serious consideration. So instead of trying to dismiss your partner's feelings, rationalize them or soothe them away, accept that it is natural to worry, feel sad or be angry from time to time – especially if you're new parents or your children are moving on to another life stage (e.g. starting school, becoming teenagers or leaving home).

When couples start communicating better, they normally find that their fears are incredibly alike – just expressed differently. For example, Simon discovered Belinda was worried that if she didn't control every aspect of childcare and keeping the house nice, he would be stressed out and annoyed and might even leave her (after all, her first husband had done just that). Meanwhile, Simon was worried about whether he would be a good enough father and feared being squeezed out if he didn't make the grade. 'She would have completed her family and she wouldn't need me any more.' In their different ways, both Simon and Belinda were terrified of being abandoned. Acknowledging this fact was the breakthrough in their counselling.

So how do good communication skills and being assertive link with putting your partner first? If your partner is domineering and seems to put his or her or your children's needs, wants and opinions before yours, it is important to learn to stand up for yourself and put your requests in an assertive manner. If your partner is passive and puts everybody else's needs first, he or she needs to learn these skills too. Hopefully, you are reading this book as a couple and can discuss what changes need to be made. However, if your partner is not really a reader (or taking for ever to get past page 3), don't worry. By modelling the sort of behaviour you'd like to see, you will be encouraging your partner to follow suit – rather than punishing the behaviour that you don't want and starting a downward spiral where he or she retaliates with something equally unpleasant.

Here are five concrete ways of showing your partner that you are interested in his or her feelings, opinions and needs.

- *Value your partner's communication style*: In most relationships, it is one partner's job to raise issues (so they can be sorted), and the other's to contain or keep a sense of proportion (so that small problems do not spiral out of control). Unfortunately, it is easy to downplay the benefits of your partner's communication style or, worse still, think his or her way is the problem. So the 'It's good to talk' partner thinks the other is ducking the issues and the 'Let's not make a mountain out of a molehill' partner thinks the other is sucking all the joy out of the relationship. However, you need both styles for a fulfilling marriage.

- *Help your partner open up*: If your partner tends to contain rather than communicate, you can invite him or her to talk about a potentially contentious issue by acknowledging before asking. For example: 'I know it's been difficult since . . . but I'd really like to understand what it's been like for you.'

- *Take seriously what your partner has to say, even if it makes little sense to you*: This is especially important if you contain rather than talk. Ask questions, nod your head to show you're listening, get clarification, discover why your partner feels this way. Your partner's experience of being a parent will be different from yours but no less valid.

- *Keep calm*: If your partner says something upsetting, try reporting how you are feeling (for example: 'I'm angry that you said that' or 'I feel misunderstood') rather than acting out (shouting, slamming doors and making sarcastic comments) or becoming overwhelmed (bursting into tears or shutting down and leaving the room). If you are calm and report your feelings, your partner will feel it is OK to disagree and is less likely to be passive (and clam up) or domineering (and escalate the discussion into a row).

- *Fully discuss an issue rather than rush to a conclusion*: If your partner is prone to being passive, you might also like to give permission to say no: 'Are you sure?' or 'I'd much rather you were truly behind the idea.' If your partner is prone to being domineering, try rephrasing your position rather than automatically backing down. Time and again in my counselling room, I find couples resolve issues by arguing for a few minutes longer than usual.

Summing Up

When you feel taken for granted or that your partner puts you last, it is easy to think that he or she doesn't love you enough or, worse still, that there's a fundamental flaw in your relationship. However, the problems could be caused by moving from one stage of love to another, or simple miscommunication. The temptation is to keep busy and look the other way. However, suppressing or avoiding issues is never the answer. If you can talk honestly and listen, really listen, there are few problems that can't be sorted. In fact, if you take away just one idea, from not just this chapter but the whole book, I would choose this one: *Happy marriages are built on good relationship skills.* And that's an optimistic message, because those skills can be learnt.

The Shock of
Becoming a Parent

Having a child is a journey into the unknown, even if you've had one, two or more before. Not only is each birth and each baby different, but they all change the family dynamic in different ways. So however much you read and prepare or however experienced you might be, there will be surprises. Many of them will be pleasant but some will not be so welcome.

There are two approaches to the unknown. The vogue in modern self-help is to focus on the bright side, with positive visualizations of perfect births, happy babies and contented mothers. This upbeat approach is very reassuring. However, optimism can also be a double-edged sword. When your mother or more experienced friend says 'Don't worry' or 'You'll cope', there is a wonderful moment of calm. However, it only lasts a while and soon you're back looking for more and more reassurance.

'It's all going to be fine' and positive thinking in general also encourages the idea that parenting is 'natural'. So not only can it be doubly shocking if things don't live up to your rosy expectations, but you can easily feel a 'failure' or a 'bad' mother or father. Fortunately, there is an older tradition to the unknown which takes a very different approach.

The power of negative thinking

Stoicism is an ancient Greek philosophy which seeks tranquillity, not by chasing enjoyable experiences or through endless reassurance but by cultivating a calm acceptance of what has happened. Seneca (4BC to AD65), one of the most important thinkers from this school of thought, counsels dwelling on worst-case scenarios. He believed that we are most hurt by what we don't expect. If we expect blue skies, no queues and smiling faces, when things don't go according to plan it can feel that we are weighed down by personal misfortune rather than just dealing with the inevitable setbacks, annoyances and problems of being human. As Seneca wrote: 'What need is there to weep over parts of life? The whole calls for tears.' Or as the French writer Chamfort (1741–94) put it more wittily: 'A man should swallow a toad every morning to be sure of not meeting with anything more revolting in the road ahead.'

Although it's not a popular approach, I believe that facing up to any possible downside is better than pretending it won't happen. Not only does denying something never quite banish the thought from our heads, but our fears lurk in the shadows, gaining strength and power over us. More importantly, when we examine and name our fears, they are never quite as catastrophic as we imagined.

Let's return to Natasha from Chapter Two, who became pregnant nine months into her relationship. On the second counselling session, when Josh had returned to his job in India, she started to voice her worries: 'What if he deserts me?'

Her friends had told her, 'Don't be stupid' and 'He really loves you' and 'Didn't he fly all this way just to be with you?', so instead I opted for the opposite approach and asked her to flesh out what that might be like.

'It would be too horrible . . .' and she dissolved into tears.

'Would you be penniless?' I asked after a brief pause.

'No, he would never leave me short of money.'

'Are you worried that he wouldn't come to the birth?'

'No, he's booked plenty of time off work and I could get the baby induced if needs be.'

'So what is it?'

'He might be too engrossed in his phone.'

'What could you do then?'

'Ask him to switch it off?' Natasha laughed at herself. 'But I suppose I worry that he'll start to drift off into the distance and then out of our lives.'

'What would you do then?'

'My mother is very supportive. I have friends.' She thought for a second. 'I'll cope, I'll have to.'

And that's the advantage of Stoicism: it gets us in touch with our own resources, as well as connecting us to a belief that problems can be overcome, and brings a lasting calmness. In contrast, positive visualizations and positive thinking provide only a fleeting and brittle relief, which ultimately feeds our anxieties.

Fixed versus growth mindset

So let's accept that babies are not all plain sailing and help you prepare for the inevitable problems and decide how best to overcome them. At this point, I want to introduce you to another important idea which will improve the way you approach parenting and any other challenge. Carol Dweck is a social and developmental psychologist from Stanford University who has dedicated her career to studying why some people achieve their full potential and others don't. In the mid-1970s, she conducted a famous experiment into how fourth-grade students responded to an unsolvable problem in a maths test. The students who identified themselves as 'hopeless' at maths were unable to complete simple questions later in the paper – even though they had solved ones of a similar level of complexity earlier. In effect, they had retreated back to first-grade-level maths and, worse still, some took days to recover their confidence. In effect, these pupils had told themselves: 'I'm not good at maths and this proves it' and simply given up.

Dweck divided these 'hopeless' students into two groups. In the first, she challenged the idea that talents were something inherent – which you either had or you didn't have – and introduced the idea that ability is something that *needs to be developed*. She encouraged the students to chalk an obstacle up to insufficient effort ('I need to try harder') or the need for more skills ('I haven't learnt how to do that yet'). In the second group, she did a neutral session on memory. When the experiment was repeated the pupils in the first group made huge strides in the maths scores, while those in the control group continued to fall apart.

Dweck believes that how you respond to a challenge – such as becoming a parent – depends on your mindset: beliefs about yourself and your most basic qualities. Do you believe that talent is innate, fixed at birth and therefore stars in any field are born rather than made? In which case, you will tend to give up easily when faced with an obstacle or hand the problem over to someone else who does have ability in that area. Dweck calls this a 'fixed mindset'. Alternatively, you could believe that talent and ability need to be developed and nurtured. In which case, when something goes wrong, you're a problem solver who tries something else or gets advice. Dweck calls this a 'growth mindset'.

Although Dweck describes two mindsets, I think it is better to imagine a continuum, with 'fixed' at one and 'growth' at the other. To use a personal example, I'm a firm believer that effort, practice and developing skills breeds success, and certainly when it comes to important matters – like love and relationships – that we shouldn't give up. So it would seem I have a growth mindset. However, I've branded myself hopeless at maths and believe that I don't have any natural talent. My hand–eye coordination is poor and I'm no good at sport. So in these specific areas, I have a fixed mindset. Except if I stop and think, I can succeed at maths – if I put my mind to it. I have a degree which involved passing a statistics paper and I have a diploma in market research, which also involved statistics. When it comes to sport, I didn't do too badly and played tennis for the school second team. So although I have a growth mindset, I have some fixed views about myself that need to be challenged from time to time.

There is more about mindsets, how they affect your attitude to parenting, and a quiz to discover where you fall on the continuum, in the following exercise. As no mindset is completely set, there is also advice on how to improve yours.

■ ■ ■ ■ ■ ■

What's Your Mindset?

To get an insight into your mindset, look at the following questions and rate how strongly you agree or disagree with them.

1. **Talent is something that just needs to be discovered.**
    Strongly Agree / Agree / Disagree / Strongly Disagree
2. **Criticism is a gift.**
    Strongly Agree / Agree / Disagree / Strongly Disagree
3. **When I get stuck, I often think, What's the point of flogging a dead horse?**
    Strongly Agree / Agree / Disagree / Strongly Disagree
4. **I'm not overly worried by change.**
    Strongly Agree / Agree / Disagree / Strongly Disagree

5. **Effort is always necessary.**
   Strongly Agree / Agree / Disagree / Strongly Disagree
6. **I get defensive if other people make critical remarks.**
   Strongly Agree / Agree / Disagree / Strongly Disagree
7. **I tend to avoid challenges if I don't think I will do well.**
   Strongly Agree / Agree / Disagree / Strongly Disagree
8. **Although I have my weak areas, I can generally understand enough to ask intelligent questions or supervise someone else.**
   Strongly Agree / Agree / Disagree / Strongly Disagree
9. **I need to look smart and perform well at all times.**
   Strongly Agree / Agree / Disagree / Strongly Disagree
10. **I often put other people's success down to luck or money.**
    Strongly Agree / Agree / Disagree / Strongly Disagree
11. **I set goals for myself.**
    Strongly Agree / Agree / Disagree / Strongly Disagree
12. **I don't think so much in terms of pass or fail but of learning opportunities.**
    Strongly Agree / Agree / Disagree / Strongly Disagree
13. **If I'm not good at something I get someone else to do it rather than having a go myself.**
    Strongly Agree / Agree / Disagree / Strongly Disagree
14. **If I put my mind to it I found I could pass most subjects at school.**
    Strongly Agree / Agree / Disagree / Strongly Disagree

SCORE YOUR RESULTS

For questions 1, 3, 6, 7, 9, 10 and 13, 'Strongly Agree' scores 3, 'Agree' 2, 'Disagree' 1, 'Strongly Disagree' 0.

For questions, 2, 4, 5, 8, 11, 12 and 14, 'Strongly Agree' scores 0, 'Agree' 1, 'Disagree' 2, 'Strongly Disagree' 3.

The closer you are to the maximum score of 42, the more you

have a fixed mindset. The closer you are to the minimum score of 0, the more you have a growth mindset.

28+: FIXED MINDSET

If you think that intelligence and ability are static and 'you are the way you are', you are likely to approach becoming a parent in the same way. You will need to look smart and perform well and thereby prove that you are a natural mother or father. That's great, but there is a downside. Sometimes you will avoid challenges – often easier for fathers than mothers – as it might affect your self-image, or stick to what you know you can do well. Equally, you can give up easily when faced with obstacles because you tend to see effort as fruitless. After all, what's the point if you'll just be back at square one? Once again, it is easier for men to bow out and tell their wife: 'I don't know' and imply 'You're the expert' or 'You're a woman so you should know', as if knowing how to care for a baby is something that women are born with. Obviously, it goes without saying that any feedback, for both men and women with this mindset, is heard as negative. This is because someone is not commenting just on how you bathed your baby but on whether you are a good parent or not.

Advice: When men have a fixed mindset, they can easily become a helper for their wife rather than a co-partner for looking after their baby, and set up a lifetime of being 'reserve parent'. (It goes without saying that this will have a detrimental effect on their relationship in the long term.) Women with this mindset can become very isolated, not only because they find it hard to ask for help – for fear of what people might think – but also because other people keep quiet when helpful advice is heard as 'sticking your nose in'. If this is you, to move more towards the middle of the scale, think back to times in the past where you have persevered with something important and achieved a reasonable competence.

Remember, there is no need to be a 'perfect' mother or father – just good enough.

27–15: COMBINATION MINDSET

A lot of people fall somewhere in the middle between a fixed and a growth mindset. In our specialized world, where we don't have to excel at everything, this is perhaps a good place to be. For example, I employ an accountant to file my tax returns. Of course, it's a hangover from school where I decided 'I'm not good at maths', but it is also pragmatism: I'm better putting my energy into writing books and seeing clients rather than struggling to get my figures right. After all, there is a certain amount of truth in the fixed mindset that doing something well shouldn't involve so much sweat. However, as Dweck says, 'the fallacy comes when people generalize it into a belief that effort on any task, even hard ones, implies low ability'.

In addition, the closer you are to the fixed mindset, the more likely you are to feel threatened by the success (or happy children) of others, as they become a benchmark to make you look bad. Under these circumstances, you are likely to run down other people or make poisonous remarks: 'Of course it's easy for her, with all that money.' Meanwhile, the closer you are to the growth mindset, the more other people's success is a source of inspiration rather than a threat.

Advice: There is one key skill to help you move more towards the growth mindset end of the continuum: dealing with criticism. Try not to judge whether comments are helpful or not so helpful – because that will make you defensive or misunderstand what's being said. For example, you might hear: 'You were too preoccupied with work on holiday' while the real message might be 'The kids really enjoyed it when you played badminton and messed around in the pool with them but were disappointed that you brought work with you.' Often criticism comes with some jam – a compliment – so don't miss out on that. Once you've really listened, heard the whole message and weighed up the truth (did you really need to work?) you can fully respond. On many occasions, criticism is a gift, as it helps us look at ourselves and our motivations from a fresh perspective.

UNDER 15: GROWTH MINDSET

If you think intelligence and ability can be developed, you are more likely to embrace change, since you view obstacles as something that can be overcome, a chance to develop new skills or refine existing ones. With this mindset, problems are not a sign of failure but an opportunity. Not only will you see effort as something necessary, but setbacks can be treated more philosophically. So a crying baby seems less a personal failure but more stoically 'these things happen' or 'some babies cry more than others'. When it comes to solving these problems, you are more likely to accept feedback and learn from criticism because it is not about you but about your current abilities (and those can be improved).

Advice: Although it is really helpful to have a growth mindset, don't lose sight of how much our culture pushes the fixed mindset and downplays the hard work behind success. On TV talent shows, successful contestants are painted as being as ordinary as possible – so we can relate to them – but this means that details like being at stage school or having studied music at the Royal Academy are edited out of their back-stories. So when you're tired, stressed and worried by the demands of a small baby, it is easy to fall into the trap of thinking other people have inherent skills, and lose touch with your growth mindset. Good parenting is the result of trial and error and nobody 'just knows' how to do it.

■　■　■　■　■　■

Common shocks

Life is full of ups and downs and even the most joyous events – like having a baby – involve disappointments and problems. In the spirit of Seneca, let's look at some of the possible obstacles so it won't seem quite so shocking if they do occur and, equally importantly, to help you get in touch with your growth mindset and be ready to overcome them.

CHILDBIRTH CAN BE TRAUMATIC

Even a natural, uncomplicated birth is a massive physiological challenge for a woman's body and it takes time, rest and a slow rehabilitation to recover. In 1931, W. Blair Bell, the first president of the British College of Obstetricians, estimated that 10 per cent of mothers were 'more or less crippled as a result of childbearing'. Seventy per cent of new mothers had lesions and 35 to 40 per cent of these lesions were disabling. Although much has changed since the experiences of our grandmothers and great-grandmothers, as recently as 1991 the Health After Childbirth report (which followed the health of eleven thousand new mothers) found that 47 per cent had at least one health problem (such as backache, frequent headaches, migraine or bladder problems) six weeks after giving birth. More alarmingly, two-thirds of these new mothers still had problems thirteen months after giving birth. Today, mothers are given more choice and benefit from the latest advances in aftercare, but childbirth remains a physically challenging experience.

Why it is a shock: In our celebrity-obsessed culture, we have almost become inured to how much time and space is devoted to poring over women's bodies and analysing their failings. However, there is a new phenomenon: hot famous women and their babies. Magazines and the Internet are full of supermodels and celebrities who have dropped sixty pounds and got their figures back after giving birth with just 'cardio and sculpting sessions five times a week'. One celebrity trainer made a DVD showing other mothers how to achieve this goal just six weeks after her daughter was born by Caesarean section. In the USA, the phenomenon is so widespread that a new term has been coined for these 'super' mothers: Momshells (a combination of 'mom' and 'bombshell'). Not only does this culture leave lots of ordinary mothers feeling guilty, but it creates an expectation that women will recover quickly from giving birth, so family and friends leave them to care for their baby alone – even though many feel physically and emotionally shaken.

Turn it around: There are two ways to confront this problem. First, stop reading celebrity magazines or visiting websites that pore over other women's imperfections. Although you might think seeing famous women looking flabby will make you feel better about your own body, the boost is only short-lived and ultimately feeds self-loathing. 'I worry more about my body now than I did before,' explained Gemma just three weeks after giving birth. 'I compare how I look to other new mums to gauge how we're coping with the roller-coaster journey.' Keep reminding yourself that most mothers take months to reshape their bodies after pregnancy and your figure is not really a guide to how well you are coping with motherhood.

I know I'm asking a lot but please don't compare yourself to other mothers or fathers. If you can pull off this trick, it will make your life much easier – especially as the Parenting Olympics have only just started. (Next it will be whose baby is sleeping best, eating most, crawling first, and before you know it getting a place at the best university.) Just because other people have entered the competition doesn't mean that you're obliged to join in. Keep quiet when other parents are boasting, walk away or turn it into a private joke between you and your partner. It will help you enjoy this special time – rather than missing something because you've been too busy looking over your shoulder.

Second, if you are a new parent and did not expect to need extra support, it's not too late to ask – especially if there were complications from the birth. Don't feel guilty or ashamed. In the eighteenth century women were considered ill and therefore should 'lie in' at special facilities while other people did the chores and mothers could bond with their babies. Even today, in Malay villages new mothers spend forty days being cared for away from their family (by other women) before rejoining their communities. In some Asian cultures – especially China – confinement is still popular, with post-partum houses being set up in US cities to cater for new immigrants who don't have practical support from their families.

Speak to your mother, father or in-laws and explain that you need some extra muscle – just a few hours a week can make a huge difference. Remember the friends who said, 'Let us know if there's anything we can do' and turn their offer into something concrete. Lots of people in your circle will want to help but could feel awkward about offering, or not be aware that you need help. Even if it is only an occasional afternoon or evening visit, this can still be a boost and make you feel emotionally supported even if no longer-term practical assistance is offered.

YOUR CAREFULLY CONSTRUCTED IDENTITY CAN CRUMBLE

Children can provide a sense of purpose and belonging and make us feel needed, but they can also turn our lives upside-down. It is particularly destabilizing when the stories we tell ourselves, to make sense of the world and our place in it, are challenged.

For example, Karen, thirty-eight, had always believed 'I can cope with whatever is thrown at me' and her career in IT had given her plenty of examples. 'When everybody else is running around screaming, I can keep calm, go back to basics and slowly work through everything and isolate the problem.' It wasn't just work that had forged this identity, it went right back to her childhood. 'My mother was a borderline alcoholic and my father was away on work a lot. I was the eldest of three children and we could never predict how my mother would be, so from about the age of seven I'd fix my brother and sister breakfast, help them get dressed and ready for school.' When I asked her to imagine herself having superhero qualities, she pictured herself as Atlas holding up the world. Unfortunately, her husband had a great career opportunity just two weeks after their second son was born and he needed to be out of the country for six weeks. In the debate over whether he should go, Karen's arguments were formed by her Madam Atlas identity: 'I can cope.' The result was that her husband went off with her blessing. Unfortunately, Karen found that she couldn't manage alone with a toddler and a newborn, and slipped into depression.

Although most men continue to work full-time – which props up their old self-image – their identity can also be severely challenged by the arrival of a child. Karen's husband, Edward, thirty-six, had always seen his job as regulating the mood in the house. 'If there's a bad atmosphere, I try and suck it up, keep positive and help everybody else get on to an even keel. Normally, it works because I've got a sunny disposition, but I couldn't shift the black cloud over Karen. I felt help-less and for the first time ever a bit hopeless too.' When I asked Edward to name his superhero, he dubbed himself 'the Great Absorber' (he had also tried to keep the peace between his parents, who were always quarrelling). Edward was feeling particularly bleak when he arrived in counselling. 'If I'm not the Great Absorber, who am I?' he said.

Other common identities that babies and toddlers challenge include 'I'm in charge' and 'my beautiful life' (where looking good, nice clothes and a beautiful house are paramount to your identity).

Sometimes the shock comes when the children are older, go off to school, become teenagers or leave home. If you are the principal carer, being a 'great mum' or 'superdad' can be the core of your identity. So what happens when the children don't need you so much?

'I suppose I was one of the first dads in our town who gave up work to look after our three children,' says Mike, forty-three. 'My wife had a career with a pension fund and promotion prospects while I just pushed paper round a desk for local government, so I was pleased to leave it all behind. It was strange at first because the mums at the school gates were a bit wary but I got involved with the school – listening to the little ones reading – and quickly made a circle of friends. They were always so complimentary – "I wish my husband was like you" – and when I helped our eldest bake for home economics, you'd think I'd invented a cure for cancer. The kids really liked me being at home and my wife was relieved that I took up the most of the strain. I suppose I became "Wonder Mike", the man who knew the name of all the children's teachers. Except the eldest is going off to university and the youngest goes up to middle school and I'm no longer needed so much. If I'm not "Ideal Dad", who am I? What do I want to do with the rest of my life?'

Why it is a shock: This generation is particularly ill-equipped to become new parents. While our grandparents came from large, tight-knit families and most daughters would be expected to care for younger siblings or help their aunt with her children, many expectant mothers and fathers today have no experience of being left in charge of a baby. A significant number have not even held one before being handed their own. In the meantime, the hysteria about abuse means that only people who have been vetted are allowed anywhere near children and the average person's contact has been further reduced. In addition, we have our children much later. Therefore, we have had longer to create myths about ourself and our role in the world, and they have become more deeply entrenched. No wonder the transformation from being childless to a parent can be difficult, and the journey out of the parenting years equally fraught.

Turn it around: It is healthy to update your self-image from time to time, but first you need a clear idea of how you see yourself. Ultimately, problems arise when you have a narrow or too rigid self-image.

Think about the questions I asked Karen and Edward and how you might respond: if you had superhero qualities, what would they be? If you were a superhero, what would you be called? Where does this image come from? How accurate is it today? How realistic is it?

Next, consider what might happen if you failed to live up to this identity. Would it really be the end of the world?

Some new mothers and fathers get a pleasant surprise and find being a parent really suits them, providing a significant boost to their confidence. This can often be the case for people who have been striving to find their place in the world or whose career was not particularly satisfying. In these circumstances, new mothers and fathers can become so fixed on caring and get so great a reward that they lose sight of some of their other identities – like partner (which can be a nasty shock for their husband or wife).

If becoming a parent has been challenging to your carefully constructed image of yourself, don't try to be everything to your child. concentrate on your strengths and be prepared to delegate from time to time. Karen learnt, slowly but surely, that it was OK to ask Edward for help when she needed it – rather than seeing this as 'failure'. The biggest turning point was when she went away for a short holiday on her own. 'It not only gave me a chance to catch up on my sleep and truly relax – possibly for the first time in years – but I learnt that the world didn't collapse if I wasn't there to hold it up.'

UNCONDITIONAL LOVE IS DIFFICULT

There is a nasty secret that most parents would rather die than confess: sometimes they resent their children. The taboo is so strong that many people won't even admit it to themselves. After all, parents are supposed to love their child unconditionally from the moment they set eyes on him or her. Unfortunately, there are always conflicts between the needs of a parent and a child and we wouldn't be human if we didn't resent the self-sacrifice from time to time.

Fiona, a thirty-three-year-old musician, has a nine-year-old son and although she expected support from her partner, he disappeared out of their lives – beyond occasional access visits – a few months into her pregnancy. 'I love my son – don't get me wrong, he's the centre of my life – but he significantly curtails my options. I'll have this idea for a new song and I'll want to be getting on with it. However, my son will want me to play and I can't always say, "Why don't you go across the road and see what Granny and Grandpa are doing?" Most of my creative friends don't have children, so I don't get to see them that often (as there's only so many times I can ask my parents to babysit) and I don't really fit into the "young mothers" dinner-party circle where they only want to talk about new kitchens and holidays in Tuscany.'

Why it is a shock: We are brought up on images of the Madonna and child, not only on Christmas cards but updated versions in adverts and across popular culture. The message is always the same: self-sacrificing, accepting, devoted. Yet, before becoming a parent, we are encouraged to set goals for ourselves, focus on them and be ruthless in our determination to reach them. What is prized most is being autonomous and independent, having the ability to control the agenda. Going from standing up for yourself to self-sacrificing is a 180-degree turn and you're expected to achieve it on just 'unconditional love'. However, parents – and even more shockingly, mothers – still have needs too.

Turn it around: It is fine to resent your children. It does not make you a bad mother or father. In fact, it could make you a better one. Any feeling that is suppressed does not simply disappear but either gathers power in the shadows or simply pops up somewhere else. In fact, this is one of the biggest causes of bitterness that I see between new parents. No mother can easily say, 'I resented my baby today' and after all, it's not his or her fault that you're tired, stressed and upset. He or she is small, innocent and needy. So it's much easier to take your resentment out on your husband, who 'doesn't understand' or has been 'having fun' at work all day. Similarly, a husband can't come home and see his wife and baby in their dreamy little world of two, breastfeeding, cuddling or tickling, and not feel a little bit excluded. He can't say, 'I'm jealous', because what sort of monster would resent his own child? So he takes it out on his wife by being snappy, or behaves in a passive-aggressive manner (for example playing games on his computer or drinking too much).

The week after I told Fiona that most parents resent their child from time to time, she felt like a weight had been lifted off her shoulders and we could begin to negotiate a compromise between her own needs and those of her son.

'In the evening, he'll be after my attention but I'll want to get on with my stuff. For example, I'll try to catch up with my friends on Facebook (because I never see them in the flesh) and he'll always be interrupting,' she explained. 'I worry what will happen when he goes to bed later and my time is completely swallowed up.'

I had the picture of neither party feeling satisfied. Her son never quite had her undivided attention (no wonder he was needy) and she could never be anything else than in Mum mode (no wonder she felt resentful).

'What would happen if you put down your work or whatever when he came home and focused entirely on him, listened to what he'd done, asked questions and maybe did something together for an hour?' I asked.

Fiona admitted she only had half an ear on his stories about school, because she was working or 'looking for something more interesting online'.

'Afterwards, he has to entertain himself for a while, watch TV, read or get on with his homework and you can focus on your stuff.'

The experiment was a huge success and, what's more, Fiona began to include her son in some of her weekends away, when there were other children around. Their relationship became even closer but first she had to admit that she had different needs from her son and sometimes resented her sacrifices.

YOUR PARENTS RETURN TO CENTRE STAGE

We spend our teens and early twenties distancing ourselves from our parents, becoming our own people and creating our own lives. The journey back into the fold starts with getting married, which turns a private arrangement (like living together) into something public as you join each other's extended families – albeit at a manageable level like Christmas and cousins' weddings. However, having a baby brings your parents back to the centre of your life – providing support and advice (whether asked for or not). This could be financial help, babysitting, an experienced shoulder to cry on or even all going on holiday together, but what used to be an arm's-length relationship has become a decidedly more intimate one. This can be wonderful, but it can also bring up issues that you thought long buried, or make existing problems more acute.

Why it is a shock: Having a child brings back your own childhood and all the raw emotions associated with it. 'When I held my son in my arms, I couldn't stop crying,' explains Derek, thirty. 'He seemed so small, so trusting, and he needed me to be there to look after him.' Unfortunately, Derek's own father had always been a shadowy presence – more a mate than a father – who had left his mother before he was a year old and had a series of transitory relationships with other women. 'I'd always thought, I don't need a dad because my mum is amazing – a mum and a dad rolled into one – but now I feel this great big gaping hole. I phoned my dad and he did congratulate me, but joked that I'd got the full ball and chain.' Worse still, Derek wondered how he could be a good father when he'd never had a father himself.

It is also easy to dump your old childhood fears on to your baby. For example, Carrie, twenty-nine, had been labelled 'the ugly one' by her mother (in comparison with her younger sister, who was 'the pretty one'). 'When the midwife told me I'd had a baby girl, my heart gave a huge lurch. Would she be ugly like me? And her face was all crumpled and she had a bit of jaundice. The midwife thought I was crying with joy but the tears were about all the jibes she'd get in the playground, because people can be cruel. It took a couple of days to realize this was not about my daughter, who after she'd recovered from the trauma of arriving in the world is a really cute baby, but me and the messages from my mother. I know she didn't intend to be mean but how could she?'

Turn it around: Although you might revert to your old relationship with your parents – and regress every time they walk through the door – it is important to recognize there has been a shift. You and your partner and your child are at the core while your parents' old omnipotence as 'Mum' and 'Dad' will dwindle as they become 'Grandma' and 'Grandpa'. What's more, you have an extraordinary opportunity to heal the scars from your childhood and transform your relationship with your parents.

If there are incidents from the past that you need to discuss with your parents, it is best to approach them as questions: 'What was happening in your life when I was born?' rather than accusations: 'You never had time for me.' As a parent yourself now, you might find it easier to understand their perspective and view past traumas from another angle.

However, I find in most cases that there is no need to confront your parents and that improving your day-to-day communication is enough. To achieve this goal, I use TA (transactional analysis), a way of looking at how we interact based on the ideas of Canadian psychologist Eric Berne (1910–70). He believed that we have three modes of operating: Parent, Adult, Child. It is important to stress that we need access to all these parts of our personality – the Parent nurtures, the Adult solves problems, and the Child is creative and fun. The problem arises when people get stuck in one particularly poisonous transaction: Critical Parent and Adapted Child. We all immediately recognize the Critical Parent ('I wouldn't do that if I was you' or 'Here you go again') but Adapted Child needs more explanation. It includes sulking, throwing a tantrum, people-pleasing (going along with something even when you don't agree), rebelling, playing the martyr and passive-aggressive behaviour (slamming doors or agreeing to do something but never getting round to it). Often in a disagreement with someone – like your mother, partner or work colleague – you will flip backwards and forwards between Critical Parent and Adapted Child. Here is an example:

> *'I've been waiting here for half an hour. You could have called.'*
> (Person A is playing Critical Parent.)
> *'I've had a horrible day and now you're having a go.'* (Person B is playing 'poor me' and being Adapted Child.)
> *'I don't know why I say anything.'* (Person A has switched into 'martyr' mode and therefore Adapted Child.)
> *'If you didn't leave everything to me, perhaps I would be on time.'* (Person B is now Critical Parent.)

As you can imagine, this type of interaction can go on for hours, even years. Fortunately, there is an alternative: if you go into Adult, the other person will switch into that mode too. By Adult I mean rational, questioning, problem-solving and assertive. For example: 'What are the facts?', 'What seems to be the problem?' and 'How can we solve this problem?' Adult is also about what's happening now or in the near future, rather than the past. It also avoids loaded words like 'always' and 'never'. Here is an example of how staying in Adult mode

– even when the other person responds in Child – will encourage them to match you in Adult:

> *'How could we ensure that everybody has a good time when we come over to yours on Sunday?'*
> *'It's nothing to do with me, your wife is always so sensitive.'* (This person is sounding sulky and definitely in Adapted Child.)
> *'What could we do differently?'* (He has resisted the temptation to slip into Critical Parent.)
> *'I don't know, I've tried everything.'* (This is 'poor me', or 'helpless me' and still in Adapted Child.)
> *'How could I help?'* (By using a question, he is sticking to Adult.)
> *'Perhaps if you arrived earlier, so we weren't having to sit down immediately for lunch, we could take the children to the park and burn off some energy.'* (Finally, this is an Adult response.)
> *'That sounds a great idea, let's try it. How much earlier are you suggesting?'*

So next time you feel yourself slipping into an Adapted Child or Critical Parent dynamic with your mother or father, check yourself and switch into Adult mode. It might take a couple of statements in Adult but your mother or father will respond and switch into Adult too, and slowly but surely your relationship will change. (There is more about TA in my book *Help Your Partner Say Yes*.)

■ ■ ■ ■ ■ ■

Telling the Story of Your Childhood

Your childhood has shaped not only you, but your understanding of what it means to be a mother or a father and your fears about the future. To help turn these from something nebulous into something concrete that can be discussed, I'd like you to tell your partner a story about a fierce moment from your childhood and listen to him or her as he or she tells you a similar story. What do I mean by 'fierce'? It could be something dramatically charged (for you or somebody else in the story). It could be the moment that everything changed, or its power might come from being very ordinary but emblematic of something that happened over and over again. Don't take too long thinking about it: if something pops into your head, go with it and tell the story. Here are a few pointers:

- How old were you?
- Set the scene. Where were you? Who was there? What time of year was it? What could you see? (This will not only draw your partner into the story but help you step back in time and inhabit the story.)
- What happened?
- How did you react? Why did you do that? How did you feel?
- What about the other people? How did they respond to the incident and to your reaction?

When you've finished telling your story, let your partner ask questions and truly understand the significance of it. Ask what strikes him or her as interesting. Consider why you chose this story, what it reveals about your role in your family and the messages you were given as a child. Finally, return to the issues that have been troubling you over the past months – especially if you're about to become a parent for the first time. What light does this story shed on those concerns?

Next, listen while your partner tells his or her story. Once it's over, think about the following questions:

- How much do you recognize the dynamics revealed by the story?
- What surprised you?

- What is missing?
- What are the differences between your family and your partner's family?
- What does the story tell you about being a father or a mother?

Finish off by thanking each other for the story and, as it's probably been quite emotional, give each other a big hug. Remember what you told each other and use it to understand why you both behave the way you do. It is easy to think that your partner does something because 'he's selfish' or 'she doesn't love me enough', but more often than not it's because your partner is wrestling with his or her ghosts rather than deliberately trying to annoy you. Knowing the real reasons for any behaviour will allow you to respond more sympathetically and, instead of a row, set up a discussion about other ways of a tackling the issue.

■ ■ ■ ■ ■ ■

Help! I'm turning into my parents

One of the biggest shocks about becoming a parent is finding yourself doing the things your parents did and using the same put-downs you promised yourself you'd never inflict on your own children. To illustrate just how deeply the parenting we received is ingrained, and how strongly it informs the parenting we give ourselves, I'm going to use a personal example.

My sister and her two children were visiting our parents and I'd joined them for the weekend. My niece was about ten or eleven and, despite a normally sunny disposition, she was being extremely cranky. It felt like one false move and she would explode, so everyone had been putting themselves out to accommodate her. If she wanted to play cards, we'd play cards, and if she wanted to go to the swimming pool and jump off the top board all day, that's what we did. On the final morning, my niece and I were alone in the kitchen. We couldn't follow her desires to the letter and she stuck out her bottom lip: 'We never do anything I want.' In my defence, I was sitting in my mother's seat at the table where I'd eaten every meal from seven to eighteen, but instead of allowing my niece to open up or asking a question –'Why do you feel that?' – I did exactly what my mother would have done. Despite all my training and my awareness of this trap, I laughed. A horrible, mocking laugh. It seemed to come from nowhere and it was out of my mouth before I could stop it. OK, it was slightly funny after two days' dancing attendance, but I didn't really know what was going on in my niece's life beyond this weekend, and I didn't even understand the last few days from her viewpoint. Instead of allowing her to express her feelings, I stopped her dead in her tracks. The same message I'd been given when I was young: shut up and get on with it. (No prizes for guessing why I decided to become a therapist!)

I want to stress that I'm not blaming anyone – I know my mother was on the receiving end of that laugh from my grandmother, and who knows how many previous generations had used it before that. However, understanding your parents' parenting style (and looking out for the same behaviour in yourself) is better than simply copying it or being so determined not to make the same mistakes that you fall into a different trap.

In a moment, I will go through eight common problematic parenting styles that I've identified and explain how they might have affected you. The first four tend to be exhibited by fathers and the second four by mothers, but they can be adopted by either men or women. If you have trouble recognizing which category your parents fall into, try completing these sentences:

'Mum will always . . .'

'Dad will always . . .'

If you're still finding it hard, because your parents were loving and supportive, don't think of just their everyday parenting style but how they behaved when tired or stressed. However much we understand their behaviour as adults, the words or actions will still have hurt and left wounds. I know this is difficult. A lot of my clients feel guilty about criticizing their parents, because they did their best, but it is important to have a balanced picture of your childhood. So what are these eight problematic parenting styles?

SUPREME RULER

This is the man who would be king. He works hard and his wife and kids should be grateful and behave like loyal subjects. Therefore, he rules by decree and if there's any dispute it's settled with 'It's my house' or 'I pay the bills.'

The effect on you: This parenting style has a greater impact on sons than daughters, who are likely to grow up and expect the same deference from their partner and children. This is less of a problem when a couple don't have children as there is plenty of money (so he can be a benign ruler) and enough free time to pursue both individual and couple goals (so who's in charge is less an issue). However, many men don't feel ready to have children in their twenties and thirties and their wives sense this deep down, and – especially if he is a Supreme Ruler – will try and keep the impact on him (especially the messy, exhausting parts of parenting) to a minimum. Unfortunately, this can lead to women feeling resentful or, when they fail to pull off the impossible, becoming depressed.

CRITICAL

This father, and sometimes mother, is full of frustration and anger because 'nobody can do anything right'. He is not only a perfectionist but he has a talent for spotting what other people have done wrong. His comments might be meant as helpful – because he wants you to do things better – but the tone is always dismissive and undermines his wife's and his children's confidence.

The effect on you: Both sons and daughters can be left feeling not good enough or worthy of praise, time or tenderness. Not only will they be sensitive to any criticism themselves – because even the mildest reproach will be heard as a character assassination – but they are likely to be critical of others too.

PASSIVE

He gives his power over to his wife, children or his boss. At home, he does not interrupt, interact or show much interest in what his children have been doing. If he did complain he would be ignored or beaten down, so he disappears into alcohol, TV or his garden shed.

The effect on you: The sons of these men grow up to hate passivity in other men, their sons and themselves. They take on too much, won't let others share the burden and behave like a Supreme Ruler; or, if they lose their job or feel defeated by life, their self-loathing becomes overwhelming and they become severely depressed or self-medicate with alcohol, pornography, computer games, etc. Daughters of passive men will often grow up with such an abhorrence of passive men that they will either marry Supreme Rulers or be so finely tuned to passivity in their partner or son that they will spot the slightest slip, exaggerate it in their minds and get angry out of all proportion to the crime.

ABSENTEE

This father is not there. It might be through work commitments or divorce but he misses sports days, school concerts and other red-letter days because he is too busy or has other priorities. He might think he's doing the best for the family by paying the bills and providing a good lifestyle, but the message he gives is one of indifference.

The effect on you: These sons have no idea how to be a father because they received little fathering themselves. They will either go to the opposite extreme and become Superdad (and over-involved in their children's lives) or throw themselves into the role of being chief provider and spend so much time at work that their marriage suffers. If they are not careful, they are trying so hard not to be their father that they become him anyway. Daughters of absentee dads have a tendency to fall for men who are either emotionally or physically unavailable and likely to leave them carrying the majority of the day-to-day responsibility for raising the children.

SMOTHERING

This mother, and sometimes father, is always there for the children. She is still tying their shoelaces years after they can do it themselves, ready to fight their battles with friends, teachers and bosses and interested in every corner of their lives. I once had a client who was about to drive two hours to her daughter's university to search for her daughter's passport because she was too busy to do it herself. Fortunately, the daughter found it behind a bookcase and saved her mother the journey.

The effect on you: There is a high possibility that you could become too involved in your son or daughter's life – especially as modern parenting culture encourages this phenomenon. The sons of smother mothers, in particular, can have a high sense of entitlement and become Supreme Rulers. If you rebelled as a child and pulled up the drawbridge so that your mother could not invade your emotional space, you will be self-contained and tend to keep other people at a distance. In which case, the experience of having a baby and its overwhelming emotional demands can be very frightening.

CONTROLLING

There is only one way to do things and that's the Controlling parent's way. They know best what time to set off for school, who makes the right friends and how to do your school project. Although fathers can be equally Controlling – see Supreme Ruler – they tend to be most interested in the areas where their lives directly intersect with their son's or daughter's (for example mealtimes or bedtimes). By contrast, mothers are interested in every part of their children's lives, both emotionally and practically. For example, I had a client – a successful career woman in her forties – whose mother was forever trying to get her to buy a different bedspread because she thought white too impractical. It is always tempting to go along with what a Controlling parent wants, partly for a quiet life but mainly because doing something different is taken as a personal affront, and who wants to upset their mother?

The effect on you: You are likely to want to be in charge too – especially as this is encouraged by contemporary culture – and feel very uncomfortable when events spiral out of control. It is especially challenging when your baby won't stop crying or your partner has different ideas about child-rearing. It is easy to become very black and white, where you are right and your partner wrong, rather than just two people with differing opinions.

MARTYR

There is a lot of crossover between this kind of mother and both Smothering and Controlling ones – especially if she doesn't get her own way: 'After everything I've done for you . . . but it doesn't matter. I'll be fine on my own.' Sometimes, these women have good reason to feel like a martyr – perhaps life has dealt them a tough hand and they are coping with illness or bringing up their children alone because their husband is Passive, an alcoholic or Absent. Whatever the circumstances, rather than being assertive and asking for what they need, both martyr mothers and fathers manipulate other people by playing the 'poor me' card, or shutting up and getting on with things (but deeply resenting all the sacrifices they are making).

The effect on you: This parenting style has a greater impact on daughters than sons, and like Passive parenting (which affects sons more than daughters), you will do your utmost not to fall into this trap. However, when you're tired and overwhelmed (something that's not uncommon after having children), you are likely to find yourself behaving just like your mother.

TIMID

These women are frightened of the world and tend to lead small lives – normally centred around the home. They always see the worst and are pessimistic or anxious about how something might turn out. Sometimes they have good reasons to be frightened, because they are trying to hide the full effect of a husband's infidelity, gambling or violence from their children. Often timid mothers have a different relationship with their children when their husband is not around or, if he is Supreme Ruler or Critical, try to appease behind the scenes.

The effect on you: The children of Timid parents tend to be cautious themselves and become anxious mothers and fathers – once again this is encouraged by our modern media and the saturation coverage of every child who is missing, murdered or abused.

The power of a fulsome apology

If reading about parenting styles has made you cringe because you have inadvertently reproduced your father or mother's behaviour with your partner or your children, please don't be too tough on yourself. Everybody makes mistakes and what counts is how you recover. That's why I am a great believer in the fulsome apology. There are three parts to it:

1. Identify the unhelpful behaviour.
2. Identify the impact on the other person.
3. Express your sorrow.
   For example: 'I'm sorry I laughed when you said nobody does anything you want. It must have made you feel belittled/not taken seriously. I really regret it and want to apologize.'

There are two ways that people lessen the power of a fulsome apology. The first is explaining the behaviour. By saying, for example, 'It's something my mother did to me', you sound like you are making excuses or asking for sympathy. The second is going overboard with expressing sorrow. For example, 'I haven't been able to sleep properly' or 'I've been so worried.' Instead of the apology being something about the other person, it has become about you (and he or she could feel obliged to forgive you).

Don't worry about whether your apology is accepted or not. Give the other person the chance to respond but if he or she has nothing to say, let the topic drop. (If you don't normally apologize, the other person could be in shock!)

It is particularly powerful when a father or mother apologizes to a child – for example, 'I'm sorry I lost my temper. It was nothing to do with you and it must have made you feel that you'd done something wrong. That's not the message I wanted to give you and I'm sorry' – because it models the sort of behaviour you would like them to use with their brothers, sisters and friends.

In addition, a fulsome apology provides the opportunity to move on and, if you fall into the same trap again, gives the other person permission to address your unpleasant behaviour.

Second child syndrome

It should be much easier to cope second time around. After all, you've already made the transition from couple to family. You know what to expect and have less to fear. However, when I take a history of a couple's relationship, it is often the birth of their second child that's been the moment that things have started to unravel. So why should the arrival of a second baby be such a turning point?

Firstly, every child is different. Returning to Donald Winnicott, the leading paediatrician and psychoanalyst who coined the term 'the good enough mother', he wrote: 'Almost from the start, the new baby has his own ideas, and if you have ten children you will not find two alike, although they all grow up in the same house – your household. Ten children will see ten different mothers in you.' Sometimes, you can be lucky the first time around and have a child that complements your personal strengths, but find your second one more of a challenge – perhaps because he or she shares some of the character traits that you dislike in yourself.

'Our daughter needs a lot more of my wife's attention,' says Owen, thirty-six. 'Although she's three, she's still sleeping in the bed with us – rather than in her own room – because otherwise there are tears and tantrums. I worry about my son, who's six: he knows that she sleeps with us. We can't hide it from him. What incentive is there for him to grow up when his younger sister gets all the special treatment?'

A second baby means significantly less couple time, and transporting two small children can be a nightmare. If you decide to go somewhere without them, it is harder to find someone to care for two children than for one. 'When our first child was born, we'd just put him a carry-cot and take him with us,' says Jessica, twenty-seven. 'He'd normally be sleeping and it was never a problem – even if we were going to a restaurant. With two children, the amount of paraphernalia is extraordinary. You can see our childless friends raising their eyebrows as we cart more and more stuff through their door. One of them is on solids and they both have to eat early. And who wants Sunday lunch at midday? My mother is happy to look after them but since the youngest started crawling, my stepfather has been making noises about "expecting too much". So I don't like to leave them there for too long. Slowly but surely, we're losing touch with anybody who isn't firmly immersed in baby world.'

Your love life takes more of a hit after the second child – especially if you've decided that your family is complete. That's because it takes a woman's hormones about eighteen months to return to normal after giving birth. The bonding chemical that helps us feel close to our partners and in touch with our sexual feelings – oxytocin – is diverted into the bond between mother and baby. It doesn't mean that a woman won't be sexually responsive, but she won't be spontaneously horny. Unfortunately, eighteen months is also the amount of time most couples leave before trying for another child, and the whole process starts again. 'One of the main reasons that I agreed to try for a second child is at least I'd least get plenty of sex,' explained Jake, thirty-eight, 'but my wife got pregnant almost straight away so I felt really cheated, and as we can't afford a third child, I sometimes worry that I'll never have sex again. OK, I know that's an exaggeration, but when will I have carefree sex again – without my wife having one ear on the baby monitor?' (There is more on this topic in Chapter Seven.)

The second child can also be a tipping point where a woman decides that working full-time is too stressful or decides to give up working altogether. 'It wasn't just that I had no time to do anything, and when I was at work I was thinking about home, and when I was at home I'd be thinking about work, but I seemed to be such a one-dimensional person,' says Sandra, forty-three. 'I hadn't read a book from one year to the next. When we went to a dinner party, people would be talking about a film or something in the news and I wouldn't have the first idea how to join the conversation because I was so out of touch. Finally, when I did the calculations, I found I was almost working to pay for childcare. It seemed a no-brainer.'

However, there is a much deeper reason why having two children can be problematic, and it goes right back to your own childhood again. 'My earliest memory is waking up on Christmas morning and wondering why my mother wasn't there when I opened my stocking. My father reminded me, "She's gone to the hospital to fetch your baby sister." I still remember the new garage I got and just as clearly thinking, I don't want a sister,' explained Anthony, thirty-seven. 'When my mother did return – and I'm a bit hazy about how long afterwards – she was really tired and all she wanted to do was sleep. Fast-forward a few months, and I must have had my nose put out of joint because I remember coming back from somewhere and my sister had piled one brick on top of the other and my mother and father were really excited. So what? Anybody could have done that, I thought, but there was also this dawning realization: I've got competition now.'

Anthony had scarcely thought of these events until his wife gave birth to his daughter and all the old feelings came flooding back. 'I don't know if I was jealous on behalf of my son or it was about me, but I felt angry for no reason at all.' Like many clients in a similar situation, Anthony found it hard to accept the link between how he felt as small child and today. 'It doesn't seem to make sense that something so small – like seeing my sister playing with my bricks – will have such a big impact.' I know it does not make *logical* sense, but we're dealing with emotions from when we were small and beyond reason.

In effect, having a second child creates the sort of family that most of us were brought up in. A mother, father, sibling and us: four of us. This gives a chance to replay all the old dynamics and unfortunately some people end up feeling defeated, excluded, blamed all over again. What's more, if your parents favoured your brother or sister, there was a crisis that consumed their attention or they simply ran out of energy by the time you were born, it can seem that love is finite, rather than something that expands for however many people there are in the family.

Under these circumstances, love will appear rationed and your deepest and darkest fear is that once you have a baby (and especially two babies), your partner will have less love available for you. 'I've never really thought of it but I suppose when it was just my wife, my son and me, it was an even competition [for my wife's attention] but once we had our daughter it was two against one,' Anthony explained. 'No wonder I've been down, bordering on depression.'

Although I've outlined the possible pitfalls, it is important to stress that they won't necessarily happen to you. Especially if you are aware of the problems and take the precautionary steps that I'm about to outline.

How to put your partner first

It takes time to fit into the role of being a mother or a father and being parents together. In essence, there is *her* journey, *his* journey and your relationship's journey, and the adjustments won't necessarily happen all at the same time. A woman has nine months to turn into a mother – maybe even longer if she played with dolls as a child. In contrast, a man turns into a father all at once. Everything is made doubly difficult if the new baby brings up old feelings from his childhood and he worries that there is not enough love to go round. If his wife is enveloped in the dreamy symbiotic world of mother and child and all her other versions of herself have been subsumed into this one identity, it can be a recipe for disaster.

Of course, it is hard to put your partner first – especially if you are a new mother. After all, how can you prioritize the needs of a big lump of a man over a tiny helpless baby? Don't worry, I'm not going to ask for much. In fact, it is more symbolic than anything else. I want you to go out as a couple and leave the baby or children behind and do something entirely devoted to adult pleasures – even if you can't do it often, make a point of putting a date in the calendar and making it a firm commitment. I'd also like you to make an effort to dress up and look nice for each other. In effect, I want you to say, by your actions, 'I care about you and we're not just mother and father but a loving couple too.'

Isabel, twenty-nine, loved being a mother and was so wrapped up in her second baby that she joked she never wanted her children to leave home – or at the very least they should buy the house next door! However, after a little persuading, she did agree to visit the local wine bar while her mother babysat. 'If there was a problem or we decided that it was not a good idea, I could have been home in less than five minutes,' Isabel explained, 'and I agreed to go for one hour only.' It was really hard and for the first fifteen minutes Isabel had to fight the urge to flee. 'I kept thinking of that lovely milky smell of freshly bathed, fed and sleeping baby, and I wanted to rush home and take a deep breath. Why did I want to be anywhere else than with my baby? But I told myself, Don't be stupid. It's only an hour and if gets too much Terry will understand. It's not like you're addicted to your baby! Although, for a moment, that's how it felt. I had this ache, this need to hold her. Fortunately, it soon passed.' Isabel discovered that it was really nice to be alone with Terry again. 'In many ways, it was like old times when we were first courting. In fact, we stayed out for an hour and a half and agreed that we would do it again sometime.'

Ultimately, it doesn't matter what you talk about – although I'd prefer it wasn't about the baby – as long as you have some couple time in the first three months after the baby's arrival. If this is not possible, please tell each other: 'I love you and although I love our baby, I do miss time alone together and I want to make it a priority that we have some couple time – and really soon.' In this way, you're letting the other know that they *are* important to each you – rather than expecting them to know – and giving permission for the topic to be discussed (rather than swept under the carpet).

While my last request is often harder for women, this next one can be harder for men. With your mother and father returning centre stage, you need to prioritize your partner over your parents.

Nigel, thirty-six, had a three-year-old son and a six-month-old baby daughter and his mother would kindly look after them from time to time. On one occasion, Kim, his thirty-four-year-old wife, went to collect the children. The boy started playing up and Nigel's mother admonished him. 'Why did you have to start misbehaving when Mummy arrives? You've been such a good boy.'

In their next counselling session, Kim was furious. 'What was she trying to say? That I'm a disruptive influence on my own son?'

'Not at all, it's just that they were excited about you coming back and she was just trying to calm them down,' Nigel tried to soothe her.

'That's right. Take her side. Like you always do.'

'She does a lot for us and we should be grateful.'

It was clear that Kim believed Nigel was prioritizing his mother's feelings over hers. Nigel, of course, denied it.

'What would happen if you spoke to your mother?' I asked Nigel.

He looked doubtful and I could understand his reticence.

Mothers are powerful people in their sons' lives, and seeing her interact with your own children is bound to bring back unconscious memories. It is easy to be robbed of adult skills (negotiating, compromising etc.) and return to being a child (people-pleasing, sulking etc.). In the meantime, men think their wife 'knows I love her and will do anything for her'; they imagine their relationship is protected and therefore they can 'temporarily' forget about her needs and concentrate on appeasing their mother. Unfortunately, their wife is feeling vulnerable, unsure of herself and easily undermined. In her mind, his behaviour is an act of betrayal.

After a long discussion, Nigel did decide to talk to his mother and tell her that Kim was upset about her comments. He would explain that they understood that she might need to reprimand their son when she looked after him. However, when their son was misbehaving and they were around, they would sort it themselves.

Especially if you've just had a baby, your priority should be putting a boundary round your new family unit. Obviously, it shouldn't be so high that no outside influences or advice can penetrate, but equally it shouldn't be so low that anyone can wander in and make supposedly helpful comments.

Whether it is your parents or your partner's parents who are causing the rift, it is important to work as a team. So how do you achieve this goal?

- Start by discussing what you both agree on. (This shows that you're both on the same side.)
- Ask your partner how he or she is feeling at the moment. (This demonstrates that you're interested in your partner's emotions and accept that he or she might have cause to be upset.)
- Give your partner a chance to explain why he or she feels this way. (You might also learn something new about him or her.)
- Communicate your thoughts about the situation. (Although it might be helpful, in the long run, to see things from either your mother or father's or your in-laws' perspective, leave it until everybody is feeling calmer.)

- Give yourself time to reflect. Finally, you are both ready to process any advice and decide whether to reject the outside influence or take part of it on board.

Summing Up

Children turn your life upside-down and, however much you try to prepare, there will be shocks and setbacks. If you're not careful, instead of supporting each other, you can end up feeling alone or, worse still, blaming each other. So instead of coming down hard on yourself or your partner for any perceived shortcomings, accept that you will both occasionally get things wrong. Parenting ability emerges over time, through tackling challenges and overcoming difficulties. When you're feeling tired and stressed, it is important to tell yourself that this phase won't last for ever and to be kind to each other.

Unfortunately, having children brings back problems from your own childhood – which you thought had long since been buried – and forces you to focus on your current relationship with your parents. Fortunately, there is also the potential to heal old wounds and right old wrongs.

What Babies (and Children) Need

Babies are small and helpless and sometimes it feels like their needs are endless. They have to be fed, winded, changed, picked up, put down, rocked to sleep. There's so much paraphernalia that has to be bought too, from nappies, wipes and changing mats to folding buggies and car seats. And that's just the beginning: soon they will be crawling, and then toddling off and exploring the world. It's not just their physical needs but their emotional welfare you need to consider: you want them to be happy, mix well with other children and succeed at school. In fact, if you have a quiet moment with your baby in your arms, it's easy to be overwhelmed by all the responsibilities and how much this tiny creature relies on you. You want to do your best for your son or daughter, your very best (and possibly be the sort of parent you wished your parents could have been). But where do you start? What makes a good parent? How do you know if you're doing OK? There are so many components to the job of parenting, and so many competing definitions of what being a successful parent means, I've decided to boil down what babies and children need to its essence. In this way, you can decide what is truly important and not be distracted by the peripheral parts of parenting.

Your child's emotional needs

Have you ever seen a small child running down the street full of joy and the excitement of being alive? They're probably two or three and going faster than their little legs will carry them. It's almost inevitable that they'll fall over and start to cry. Perhaps they've scuffed their knee or the damage is to their pride or it's out of simple frustration, but they've burst into tears. Hopefully, one of their parents is watching, picks them up and soothes them. In a couple of minutes, the child is laughing again and either walking beside their mother or father or running off again – probably a little slower.

This small drama is good parenting in a nutshell as it demonstrates the two key elements: helping your children regulate their emotions and fostering their independence. The first is important because small children don't have the ability (knowledge, experience and a developed enough brain) to soothe themselves. The second is vital because, much as we love our children, we bring them up to leave us. We don't want them still living on our sofa at forty!

Unfortunately, this simple scenario of the child falling over and being picked up is harder than it seems. Many parents are tired and stressed and instead of lovingly rescuing their children are annoyed: 'I told you to look where you were going but did you listen to me?' or 'That will teach you.' They might even give them a smack for being disobedient. Others will pick their child up but tell him or her not to make a fuss out of nothing: 'Big boys don't cry' or 'It's only a graze. Look, there's nothing there.' Instead of helping their son or daughter regulate their emotions, these parents are effectively saying, 'Don't feel.' Occasionally, I see parents who try the philosophical approach and tell their child: 'Crying won't make it better' (basically they're encouraging their son or daughter to rationalize away their feelings). Other parents are too busy talking to a friend on the phone or catching up on some work. Their son or daughter bursts into tears and gets no reaction, so they have to exaggerate their upset and start to wail before getting any attention (and therefore are encouraged to set their internal upset thermostat so high that they need lots of soothing before they can feel safe again).

Not only is it important for parents to pick up their children when they fall, they also need to let them run off in the first place. Right from the moment babies can crawl and toddlers can walk, they want to test their independence and explore the world. However, they also need to feel safe. So our small child running down the street is probably looking back over his or her shoulder to look for Mum or Dad and checking they are still there. Unfortunately, it is hard to let our children make mistakes. We want to run after them and grab their hand before they fall over, or keep such a tight eye on them that they don't escape in the first place. After all, it's a dangerous world, with speeding cars, aggressive dogs and sharp objects. Obviously, we have to look out for children's safety – because in the same way they can't regulate their feelings, they can't judge risk – but it is equally important that we don't pass on our anxieties either. (The speeding cars are the other side of the park railings, the dogs are more interested in chasing sticks, and it's highly unlikely that our child will trip and hit his or her head on the bench.)

Returning to my example of children running down the street and being lovingly picked up: their parents have offered everything they need. First, the chance to test their independence and learn an important lesson for the future: I go faster running downhill and therefore I'm more likely to fall over. (It will stick much better than shouting, 'Be careful!') Second, when things have gone wrong, their parents have kissed it better, rubbed it better or given them a hug. (They've learnt it's OK to express their distress; someone will attend to their needs and help them regulate their feelings.)

Don't worry if once or twice you've been slow off the mark picking up your son or daughter – you can't have eyes in the back of your head. What matters is not one particular occasion but the pattern. If you're still concerned that you might not have been helping your child regulate their emotions or develop age-appropriate levels of independence, it's never too late to change, and when they're young small adjustments in your behaviour will reap big dividends.

So let's look at the key stages – baby, toddler, child and teenager – and how to regulate emotions and encourage independence.

BABIES

There are hundreds of ways of successfully caring for a baby across many different cultures and times. Ultimately, it doesn't really matter if you breastfeed or not, return to work or stay at home, or any of the other current controversies. What counts is that your baby feels safe and the care is reliable, predictable and available.

John Bowlby (1907–90) was a British psychologist famous for his pioneering work on child development and in particular the importance of parents in providing a secure base for their baby. 'These early attachment experiences then determine how one views the lovability and worthiness of the self, what it means to be cared for and care about others, what to pay attention to and what to forget, how to manage emotions and how to behave, what to expect from other people.'

In many ways, looking after a baby is an interactive project. Your son or daughter arrives in the world with his or her unique store of genes that will be triggered and shaped by the world around him or her – which principally is you. Equally, you will be shaped by his or her needs and demands. Perhaps your baby is more sensitive and reacts more strongly to stimulation than others and therefore needs careful handling. Maybe your baby is calmer and more robust and you can pass him to almost anybody to hold. Slowly but surely you will get into the rhythm of each other and begin to customize one another.

So although you might think experts hold all the answers – and certainly we can help by teaching skills and providing fresh insights – you and your partner are the real experts on your baby. After all, he or she is shaped by hours and hours of interaction with you, and his or her brain and emotions are being programmed by your personality and your family's way of doing things.

HOW TO HELP REGULATE

Feelings in babies start in a very basic way. They are either content or distressed, comfortable or uncomfortable. Your job is to help your baby bring these intense emotions down to a more manageable level (so when they're older they can learn to do it for themselves). The obvious ways of regulating your baby are touch and sound – holding, stroking, singing, cooing, playing, talking in a sweet soft voice, making eye contact. If you are calm and can tolerate his or her uncomfortable feelings, your baby will slowly synchronize with your relaxed, regular heartbeat and feel comfortable again. That's why it is particularly effective to hold your baby close to your chest.

However, if you are angry or hostile and pick up your baby abruptly or so tightly that it is stifling, his or her distress will be amplified by yours (and potentially yours by his or hers). Conversely, if you are insensitive to your baby's crying, you will upset the delicate programming that's starting in his or her brain. (These babies get no help bringing their distress down to a manageable level – beyond crying themselves to the point of exhaustion.)

Even from a very young age, babies are trying to make sense of the world around them and work out the difference between a smiling or a cross face. If mothers and fathers act in predictable ways, babies begin to learn the pattern: If I cry, someone will pick me up gently. Their brains are being programmed with an important message: It's OK to have these horrible feelings because they can be attended to and managed.

Equally importantly, they learn that if they gurgle happily, other people will mirror back those good emotions and support them. Slowly but surely, they are getting introduced into the human race and learning what to expect from other people.

HOW TO FOSTER INDEPENDENCE

Small babies are still very much part of their mother. She provides the milk to feed them and boost their immune protection. Her heart and blood pressure help regulate theirs. Her touch helps stimulate their muscles and encourage growth and, as I've already explained, disperse their stress hormones. So in many ways it seems extraordinary to talk about fostering independence at this stage. Yet being a mother can become a form of slavery, where you are not free to come and go. It is hard to be happy and contented if you can never step away, take a break and mentally regroup (and as babies mirror their mothers, they won't be contented either).

So please, after the initial newborn stage, foster a little independence – which could be more your independence from your baby – and allow other people to help out. Remember, what counts is that the care is reliable, predictable and consistent. If you're a mother, that could be your partner. If you're a father, step forward and become part of your baby's support team. If there are other people who are happy to assist, please welcome them with open arms.

Moving on to helping your baby feel safe – even when you're in the next room: use your voice as a transitional object (something to take the place of the physical parent–child bond). I recommend singing or giving your baby a running commentary: 'I'm just going into the next room to fetch some nice wipes to take all that goo off your face' or 'Where are those wipes? Where are they hiding?' followed by 'Guess who's coming back in a moment?' Make the tone of your voice upbeat and exciting – as if this is most thrilling news ever – because babies only hear messages as positive or negative (and you don't want there to be any confusion).

Another idea is playing peek-a-boo with your baby. This is where you disappear out of his or her eyeline, like behind the stroller, for just a second and then pop back up again. You need to play it several times, so your baby can predict the pattern. First, you will disappear (potentially frightening) and then you will reappear (reassuring). Even at this early age, they are learning to cope with separation, something that will stand them in good stead when they are adults: what we fear (abandonment) can also be thrilling and have a positive side (independence).

How to Regulate Yourself

Understanding how your mood impacts on your baby can be a little unsettling. There's no problem when you're feeling relaxed and happy, but life isn't always like that. What about the times when your partner is yelling, 'Where are the keys?', your toddler is scribbling over some important paperwork and you've only had three hours' sleep? In fact, how can you regulate your baby's emotions when you're not quite certain how to regulate your own?

Don't worry, most people are equally shaky on this concept, but mastering it will not only help you raise a happy child but also improve your relationship with your partner and make you feel more grounded in your own skin.

1. Think for a moment: how do you currently soothe yourself or take the edge off your stress? Write down as many as possible ways on a piece of paper.
2. Divide them into positive ones (which not only work at the time but have no long-term unwanted consequences) and negative ones (which temporarily make us feel better but often come back and bite us). For example, positive ways of soothing include taking a couple of deep breaths, counting to ten before

speaking, soaking in a hot bath, making a cup of tea, having your hair done, talking to a friend on the phone. Negative ones might be stuffing your face with chocolate, drinking a bottle of wine, switching off (for example, not engaging with your partner's lost keys) or shouting at your partner: 'How should I know where your bloody keys are?' (which gets the anger out but makes matters worse).

3. Think: how could you expand the positive ways of soothing and cut down on the negative ways?

4. Look at whether you are still expecting your partner to regulate your feelings – much as you were soothed by your parents when you were a child – and getting angry when he or she fails. (For example, the partner who had lost his or her keys wants the other one to find them and make him or her feel better.) Of course, our loved ones can help soothe us from time to time – especially in times of adversity – but ultimately we must take responsibility for regulating ourselves.

5. Next, offer yourself the same deal that you're going to offer your baby. You don't question whether your baby has the 'right' to be distressed or happy, and I'd like you to accept and acknowledge your feelings too – especially the negative ones, which most people would rather ignore or suppress.

6. Identify the emotion and mentally tell yourself: I'm feeling … For example, 'I'm annoyed with my partner (for demanding that I put down everything and find the keys).' You'll be surprised how difficult this can be – partly because we go to extraordinary lengths to avoid difficult feelings and partly because we seldom stop and think. However, it is useful to know if you are simply annoyed, rather than angry, bitter or boiling over with rage.

7. Repeat the feelings to yourself. Just by naming them, you will begin to feel calmer.

8. Finally, you're ready to discover what your feelings are trying

to tell you – because negative reactions are there for a reason – and start to act on them. Returning to our example, the couple could decide mornings are too rushed and it might be easier to prepare as much as possible the night before.

Remember, it takes time and energy to become more in tune with yourself. However, you need to understand your own feelings to be able to read your baby's.

■ ■ ■ ■ ■ ■

TODDLERS

There is a massive amount of development in the brain between six and twelve months old. All the neurons – the nerve cells that communicate information – are there at birth, but it takes time and exposure to the world to begin to connect them and make them work. Around toddlerhood, the frontal cortex begins to mature and babies can register fear, followed by sadness, shame and guilt (which are there to help us control our behaviour and fit into our family).

It goes without saying that these are difficult and painful feelings and toddlers need to learn to accept and tolerate them, and discover that there are ways of dealing with them. (I will explain how in a moment.) It is not just negative emotions: toddlers need help dealing with the other end of the spectrum – like joy and excitement.

Dr Allan Schore is a leading researcher in neuropsychology on the clinical faculty of the Department of Psychiatry and Biobehavioral Sciences at UCLA, and has been studying how psychological and biological factors interact during the first two years of life. 'Much of my work is now not only swinging around trauma and negativity but also the positive emotions of interest, excitement and enjoyment. Joy has something to do with the quality of life and the pole or opposite of joy would go to shame. The attachment to the mother is therefore not only minimizing negative states but she's maximizing positive states.'

Unfortunately, lots of parents are not comfortable with strong feelings themselves – whether positive or negative – and if you can't bear those feelings in yourself, you won't be able to bear them in your children. So these parents tell their offspring: 'Shut up' or 'Don't try it on with me' or 'There'll be tears before bedtime.' In effect, the toddlers have to regulate their parents by being good boys or girls (and not getting too excited or too upset). On the surface, these children seem calm and pliant, but their emotions are going through the roof. As there is nobody to regulate them, they have no option but to switch off or dissociate themselves from their feelings – which stores up problems for the future.

Another common pattern at this stage, which has equally far-reaching consequences, is parents who are sometimes concerned and sometimes switched off. These toddlers are also forced to register the state of their parents' minds. However, rather than suppress their feelings, they exaggerate them in a bid to get their parents' attention. They end up becoming overly aware of their feelings, and crying hysterically or throwing temper tantrums. These are horrible for their parents – who are equally ambivalent about sadness, shame and guilt themselves – so rather than calmly helping their sons and daughters to regulate their emotions, they will try and suppress them (by blocking the upset with sweets or some other treat, or alternatively shouting at their child). The result is that the toddler's feelings are like a car speeding out of control when suddenly the brakes have been slammed on.

HOW TO HELP REGULATE

Every toddler has tantrums. Sometimes it is frustration that their arms can't reach something, or they are tired, but more often than not they are upset and don't have the words or skills yet to express themselves. So although it is tempting to try and discipline or reprimand them, you are wasting your energy (and probably winding yourself up, and because your toddler mirrors your mood, making the situation even worse). Think of your child's brain as being only partially wired and the strong emotions have tripped the fuse. The lights can't come back on until everything has calmed down. So how do you achieve that?

In many ways, the first step is the hardest: put your stuff to one side. I know toddlers choose the worse place possible – like the middle of the supermarket – and you're aware of all the other shoppers thinking: He doesn't know how to control that kid or Why is she dragging that child round the shops rather than taking it to the swings and slides? It doesn't matter what they think (and most probably these are your issues put into other people's mouths). So stop weighing the apples or looking at your watch and worrying about getting to playgroup on time. Instead of getting upset or thinking about the inconvenience, frame the tantrums as an opportunity to help your child's development. Crouch down so you're at the same level and look your son or daughter in the eye.

Next imagine what your child is feeling and why, and put it into words: 'You're *angry* because *you wanted the sweets*' or 'You're *upset* because *you want to go to the park.*' I call this technique 'Acknowledge and Name', because you're going to acknowledge the upset and name the feeling. If you have no idea why your child is throwing a tantrum, just concentrate on identifying the emotions. Keep your voice calm, low and soothing and repeat your sentence until you have his or her complete attention and their emotions have begun to return to normal. It's at this point that you can begin to reason or explain: 'We'll have tea when we get home and we're going to have sausages, you like that.' Alternatively, you can distract – for example, let your child play with the little mirror from your handbag or have a game of I-spy.

A hug is also a good idea as it physically and emotionally holds a child and shows that they are equally acceptable when they're upset as when they're happy, and even more importantly that you care about their feelings (and not just the nice ones). In addition, you have also helped your son or daughter begin to name, understand and deal with difficult emotions.

HOW TO FOSTER INDEPENDENCE

Toddlers need to explore, but they have no knowledge of the world and how dangerous it can be. So how do you balance their need to be free and discover things for themselves with your need to keep them safe? I know this is a controversial idea but I'm a big fan of playpens as they allow children independent play – without us forever joining in and showing them how to put one brick on top of another or which shape goes through the hole. Lots of parents are uncomfortable with walking reins, tethers and wrist links, but they give children a degree of autonomy and mean your whole communication is not 'Hold my hand', 'Put that back' and 'Come over here.'

You can help your toddler begin to decide for him- or herself what is right or wrong by using 'no' sparingly. (I'm sure you know lots of kids who think they have double-barrelled names: Jamie-No or Lucy-No!) If your toddler is about to do something that you want to stop – like reaching up to a coffee table to grab a glass of water – make a small 'Ahh' noise in the back of your throat. It acts as a mild corrective and your son or daughter has the option to decide to stop for him- or herself. You'll be surprised how often it works (please praise if it does) and you can keep 'no' for when you really need it.

In safe environments, like a park, let your toddler run off and decide for him- or herself what is an OK distance. If you're concerned that your child has gone too far, instead of running after him or her, try calling out his or her name and getting his or her attention, and then pretend to run in the opposite direction. Guess what? Your child will turn round and chase you. It seems like a fun game but you're also teaching him or her to watch you.

Improve Your Toddler's Emotional Dictionary

The more words your son or daughter knows, the better he or she will be able to express him- or herself. Unfortunately, even as adults we are not always clear what is an emotion and what is a thought. Often in my counselling room, I ask people to name the feeling and they will say: 'I feel he hasn't heard a word I've said' or 'I feel she is blanking me.' I have to push to get them to name the feeling rather than explain the thought. For example: are they upset, angry, misunderstood? Look at the list below of common uncomfortable feelings and try to put them into your everyday vocabulary, so they trickle down into your toddler's brain. For example, use these feeling words to discuss characters in the book you're reading to your child or the programme that you're watching together on the TV. When he or she is having a tantrum, don't worry whether he or she knows the word yet; here is a great opportunity to learn.

Afraid	Upset	Lonely
Anxious	Annoyed	Left out
Ashamed	Angry	Confused
Nervous	Frustrated	Disappointed
Sorry	Misunderstood	Jealous
Unsure	Worried	Sad

CHILDREN OVER THREE

Up to this point, children have principally seen the world through their parents' eyes. Their family's way of doing things is the only way. (If they've been to a nursery or a childminder, this becomes an extension of their regular routine, and the people part of their extended family.) Even when your child has gone into unfamiliar surroundings – like a mother-and-toddler or a playgroup – either you or your partner has been there or only left him or her for a short while. So this is the age when your son or daughter begins to be exposed to the wider world and learn the rules (which could be different from yours). They will soon be going to school, making new friends and discovering different ways of doing things. Three-plus is a time of transition from babyhood (and complete dependence) into being a small child (and the beginning of independence), and children can swing wildly from one extreme to the other. This can be bewildering for parents, who never know quite what to expect, and underlines the importance of regulating children.

HOW TO HELP REGULATE

There is so much to discover and so much information to process, it can be overwhelming for a small brain. It helps to have a regular routine of what happens when, so children know what is expected of them. In effect, there is a time to get up, to dress, to have breakfast, to clean their teeth, and so on. When everything goes in a predictable order, children can focus on the new and surprising stuff – rather than encounter it with their brain already overloaded from making sense of how the regular things are being done today. In effect, routine is safe and calming because children know where they are.

The best way for children to learn is through positive feedback. Unfortunately, we tend to take for granted what's going well and focus on what isn't. Recently, I witnessed a mother having coffee in a café with her two daughters under five. She wanted to listen to the conversation between the woman behind the counter and another regular customer and pitch in with the odd comment herself. So when the children were eating their crisps and talking to each other, she ignored them. When they started kicking each other or stealing each other's crisps, she gave them her undivided attention: 'Sit up straight', 'Don't do that.' In effect, she was rewarding their bad behaviour (because children would rather have negative attention than none at all). It was not very long before both children were in tears and the mother was exasperated. I wonder what would have happened if she had praised what she'd liked: 'You're sitting up really nicely at that table' and 'You're eating your own crisps, that's really polite.' Not only would she have taught her children what was expected in these un-familiar surroundings but she would also have had the chance of a bit of un-interrupted adult conversation. In addition, her children would have had a clear sense of the rules and been able to regulate their own behaviour rather than being forever corrected.

One of my key messages to clients in unhappy relationships is how carrots work better than sticks. It's even more important when dealing with children rather than adults. Try and make the feedback as detailed as possible, so your child knows exactly what they've done right and why you are pleased. For example: 'You put on your own clothes this morning, that was really helpful' or 'You hung your coat on the hook when you came home, that was really tidy.' This technique is called 'descriptive praise' because you describe the good behaviour (and thereby encourage your children to do it again) rather than just give empty compliments like 'What a clever boy' or 'You're a wonderful girl.'

Stephen Grosz is a psychoanalyst and lecturer at University College London. In his book *The Examined Life* (Chatto & Windus), he quotes research by Carol Dweck – whom we met in the last chapter – into children's reactions to praise. One group were complimented for their hard work ('You did really well, you must have tried hard') and the other were praised for their talent ('You did really well, you're so clever'). Unfortunately, the children who were praised for being clever worried more about failure, took fewer risks and experienced a drop in their self-esteem. No wonder Grosz was anxious when he overheard a nursery assistant's empty praise for his daughter's drawing: 'Wow, you're really an artist.' So he set himself the task of solving the problem: if praise alone doesn't build confidence, what does? He found the answer watching an eighty-year-old remedial teacher at work. When a four-year-old boy in her class stopped drawing a picture and looked up, Grosz thought he was looking for praise, but instead the teacher commented on the drawing: 'There's a lot of blue in your picture.' It encouraged the boy to explain and draw more. 'Unhurried, she talked to the child, but more important she observed, she listened. She was present,' writes Grosz. 'Being present builds a child's confidence because it lets the child know that she is worth thinking about. Without this, a child might come to believe her activity is just a means to gain praise, rather than an end in itself. How can we expect a child to be attentive, if we're not attentive to her?'

HOW TO FOSTER INDEPENDENCE

Another way of building children's self-confidence is letting them do things for themselves. So although it is quicker, for example, to button up their coat yourself, it is better if you let them get on with it. Follow it up with a bit of descriptive praise: 'You did up all your own buttons, you're becoming a big boy.' Don't go over the top, for example, 'You're so talented' or 'the best girl in the world', as children know when the praise is empty and you'll have no superlatives left for something genuinely spectacular.

What tasks could your children perform? Even young ones can straighten up their duvet in the morning, dry themselves after a bath, put their toys away or lay the table for tea. Doing small jobs gives small children agency (by which I mean having some control over their environment) and fosters independence. Once you've established a family routine, your children will start to adopt it as their own – rather than forever being told 'Do this' or asked 'Why haven't you done that?'

You can encourage children's cooperation (and increase their agency) by helping them to think ahead. Adults have a list in their head of tasks to complete: stop and buy some milk, get home, prepare tea, do my emails and be ready to go out by seven. Children, however, live in the moment, which is one of their great charms but causes stress and arguments when they want to play but you need to rush them out of the door. No wonder there are tears and tantrums and you lose your temper.

I witnessed a good example of how thinking ahead builds cooperation when travelling by train with my new puppy. Pumpkin was just over a year old, cute enough to be a magnet to small children but steady enough for him to be safe. A three-year-old girl in our carriage was completely entranced, becoming more and more confident about stroking him and putting her arms round his neck as the journey progressed. Her mother was aware that her daughter wanted to continue playing with Pumpkin (and possibly take him home too!). There could have been an ugly scene. However, she helped her daughter think ahead by saying, 'It's our stop next and we'll have to get off, so give Pumpkin a last stroke.' Children often get upset because our instructions come, for them, out of the blue and they find it hard to switch from one activity to another. Fortunately, her mother had given her daughter enough time to prepare. A couple of minutes later, she explained what needed to be done next. 'Let's get you into your pushchair, so we can get off the train easily.' Rather than having to be lifted into the pushchair, the child undid the straps and climbed in herself – without complaint – and was ready to leave when we arrived at their station.

You can further help your children 'own' what comes next by asking them a question so they can think ahead for themselves, rather than just be told. For example, you could say: 'We're coming to our station. What do you do before we get off the train?'

PLANNING REALISTICALLY

This next idea comes from puppy-training – I know this will sound strange but stay with me. One of the most important tasks is to get your puppy to walk to heel, without pulling on the lead. If you don't get it right, you'll spend the next twelve-plus years being dragged behind an excited dog (something I know from experience). The book I bought advised that when my puppy pulled I should stop immediately and wait until he sat down. When his bottom was on the pavement, I could start walking again. (Interestingly, the advice was to let him discover the key to moving ahead for himself – rather than saying, 'Sit' – as this would make the lesson sink in faster and better. A bit like asking questions to your children on a think-ahead rather than forever telling them what to do.) So far, so good, but the crucial advice that helped me crack walking to heel was 'Never go anywhere with a puppy when you're in a hurry.' With my previous dog, I'd be rushing to the post office before it closed and let him get away with pulling, not sitting at the kerb when I crossed the road, or lunging at a passing leaf. The more I let him get away with things, the worse his walking to heel became and the more likely he was to pull next time we were out together. In effect, I had set myself up for a lifetime of pulling on the lead.

So here's this tip in a nutshell: 'Don't go anywhere with a small child in a hurry'. They know when you're up against the clock. They know you will buy them off with sweets. They know you will put up with bad or whiny behaviour – because you haven't got time to sort it out. (You're also too busy clock-watching to help your child think ahead or praise any helpful behaviour.) Obviously it is impractical to *never* go anywhere with a small child when you're in a hurry. However, you *can* plan realistically and not try to fit too much into your day. Remember, small children live in the moment: you don't need to stuff their day with exciting activities (because they can learn so much from something simple like going to the local shops – if you use your imagination) and they're at their best when not harried and hurried. So do less and take longer over it.

CHILDREN SIX-PLUS

With better coordination, strength and motor skills, children are developing quickly: trying different sports, learning to read, write and draw. They are also beginning to find their own interests and tastes (which might be different from yours) and make their own friends (rather than play with the children of your friends). While previously their main focus might have been on How acceptable am I to my parents, siblings and grandparents?, their attention switches to their peer group. At this stage, children start to identify as boys or girls and develop strong loyalties to clubs (like Brownies, Scouts, football or drama), idols (pop or TV stars) and of course their friends. This comes hand-in-hand with a strong sense of fairness and the importance of following rules. However, if they fall out with their peer group, it can seem like the end of the world (and they need a lot of help and understanding from their parents to handle these difficult feelings). Ultimately, the most important lesson to learn at this age is that it's possible to have a disagreement but still love someone.

HOW TO HELP REGULATE

Parents need endless patience because small children are always asking difficult questions – like 'Why is water wet?' – as they try to make sense of the wider world. Although these might test our knowledge of physics, history or maths, what is most unsettling is when they question our rules and test our boundaries. It might seem they are being difficult or rebellious but they just need to understand (so they can adopt the rules themselves). Children of six-plus are obsessed with 'fairness' and their standard answer to any request is often 'Why?' or more likely, 'It's not fair.'

Don't get drawn into a debate about the rights and wrongs but ask why they think, for example, they should stay sitting at the table while eating their food. If they refuse to answer or claim they don't know, ask them to have a guess. They will probably come quite close. For example, 'I'll make a mess' or 'I'll get a stomach ache if I run around.' Praise what they get right and add any explanation of your own. Next, get them to repeat why they shouldn't get up from the table: 'I shouldn't get up from the table because I'll put sticky fingers every-where.' By repeating rules, children own them and begin to regulate themselves.

If your child refuses to answer or runs away, let it drop until they are calmer and able to think straight. At this age, children will always need to ask something, so wait for your opportunity. Put down whatever you're doing, give them your full attention and say: 'I'd be happy to answer your question but first will you answer mine: Why shouldn't you get up from the table while you're still eating?'

Praise your son or daughter if they have the right answer, or some element of their answer is correct, and ask them to repeat the reason again.

Next time they stay at the table until given permission to leave, use descriptive praise to explain why you approve: 'Well done for sitting still at the table, that was really polite.'

Children of this age still need help processing difficult feelings and often end up acting out their distress. It is tempting to discipline them or give them a good talking-to for bad behaviour – for example, shoving one of their teammates while playing football. Instead of concentrating on *what* they have done, spend a moment with them to look at *why*, and thereby acknowledge their upset.

Hopefully they might be able to name the feelings for themselves, so ask: 'What did you feel when you pushed your friend?'

If they don't know or give their thoughts rather than feelings – 'He was calling me names' – once again, ask them to guess. Be aware, they are struggling with the most toxic of all human emotions: shame. (In effect, we feel that we are not good enough or a bad person, which is the opposite of feeling acceptable and loved.) Although shame is a difficult feeling at any age, it is particularly hard between six and twelve, when we're desperately trying to fit in.

If your son or daughter can't name the feeling, provide the word for them: 'You were angry' or 'It felt unfair.'

Next, address the thoughts attached to the feelings: 'Your friend seemed to get all the passes' or 'Her dad has been giving her extra coaching' or whatever.

My rule of thumb is *accept the feelings* (we can't help how we feel) but *challenge the thoughts*. So instead of saying, 'Don't be stupid' or 'You shouldn't do that', be sympathetic and then help with the underlying problem. For example, you could ask your son or daugh-ter: 'How could you get more passes from teammates?' or offer solutions: 'Your uncle's a good coach, shall we get some advice from him?'

By following this pattern – identifying the feeling and then looking at the underlying causes – you will have helped your child learn perhaps the most important lesson of all. We should listen to our feelings – rather than ignore them, suppress them or distract ourselves – because our feelings, especially the negative ones, are telling us something important.

Once you've taken any learning from the event, that's the moment to put it right. So, for example, encourage your child to apologize to his or her friend – whatever the provocation – as he or she broke the rules (of the game or of friendship). Apologizing reinforces the idea that you can fall out, make up and still be friends.

While I'm on the subject, when you've done something wrong yourself please apologize to your child. For example, 'I'm sorry I shouted at you, that was wrong' or 'I'm sorry I lost my temper and didn't listen properly to what you said.' Not only are you modelling the behaviour that you want from them, but you're showing your children that you play by the rules yourself (rather than having one rule for yourself and one for everybody else). Ultimately, knowing that there are rules which everybody abides by makes children feel secure and less anxious.

HOW TO FOSTER INDEPENDENCE

Although children of six-plus want your physical presence less, they need more time alone with you to process their difficult emotions. That's why I recommend regular one-on-one time with each child – especially with the parent of the same sex – so your children can begin to learn what it means to be a boy or a girl, and how men and women do things. It could be reading a story each night, or bathing your child, but set aside ten minutes (every day or at least five times a week) when you can be quiet together and your child has your undivided attention. (If you can follow an activity together as well, that's great.) I know from my clients how busy families are and how much I'm asking – particularly of men, who often prioritize work. However, your children need regular time alone with you (rather than mediated through your wife) and that's much more important than all the gadgets, holidays and bigger back gardens that you're toiling so hard to buy.

Most days, these few minutes will be full of trivia. However, time alone keeps you informed about the minutiae of their lives (who's their best friend today and the name of their football coach) and provides the opportunity for important conversations and a safety net as they launch themselves into the wider world. There is a second advantage to time alone with you: fewer squabbles between siblings. This is because each child feels secure about your love and therefore is less likely to compete with their brother or sister for your attention. It might be tempting to weigh in when your children fall out with their friends or each other, but hold back on minor disputes, as this will give them the opportunity to resolve things for themselves.

Finally, it is important to give your child enough space to develop interests for him- or herself. Erik Erickson (1902–94) was a German-born American developmental psychologist who coined the term 'identity crisis'. His life's work was understanding how we develop our identity – possibly because he was born after his mother had an affair, and his biological father's identity was kept a secret. In addition, Erikson was blond and blue-eyed and raised as Jewish. At temple school the kids teased him for being Nordic, and at grammar school for being Jewish.

Erikson described the stage from five to twelve as the 'Age of Competence' as children start recognizing their special abilities and pursuing particular interests. However, he warned that if they were not allowed to discover their own talents in their own time, they would lack motivation and develop low self-esteem and lethargy.

How to Deal with Your Frustration

Everybody gets frustrated with their children from time to time. The temptation is to beat yourself up – and maybe criticize your partner too – for not being patient enough (or maybe snap at the kids and be doubly down on yourself). However, in the same way that I want you to help your children accept their difficult and uncomfortable feelings, I'd like you to extend the same courtesy to yourself (and your partner). When one or both of you are feeling frustrated, ask yourself: Why am I frustrated? What are my feelings trying to tell me? What do I need to do differently?

Here are some possible answers:

- You and your child have got out of sync with each other. Perhaps you're responding not to the needs of your particular child but what you think they should be.
- You have not given enough descriptive praise and your child is acting up in order to get your attention, even if it is crabby and distracted attention, as that is better than none at all.

- Your children are unclear about the rules and what you want from them. In your head, for example, it's obvious that they should put on their shoes and be ready for school; but have you told them, nagged them and shouted at them, rather than getting them to think ahead and own the routine for themselves?
- You have been thinking too far ahead yourself. Instead of focusing on the next step, are you worrying, for example, about taking the car in for a service after lunch or how to balance the bills at the end of the month?
- You need to remove obstacles that make it harder for your children to cooperate. For example, they are less likely to be dressed if the TV is on. What could you do to make it easier for your children to succeed?
- You have been trying to fit too much into your day and you're making yourself stressed and anxious.
- You need to look after yourself more. How can you attend to everybody else's needs and keep on giving when you're close to empty yourself?
- You find it hard to ask for what you need. Perhaps you're hoping that your partner will come and give you a kiss on your forehead and say, 'You're doing so well' or 'I love you.' Instead of waiting, possibly for ever, why not ask your partner, rather than expect him or her to be a mind reader?

■ ■ ■ ■ ■ ■

TEENAGERS

Whatever happened to that pleasant and cooperative child? It might seem that overnight your son or daughter has been replaced by a surly and dismissive stranger, but teenage rebellion is a vital part of grow-ing up. Whereas the previous stages were all about belonging and fitting in, first to your family and then to their peer group, this one is centred on asserting independence and becoming their own person. The easiest place to start is saying, 'I don't want to be anything like my parents.' Obviously, it will feel incredibly rejecting to you. However, please be reassured: it is only once your children have questioned or rejected everything that you stand for that they can begin to form their own identity. In the end, they will probably choose to adopt many aspects of your lifestyle, morals and way of looking at the world. For example, my mother was a teacher (and her mother and her grandmother too). The last thing I wanted to be as a teenager was a teacher, but here I am, forty years later, writing books and teaching about relationships! So although this is a difficult life stage, and there will be times when you feel overwhelmed, I would be more concerned if your teenager was *not* rebelling.

Diana Baumrind is a US developmental psychologist (born in 1927) who worked at the Berkeley Institute for Human Development and conducted a series of important studies of Western parenting in the 1960s. She is best known for classifying three types of parents: Authoritarian (who expect high levels of conformity and compliance with little or no discussion of the rules), Permissive (who are indulgent, lenient and responsive but place few demands or controls on their children's behaviour) and Authoritative (who are demanding but also responsive to their children so there is discussion and explanation about the rules). Although there are pros and cons for all three styles, during the teenage years, the first two can become problematic.

Small children respond well to rules; however, teenagers need the reasons for something explained (rather than being told 'Because I say so') and to feel any punishment is both reasonable and fair. Therefore Authoritarian parents have to become more responsive to their children otherwise their son or daughter might have a spectacular teenage rebellion as they try to make themselves heard and taken seriously. With Permissive parenting, children tend to be more impulsive – as they've had little external help to regulate themselves – and can engage in heavy drinking or experiment with drugs during their teenage years. It is often necessary for permissive parents to introduce a consistent set of rules so their children have something solid to rebel against.

Authoritative parents should find it easier to negotiate with their teenager – because they have been used to explaining rather than demanding. However it is still hard to find a balance between hemming in your son or daughter with restrictions and setting standards for socially acceptable behaviour. There also needs to be plenty of time to consider each decision without, on the one hand, simply giving in to your child's desire or, on the other, falling in with the group consensus of other parents.

Finally, whatever your parenting style, it is important to remember that teenagers are incredibly vulnerable because they are trying on new identities and experiencing everything, like attention from the opposite sex or falling in love, for the first time. It is easy to tease them or put them down – especially if you are not that comfortable in your own skin – but be aware that words at this age resonate stronger and longer than you imagine.

HOW TO HELP REGULATE

Hopefully, you will be giving your children a secure base to rebel against – rather than making up the rules (or bending them) as you go along. It is particularly important that you and your partner present a united front – since children, and teenagers in particular, will do their best to divide and rule.

So while you might have got away with different rules for different parents when they were younger, it is important now to agree on four central tenets.

Be consistent. Otherwise, your children will spend their energy and exhaust your patience wheedling, testing your boundaries and looking for loopholes. Remember, you hold all the main cards (like money and keys to the car) while your children's only power is to wear you down. If you give in – because they've asked for hundredth time –

you've just trained them to pester for longer, and longer and longer. It might be hard to stand firm in the short term, but you've saved yourself lots of aggravation in the long term.

No arguing about the children in front of them. Otherwise, you're handing them ammunition to divide and rule.

No making policy on the spot. Give yourself time to think through new requests and discuss implications with your partner.

Back each other up even if you disagree. This is perhaps the hardest part of parenting teenagers – as you're bound to have different opinions – but I have more advice on being a team at the end of this section.

Ultimately, teenagers need time, attention and to have their rebellion centre stage – rather than in a dark corner because their mother and father are too busy working, fighting with each other or struggling with their own issues. If it does not seem safe for your son or daughter to rebel (because they don't want to add stress to a chaotic household or are too busy 'supporting' their parents and helping them through their distress), they will push their identity issues to one side. On the surface, these teenagers will seem 'really together' but in reality their adult persona is flimsy, without the space to experiment or discover their true self. (What normally happens is that they put off having their rebellion until they are older – normally around forty – when they have a spectacular mid-life crisis instead.)

While some teenagers opt out of rebelling altogether, others find their rebellion ignored or only noticed when they go spectacularly off the rails (with drink, drugs or teenage pregnancy). I know this sounds really scary but if you have been used to giving your son or daughter plenty of positive attention (and praising good behaviour), you are unlikely to fall into the trap of giving negative attention when they become teenagers.

HOW TO FOSTER INDEPENDENCE

Although teenagers want your presence less, they need you more – in sharp contrast to babies and toddlers, who might want you more but actually need you less. While any competent adult can change a nappy or cook a child tea, you don't want to delegate the important teenage issues – like choosing exam options, monitoring whether they've fallen in with the wrong crowd and offering moral guidance.

Unfortunately, it is really hard to strike the right balance between being in charge (because parents still have better judgement about risks and the long-term implications of any behaviour) and allowing teenagers enough freedom to discover who they are and what is right for them. However, do give your son or daughter room to develop their own cultural interests – being a punk, goth, metalhead or whatever is the first draft of defining who they are. At this age, there is nothing more annoying than your parents muscling in on your music or television programmes or, worse still, trying to be friends with your friends. If you're ever in doubt, think back to your own teenage years.

I would also choose your battles very carefully. Ultimately, we can't *make* anybody – our partners or our children – do anything, and we waste a lot of time and emotional energy in the process. (Although we can influence, encourage, teach, negotiate or make a deal.) If you find yourself trying to make a rule stick as a point of principle, please stop and have a rethink. For example, Laura, forty-two, had two teenage children – a daughter of twelve and a son of fifteen – and was fed up with them leaving the back door open.

'The dog comes in from the garden with his muddy paws and goes straight up to my bedroom and climbs on to my white bedspread. I've had to wash everything three times in the last week,' she complained. 'How can I make them close the door?'

Although I expected Laura to be annoyed when I shrugged and explained that it was impossible to *make* anybody do anything, she seemed relieved. 'I've tried nagging and shouting and of course they don't work. And now I realize that I'd been setting myself up for failure.'

So we discussed the techniques for thinking ahead and Laura decided to talk to her son and daughter when she was calm.

'Ask them what they should do when they come back into the house and why. When they can answer and repeat back the policy, they begin to own it.'

Next, Laura began to think of other ways to solve the problem – like closing her bedroom door and training the dog not to jump up on the furniture – but broke off halfway through. 'It would be really nice if someone listened to something I said!' The force of that statement almost took my breath away, so I stopped her and we looked deeper.

The back door had become a *point of principle* that was important to Laura but seemed totally random to her children, and her level of upset out of all proportion to their crime.

'What would be a much more important battle to win?' I asked.

'My son tries to get away with the minimum homework and as long as he scrapes through that's good enough for him.'

'So perhaps the listening to "something" should be homework, not shutting the back door?'

When Laura began to choose her battles, she reported back that she felt less out of control and the atmosphere at home was calmer.

■ ■ ■ ■ ■ ■

Sorting out Your Specific Parenting Differences

Creating a united front can be really difficult. Not only are teenagers experts at finding your weak points and exploiting them, but many of the dilemmas they pose need an answer one way or the other – for example, can your daughter go to the rock festival or not? – so you can't agree to differ. Here are some guidelines for avoiding the worst pitfalls.

- Give each other your undivided attention. There's no point trying to talk while one person is cooking or is on the computer.
- Set a limit on how long you're going to discuss the issue. (If you haven't come to a resolution by the end of the allotted time, it probably means you're going round in circles. Stop and make an appointment to talk again.)
- Stick to one topic at a time. (Resist the temptation to throw in similar situations, even if they back up your case, because you're making it harder for yourselves.)
- Start with what you agree on. For example, 'We both want the best for our children' or 'Schooling is a top priority.'
- Avoid describing the problem (which can be heard as blaming) but focus on finding an answer.
- It is important that both of you try and find solutions, so both of you have a stake in following it through.
- Never criticize your partner's ideas, as even seemingly stupid ones can trigger better ideas.
- Give positive feedback to your partner during the discussion: 'That was a good point' or 'I agree with you there.' This will help build agreement.
- Remember, there is no right or wrong way to bring up children – just lots of different opinions which deserve to be listened to and taken seriously.

Why couples fall out over their children

When an issue keeps coming back time and time again, it is nearly always about something deeper than, for example, what time children should go to bed or enforcing saying please and thank you. In my opinion, the argument is probably only 20 per cent about the topic under discussion and 80 per cent about hidden subjects.

Sometimes one partner is afraid to talk about what's really driving their anger for fear of being rejected. For example, the row about children's bedtimes could also be about sex – because one partner feels that unless they have enough adult time together *and* get into bed themselves at a decent time then they will never have enough sex. It is hard to admit that you feel unloved and easier to try and tackle what you consider the cause of the problem than own up and discuss possible solutions to the underlying issue.

Alternatively, one or both partners is not wholly aware of what's behind the argument – perhaps they have never stopped to think or the roots are too far back in their childhood. For example, the row about 'please' and 'thank you' could be important to one partner because their own father or mother was a dictator and extreme politeness could sometimes tame the anger. To the other partner, whose childhood did not make them feel anxious, this attitude makes no sense or, worse, seems over-the-top or stifling.

So if you're having repeat arguments, look at the following issues that lie at the bottom of most couples' hidden agendas.

MALE V. FEMALE PARENTING ENERGY

I'm going to state the obvious again, so please forgive me. A baby comes out of a woman. To her, he or she is a part of her and seems vulnerable in the big outside world. To a man, conversely, a baby is a separate and independent being. Therefore, when it comes to caring for children, men and women can end up having fundamentally different approaches and two different parenting energies. I label them 'male' and 'female'. (Although I have seen men radiate the female parenting energy and vice versa). So what are these energies? Female parenting tends to focus on *accepting* and male parenting on *challenging*.

Trevor and Louise, thirty-one and thirty-two, would frequently fall out about their two children's lunchboxes. Trevor thought his son, ten, and daughter, eight, should be making their own sandwiches for school, or when the family had a day out that they should help prepare the picnic.

'He'll get really angry if he finds out that I've done everything myself,' explained Louise. 'It can leave a horrible atmosphere over what should be relaxed family time. He'll open a sandwich and inspect it, trying to work out if the children cut the cheese and spread the pickle. Why can't he just enjoy himself? I don't mind. It's quicker and easier. I know what we've got and where it is.'

Trevor saw the issue differently. 'It's teaching them to be independent, to stand on their own two feet and not take stuff for granted. Why shouldn't they help out? It's not like any of our knives are sharp.'

'Can't you let them just be children instead of making them think about whether we've got enough bread and putting it on the shopping list? What are you so keen to prepare them for? Running their own sandwich business?'

'That's not such a bad idea.'

In effect, Louise felt that she was defending her children and accepting them as they were – especially since, as she saw it, he could be critical of their efforts. Meanwhile, Trevor wanted to challenge and stretch them.

'These are really valuable life lessons that they don't really get taught at school.'

Turn it around: It is easy to get entrenched in your position because from your perspective (informed by your parenting energy) you are right and your partner is wrong. However, children need to be both accepted (so they feel secure) *and* challenged (so they grow and develop). That's why it is important to value your partner's different parenting energy. And there's an added bonus: once you accept that your partner has a valid case (and stop defending your position so carefully) you will find a middle path, where your parenting energies are in harmony rather than competition. In the case of Trevor and Louise, they agreed that he would organize the picnics in future but with help from the children.

IT'S NOT ABOUT THE CHILDREN, IT'S ABOUT YOU

What winds you up about your children says more about you than it does about them. So before looking to change their behaviour, it's important to look at yourself first.

For many mothers their daughter's waist size can be a measure of whether they have been a success or a failure as a parent. 'My daughter is really outgoing, popular and doing well at school. It's probably only puppy fat and I hate to admit it but I would much rather she was slim,' said Lizzy, forty, about her nine-year-old daughter. Unfortunately, these adult concerns trickle down to our children. A recent poll of 1,500 children revealed that 40 per cent of under-tens worried about their weight, two-thirds of children aged seven to ten admitted weighing themselves, and nearly a quarter had been on a diet in the last year.

For fathers, their son's prowess at sport might become a measure of how 'manly' they are. So if their son 'throws like a girl', it is hard not to feel a failure as a father. Equally, their son's team's success can become a measure of their own standing in the world. 'My father didn't say anything but his silence said it all,' said George, now thirty-eight, about trying out for his father's cricket team's junior squad when he was about six or seven. 'I desperately wanted his approval, to do well and fit in with the other boys, but even at that age I knew I was different. Of course, I didn't have the words to explain what sort of different – that would come later – but I knew I was a disappointment, that I had let him down and that we couldn't talk about it.' George grew up to be gay, and although he did come out to his parents in his twenties, his father remained uncomfortable about the subject.

Although I've given examples of mother and daughter and father and son, it's equally possible for characteristics from our child of the opposite sex to hold up a mirror that makes us question ourselves. Perhaps they are shy or socially awkward or get angry in just the way that we do. Conversely, your children may grow up to be different from you – for example non-academic, or a budding capitalist while you're a trade unionist – and that can be equally challenging.

With sensitive subjects, it is often difficult for your partner to step in. For example, Lizzy's husband, Patrick, left nutrition and portion control up to his wife. 'She's really studied this subject – read everything that's been written on the subject – so I don't like to intervene.'

At least, this was the 'official' story, but I discovered that he would secretly subvert his daughter's diet plan. 'If I take her out and we stop somewhere for lunch, I'll go somewhere like a Chinese restaurant where the "sensible eating" rules are not quite so clear and we can relax and enjoy ourselves. I've also been known to buy ice creams.'

With George, his mother guessed that her husband's relationship with their son was strained. 'She would sort of over-compensate by making a fuss of me and letting me hang around the kitchen and help her,' he explained. 'I don't know if she would have voiced – even to herself – what was really going on. I don't think she would have wanted to look at why my father was so determined to "make me a man" or what that said about him. So although she never said anything against his desire on summer holidays to get me out rock-climbing or, on one terrible occasion, bungee jumping, she would show me how to bake biscuits or ice a cake.'

Turn it around: I have two positive messages to share. First, if you don't make something an issue it will not become one (and the reason that it is an issue is nearly always about you). Second, there is nothing wrong with straightforward honesty with your children – for example: 'I have a problem with my temper but I'm trying to do something about it.' What is damaging is saying nothing or pretending there isn't a problem, because the hidden subtext remains and children are really tuned into their parent's limbic brain (what you are thinking and feeling).

If the problems are down to you, that's reasonably easy to fix. Start by recognizing that you are stressing yourself out, as making a conscious effort to be calmer will have a knock-on effect on your child. Next time you catch yourself slipping back into old behaviours, stop and apologize. Not only does an apology clear the air, but it gives your son or daughter permission to talk about what previously seemed unmentionable.

If you're concerned that your child's problematic behaviour is being fed by your partner's own anxieties, that is harder to resolve. My advice would be to ask questions rather than give advice (because, however kindly meant, it will be heard as criticism).

For example, Patrick could ask Lizzy: 'How old were you when you first weighed yourself?', 'What triggered your interest?', 'How do you feel now, looking back?', 'If you could give yourself some advice as a child, knowing what you know now, what would you change?'

During the conversation, make certain your partner feels heard by trying to identify the feelings (for example: 'You felt unwanted') and repeat back statements that seem particularly striking (for example: 'You were given a set of scales for your birthday').

Aim to ask at least four or five questions and for the conversation to last at least fifteen minutes – so your partner feels truly understood – before making the links between his or her behaviour and your child's: 'To what extent do you think our daughter has similar feelings?'

Once again, don't offer solutions – even if you think you've got the answer – but ask more questions and listen to your partner's thoughts. Slowly but surely, a way forward will emerge.

DISCIPLINE

Discipline is a really difficult subject because on the one hand we want a relaxed and joyful relationship with our children, but on the other, we have a responsibility to make certain their behaviour is not anti-social. What makes the subject particularly toxic is that our parents will probably have had different attitudes and methods from our partner's parents. Finding a compromise is always going to be difficult, especially if the partner who spends less time with the children does not want his or her few hours to be dominated by rules and regulations.

'My job can involve evenings and some weekends,' explains Ethan, thirty-two, father to two boys aged eleven and nine, 'so when we have time together I want it to be special. I know I bend the rules – like sweets before their tea – but it's not like it's very often, so I don't see the problem.'

'But it's not just bending the rules, it's undermining them,' his wife Matilda, thirty-one, cut in. 'There are times when I've sent our youngest to his room to cool down and reflect on his behaviour but you go in and have "a little chat".'

'He was genuinely sorry and I thought he'd been in there long enough.'

'Sometimes it feels like I have three children, not two. Life can't be all putting on puppet shows and kicking a ball round the garden. They need to do their homework too, but do you ever insist on that?'

'I back you up.'

'But it's me telling them to come in and start their schoolwork. Why should I always be the Wicked Witch of the West?

Turn it around: Instead of focusing on disciplining your children, it is better to avoid the bad behaviour in the first place. If you have been using descriptive praise and thinking ahead, and helped your children name and acknowledge feelings, they should be more co-operative and a pleasure to be around. If you understand that they play up because they are overwhelmed by difficult feelings (and don't have the ability to regulate themselves yet), or over-tired or fractious because their regular routine has been disrupted, then you will be able to look at their 'naughtiness' in a different light.

So what should you do if they are truly being badly behaved? I think it is up to you to decide how to discipline your children – after all, you know your children best and what motivates them. However, I have three general principles to share. First, it is better to offer incentives to good behaviour rather than punishments for bad behaviour. Second, I want you to model the behaviour that you want your children to exhibit. (So please try not to lose your temper and don't hit, slap, spank or use any similar physical force, as you are just teaching your son or daughter to resort to similar means when annoyed or not getting their own way with their friends or younger sibling.) Third, always follow through: don't make idle threats that you're unlikely or unable to carry out. There is more about dealing with bad and stopping dangerous behaviour in Chapter Eight.

If you're still having problems agreeing on how to discipline, use the 'Communicating Better' exercise from Chapter Two to solve your dispute. I'm going to recap and add an extra element to contain your argument.

- *Flip a coin and decide who goes first.* The winner speaks without being interrupted.
- *This is the difference.* He or she can talk for only *three* minutes – set an alarm on your phone or use an egg timer. (This will help contain your argument because discipline raises strong emotions.)
- *Summarize.* The listener doesn't think about how to respond or rehearse what he or she is going to say but gives the speaker undivided attention. At the end of three minutes, the listener repeats back the essence of what's been said (and nothing more).

- *Feedback.* The speaker can give feedback about anything important that has been missed out.
- *Swap over.* So the partner who was the listener becomes the speaker and sets out his or her case for *only* three minutes without being interrupted – except by the timer. (The advantage of the three-minute rule is that you deal with only one or possibly two topics at a time.) Afterwards the other partner summarizes what was said.
- *Keep repeating the exercise.* When both parties feel heard, you are ready to find a solution.

Finally, try to aim for a middle way – rather than one partner just giving in (for a deal to stick there has to be something for both parties). For example, Matilda decided to join in the game of football in the garden (for a couple of minutes) so she could be perceived as fun too. Ethan really liked the idea of all the family enjoying themselves together and agreed to call time (after a couple of minutes) and insist on the boys starting their homework.

How to put your partner first

There is a particularly nasty trap that lots of parents fall into – often unwittingly. They set up a sub-alliance with one or both of their children and leave their partner feeling isolated and often angry.

For example, when Matilda had come into the garden to remind the boys about homework, Ethan had rolled his eyes to the children. In effect, he was saying, 'Here comes nasty Mummy to spoil our fun.' So instead of backing up his wife, and acting as a team, he had set up a sub-alliance 'Dad and boys' versus 'Mum'. Not only did he make his children more rebellious (because they knew they could exploit the differences between their parents) but he was sending a message to Matilda: 'I care more about being popular with the boys than what you think of me.' In effect, he was putting what he perceived as his sons' needs (for fun and bonding time with their dad) before his wife and her beliefs (that homework was important).

It is not just men that set up sub-alliances with their children. George's mother had fallen into the same trap. Instead of being upfront about giving her son baking lessons, she had waited until his father was out of the house. Her unspoken message was: 'If you don't tell your father, I won't.' Sometimes the criticism is more overt: 'Your father's late home *again*' or even 'Don't take any notice of Daddy, he's just being silly.'

If you and your partner are going through a tough patch, it is very easy to lean on one of more of your children – especially as many small children will try to 'make it better'. For example, when George was about nine, he would sit on the landing listening to his mother crying in the toilet after a row with his father and push drawings he'd made under the door. Obviously George's mother would have been touched by this loving gesture. However, she was getting a child (who doesn't have the emotional maturity to understand) involved with adult problems.

My golden rules for avoiding sub-alliances are as follows:

- Don't discuss or comment on issues between you and your partner with the children. (If they ask about something, don't lie, but tell them as little as possible: 'Yes, we had a disagreement but we're sorting it out.')
- Don't use children as go-betweens.
- Don't go behind your partner's back. (Tell him or her what you've been doing – even if he or she will disagree. It is better to have these issues out in the open where they can be discussed, rather than a hidden sore.)
- Don't discuss issues about the children in front of them. (If

something comes up, make an appointment with your partner to speak when they are out of earshot.)

- However, it's fine to argue about non-child-related issues when they're around – for example: 'What have you done to the computer?' or 'Did you move my papers?' If you can argue constructively – by which I mean sticking to the point, not dragging in other examples, listening to each other, negotiating and finding a compromise – you will have taught your children an important lesson about relationships: it is possible to hold different opinions, fall out and make up but still love each other.

Summing Up

Once you have children, everybody seems to have advice – much of it contradictory. However, there are some core ideas that run through all the research. If you can stay calm, your baby will relax and the positive mutual feedback between the two of you will increase. Conversely if you are stressed and annoyed, your baby will be stressed and fractious too.

Babies and toddlers have strong feelings that they do not understand. Your job is to help them cope with the highs and lows but also to provide enough space for them to discover the world and their place in it. Don't worry if you and your partner have a different take on how to achieve this goal: by capitalizing on both of your strengths, you can find a middle way and a balance that's best for your children.

Housework and the
Responsibility Gap

Although most modern couples sign up to the idea of an equal partnership, the reality on a day-to-day basis can end up looking very different, especially after the children arrive. Only 13 per cent of married men do more housework than their wives – according to the Institute for Public Policy Research – even though the number of house-husbands in the UK has trebled in the last fifteen years. Couples do an equal amount of housework in just 10 per cent of households. Of course, men are more hands-on than their fathers were, but it is often at the fun end of parenting, while the mothers are running round in circles doing all the hard work behind the scenes.

'Julian is a great dad and the kids love him, so I'm not complaining,' said Daisy, thirty-two, and then like a lot of mums proceeded to do just that. It's almost if they are frightened to complain – for fear of a backlash from their husbands – but my counselling room, or a group of other mums, is just too tempting to resist. After all, they have a lot of pent-up feelings that need releasing. 'Take Hallowe'en as a good example. Julian was happy to come home early and help the children carve the pumpkin and escort them round the neighbourhood to trick or treat. At some households – where the dad was still not back home – you could see the mums going, "Isn't he great?", and he is.' She took a deep breath. 'But who bought the pumpkin, and the bags of sweets for the children who came to our door? Who made the costumes? Who reminded him twice the week before that it was Hallowe'en, so he wouldn't put anything in his work diary that might clash? And who makes the kids their tea on the other 364 days a year? Of course, I want him to see the kids all dressed up – this year he helped paint their faces green – and it's great that they're spending "quality" time together but I'm doing all the donkey-work to make it happen.'

It's not just the physical hard work of cleaning, cooking and looking after the children (which is beginning to be shared more) but the emotional housekeeping too. Remembering birthdays and medical appointments, sending thank-you cards, arranging play dates for the children, booking cinema tickets and checking if the babysitter is free. More often that not, this is considered woman's work and men get a free ride. No wonder many mothers are exhausted.

'I have to keep going even when I have the flu or my period pains are so bad I just want to crawl into bed and curl up,' said Sophia, twenty-nine. 'That's partly because my husband is away a lot as his work involves travel, but to be honest he can't really be trusted. OK, he can get the children up for school and give them breakfast – particularly if it's one of my working days and he's at home – but he'll send our daughter off to school in her games kit but forget to pack her ordinary shoes to change into afterwards. He'll make the packed lunch for our four-year-old for nursery school but forget to cut the grapes in half – they're a choke hazard – and I'll get a nasty note from the school. There's all these balls to keep up in the air and I can't relax because if I don't get it right everything in the family will collapse.'

When you are under such stress, it only takes one extra burden – like Sophia's mother being diagnosed with cancer – for the family to plunge into crisis. They had arrived in my counselling room complaining of bitter and destructive rows. Sophia was feeling particularly unsupported. 'I want a partner, not a third child to look after.'

Daniel, her husband, felt criticized and demotivated. 'I'll do a hundred things right and all she comments on is the bit I've got wrong.'

'But these are important things. What was our daughter going to do? Wear her hockey boots in the classroom?

So why do so many women feel like the responsible adult with no back-up plan in place? Why does the housework and responsibility gap seem to be widening – despite all the good intentions of men? But before tackling these questions, it's important to understand the full impact and how they undermine relationships.

The Toxic impact of unequal parenting

Many couples feel embarrassed about discussing hockey boots, grapes and pumpkin lanterns in my counselling room – as if they should be dealing with weightier topics – but if you can't sort out these everyday problems, there is a danger you could fall into one of the following traps.

RESENTMENT

It normally starts out over small things but resentment is a bit like a snowball rolling down a mountainside: it soon builds up size and momentum and risks crushing everything in its path. Natalie, thirty-eight, found that although her division of labour with her husband Frank made logical sense, she was growing more and more resentful. 'When it came to finding a playgroup for our son, I had the time and the local contacts so I was happy to do the footwork. I whittled it down to three possibilities and explained all the pros and cons to

Frank. He came to see the first one and said, "That's fine" and "Whatever you think best" but he couldn't get time off to see the next two. I have to admit I did feel resentment. It was like "I've better things to do", but what could be more important than our son's future?'

With playgroup being a tricky subject, Frank didn't risk asking much beyond 'How did it go?', and Natalie didn't tell him the ins and outs of the playgroup activities or the personalities and politics of what happened there. 'I didn't think he was interested. He certainly didn't care enough to come and see it for himself.'

No wonder they began to drift apart, with such a large topic becoming increasingly toxic.

It didn't take much probing in my counselling room for a much bigger resentment to come out. 'My life has been turned upside-down,' said Natalie, 'but for Frank things have hardly changed at all.'

Unfortunately, there is an even bigger resentment here. One so big it hardly ever gets spoken. Although we love our children, *we can sometimes resent the burdens and restrictions of being a parent*. However, this is such a taboo topic that it is easier to just resent our partner instead.

Turn it around: Report your feelings rather than act them out. Instead of letting your resentment, anger or disappointment leak out through your body language (rolling your eyes, sighing heavily and slamming the cupboard door) or as a tirade of criticism, tell your partner how you are feeling and then explain why. For example, 'I'm upset because you didn't notice that I . . .' or 'I'm frustrated because you didn't listen when . . .' Reporting your feelings is important because it stops your partner imagining something worse (like being bitter or vengeful). By explaining why you're feeling this way, you can also stop your partner jumping to the wrong conclusion and limit the upset to just this one particular event.

NAGGING

You've tried asking nicely. You've tried reminding when nothing happens. So the only way to get anything done is to drop pointed hints, criticize or lose your temper. And especially when you've got a head of righteous anger up – fuelled by all your justified resentments – nagging seems the only way to get things done. Even if you don't particularly like yourself afterwards, it does get results – eventually. Unfortunately, nagging also poisons relationships and sucks all the fun out of your day-to-day life.

Although nagging is seen as something women do, I find it is an equal-opportunity trap. Adam, forty, had always been a stickler for good food hygiene and would wash bananas before eating them and garlic cloves before frying them. He would often be 'reminding' his partner Miranda, thirty-eight, to wash her hands – for example, after she touched the lid of the kitchen bin to throw something away. After they had a baby, it became more of an issue.

'It seems like he's always asking me, "Have you washed your hands?" and I know hygiene is important but it feels like I'm being nagged *all the time*,' Miranda explained. 'I used to like it when we prepared Sunday lunch together. We'd have a glass of wine and chat over the week but now it is too stressful for both of us to be in the kitchen at the same time. Especially if our daughter is going to have a few vegetables or some meat from the meal, I'd much rather I cooked alone or Adam did.'

If something isn't working – and although nagging might take the edge off your resentment it doesn't solve anything – you'd think we'd stop and trying something else. Unfortunately, we think if we do it one more time or shout louder or really shame our partner, he or she will change. However, all we achieve is digging a deeper hole of resentment for both the person who nags and the person who is nagged (and it is not uncommon for both partners to nag on different topics).

Turn it around: Apologize and look to build cooperation and teamwork instead. This chapter and the next are full of alternatives that work much better than nagging, but first it is important to draw a line under old, unhelpful behaviour. You have probably said sorry a million times before but it often doesn't register because either we don't really mean it (because we're just trying to keep the peace) or it doesn't properly register with our partner. Instead try a fulsome apology – which I explained in Chapter Three. Let me recap: identify the behaviour that you regret: 'I'm sorry I have been nagging about getting home after the children go to bed.' Next, identify how it must have impacted on your partner: 'It must have made you feel unwelcome when you did arrive.' Please do *not* add an explanation – for example, 'I think it's really important that the children see more of you' – because this weakens the power of a fulsome apology as it can be heard as justification for your nagging. (Most probably, your partner already knows why you want him or her to do something – because you've already told him or her a million times. If you've realized something new, you can always explain on another occasion.) Finally, make your apology.

PASSIVE-AGGRESSIVE BEHAVIOUR

This is where someone agrees to do something to your face – 'Yes, I'll be back home by five-thirty and take care of the kids so you can go to your meeting' – but then goes their own sweet way. They will forget ('I was caught up in something else'), deliberately misunderstand ('Did you mean today?'), make excuses at the last minute ('I've suddenly remembered a meeting') or deliberately sabotage (they show up on time but let the children stay up too late and they're fractious and running round the house when you get back, or they arrange finger-painting sitting on your new sofa), so you decide it's not worth the hassle next time round. However, it's impossible to challenge someone who is passive-aggressive because he or she 'wants' to help, it's just . . . (fill in the excuse) or he or she will get round to it in a moment (it's just that moment is not going to arrive any time soon). This is one of the reasons why passive-aggressive behaviour and nagging go hand-in-hand, because when something doesn't happen as promised, the other partner has to bring it up again and again or it will just be forgotten.

Passive-aggressive behaviour is also triggered by a feeling of power-lessness. Christopher, thirty-eight, did not agree with his wife, Melanie, enrolling their eight-year-old son as a model/actor for TV commercials.

'The casting calls are like cattle markets and it involves a lot of rejection. I don't really think it's right for him,' he explained. 'My wife thinks he wants to do it, but I believe he does it to keep her happy.'

'Have you told her how you feel?' I asked.

'I've sort of said it.'

'But not in so many words . . .' I suggested.

'She pulls rank. She knows *her* son best. She spends the most time with him. And what have I done for him? I want to take him to my cricket club as they have a class for young boys, but it clashes with acting lessons.'

Not only had Christopher failed to give his opinion strongly enough, so his wife took his silence for agreement, but he had become a second-class parent (whose opinions did not count). This problem was reinforced because Christopher did not prioritize his son's acting career – in his mind it wasn't important – and failed to collect glossy promotion prints from the studio close to his office, and wouldn't take time off work to take him to an audition. So it seemed to Melanie that she was always nagging him to get things done.

There was a similar problem with their love life, but this time round the roles were reversed. Christopher would drop repeated hints and nag that he 'hardly ever got sex'. Meanwhile, Melanie would be passive-aggressive. She would tell him that she enjoyed making love and that she fancied him. However, she just never seemed to be in the mood.

'To be honest, there's nothing less sexy than being pestered to do something. Not only do I close up inside but I feel resentful and angry.'

The result was that Melanie 'gave in' enough times to keep the peace and keep the lid on the problem but increased the levels of resentment for both her and Christopher.

Turn it around: This is an opportunity to practise your assertiveness skills and give your partner permission to say no. People behave in a passive-aggressive manner because they want to keep the peace. I know it causes rows and upset in the long run but at the time they keep everything nice by saying, 'Of course, darling.' So next time you get a too-easy agreement, double-check that your partner really means it by saying: 'Are you sure?' or 'I'd much rather know how you really feel.' If the answer *is* no, you could change the request, negotiate something your partner would accept doing or arrange for someone else to do it. At least you know where you stand. If you're the partner using the passive-aggressive behaviour, give yourself time to think – rather than being caught on the hop and agreeing out of habit. Choose a quieter time and discuss your reservations with your partner. He or she might be annoyed but that will pass. In contrast, resentment – from agreeing but not doing something – builds and builds and festers.

PLEASURE IN YOUR PARTNER'S DOWNFALL

Each of the consequences of unequal parenting compounds the others. In the worst cases, resentment will breed nagging from the parent 'in charge' and passive-aggressive behaviour from the 'second-class' parent. Fortunately, most couples don't reach the fourth trap, where the 'in charge' parent secretly wants the other to fail.

'I wanted my husband to experience just how hard it was looking after our daughter,' explained Tanya. 'So I almost willed her to puke and scream when he was in charge of her. When it did happen, I would look on coldly and offer no advice or support. If things went from bad to worse, I would criticize from the sidelines and then take over and show him how to do it.'

Although deep down Tanya wanted help, support and some acknowledgement that her life had been turned upside-down, she kept discouraging her husband and casting him forever in the support role. I've had male clients who were simply incapable of looking after their small children on their own – because they had no idea about feeding routines or how to get them in and out of car seats – so had to invite their mother round or take them to their sister's house if their wives were away.

Turn it around: If you've reached this point, it is a clear wake-up call that something has to change. Although you are unhappy and desperate for help, you are going about getting it in the worst way possible. So step back and think about what would help. If you can turn it into something concrete, for example time to yourself to go to the hairdresser, that's even better. Remember the section on being assertive in Chapter Two. If you ask for something clearly in an open and straightforward manner – rather than hoping your partner will guess, or getting angry and driving him or her away – you are far more likely to succeed.

■ ■ ■ ■ ■ ■

How to Ask for What You Need

One of the most important relationship skills – which will help you be a good partner, parent and also feel good about yourself – is to be able to ask for what you need in a simple, direct and honest way. Unfortunately, we've been brought up with statements like '"I want" doesn't get', and all too often we're frightened to ask for fear of being turned down. Somehow, we believe, it is better to hint, because the rejection does not feel quite so devastating. However, not asking leaves your partner guessing (probably wrongly) or maybe even oblivious to your needs (and you're left wondering why he or she doesn't care). So what's the alternative?

- Skip the preambles, like 'I don't often ask but . . .' or 'I know you're busy but . . .' The danger is that your partner will have switched off before the request, have heard the preamble as an attack or been unwittingly handed an excuse for not cooperating.
- Skip the explanations, like 'I haven't asked for much before . . .' or 'I'm really short of time . . .' It is almost as if you're saying you don't deserve to ask beyond exceptional circumstances – which is not going to be good for your self-esteem. The other problem with explanations is that they invite a debate – for example about who is the most tired or busiest – and you get distracted from asking.
- Keep it simple: 'Please could you . . .?' or 'Can you . . .?'
- Once you've asked for what you need, make certain that you listen to your partner – rather than jumping to conclusions about his or her response. If you think the answer is a 'Maybe' or a 'Yes, but', get clarification or ask another question. This could be the time to explain why you're asking.
- If you need emotional support, ask for something specific and concrete (like a hug) so your partner does not get confused. If you ask for something general (like 'more help') they could interpret that in a million different ways – some of them more irritating than helpful.
- Don't underestimate how hard it is to ask in a clear and direct

manner, especially if you have always dropped hints or thought your partner should 'just know'. So practise asking your friends or colleagues for something. If you find that hard, practise what you're going to say in your head first. Slowly but surely, it will become second nature.

- If you just need to talk, explain what sort of reaction would be helpful. Are you looking for your partner's opinion? Do you need advice? Do you want reassurance or just someone to listen?

Why do parents end up on different sides of the responsibility gap?

It is easy to lay all the blame on men. I've heard it many times in my counselling room. They're lazy, self-centred and, well, they're *men*, so what can you expect? There is a similar dialogue in the media and on social networks too. Although there are occasional 'great dads' who are singled out for praise, the majority are simply written off. I think 'selfish man' and 'Superwoman' are really unhelpful stereotypes because, first, the real picture is more complex, but second and most importantly, labelling men as the problem just puts their backs up and makes them opt out. Instead of complaining, I think a far more interesting question is: why aren't men doing more?

MEN CAN FEEL EXCLUDED

Right from the beginning, a mother and her child are wrapped in a cocoon of care that is sometimes difficult for fathers to penetrate. The vast majority of men, after watching their wife give birth to their new son or daughter in hospital, are shown the door. There are simply no facilities for the whole family to stay together over the first crucial hours. If the baby wakes up in the middle of the night or needs something, he or she is sleeping in a cot next to his or her mother's hospital bed while the father is phoning relatives, buying nappies or celebrating down the pub. Right from the beginning, she is 'in charge' and he's off running errands. Meanwhile, breastfeeding tethers the child to the mother and all the follow-up services are naturally designed to check the health of mother and child. Even fathers who are determined to be hands-on feel uncomfortable attending clinics.

'I was the only man in the waiting room and I didn't know quite what to do with myself,' explained William, twenty-three, after the birth of his daughter. 'So I buried myself in the information leaflets on the coffee tables. Except they were all aimed at mothers and babies and the only reference to men was a poster on the wall for a domestic violence phone line. I did ask one of the nurses if they had anything for new dads and she dug around and found one leaflet.' Needless to say, he did not go back. 'I felt like a spare part, and who wants that?'

The sheer amount of contact time is important for bonding between father and child, according to research from the University of Calgary into what happens to the brains of male mice after the birth of their offspring. The scientists discovered the male mice grew new cells in the region of the brain connected with smell and memory to help recognize the scent of their pups. However, it only happened if the father mice were snuggled up to their offspring in the nest. If they were separated by a mesh screen, the cells did not grow.

MEN HAVE THEIR OWN PROBLEMS

While there are low expectations of men as child carers, there are high expectations of them as breadwinners. It is not surprising, therefore, that they put more effort into the latter than the former. In many cases, fathers are left trying to keep everybody happy and finding it increasingly difficult to reconcile the demands at work and at home.

'My line manager was reasonably sympathetic to me taking time off after the birth of both my son and my daughter,' explained Charles, thirty-five, who works for a large firm of auditors. 'However, it was made very clear that I shouldn't take more than a few days – even though the statutory parental leave is up to two weeks. "My team were counting on me" and "clients liked continuity".'

Eventually, Charles's wife returned to work three days a week and occasionally she would have a childcare crisis and ask him to take time off.

'Nothing can be put on a formal basis because it might "set a precedent",' he explained. 'It's really stressful because I never know what answer I'll get and my wife doesn't really understand the culture at my work. If I say it's not a good time to ask or I get a knock-back from my line manager, she acts as if I don't think her job is important or I don't care about the children or I'm just plain difficult. But they are always looking for cost savings, there's a real attendance culture where your bottom on the seat is more important than what you do, and I don't want to be thought a "lightweight".'

Other men will agree to something that makes sense for the rest of the family but has a huge impact on their life. Sebastian, a forty-eight-year-old lawyer, bowed to pressure and bought a house in the countryside that involved a two-and-a-quarter-hour commute to his office in London. 'We didn't want the children growing up in a city and the schools are better here but I'm often up at five-thirty for an early train. My work involves a lot of socializing so sometimes I'm on the last train home and have less than five hours' sleep. Not surprisingly, I can fall asleep on the sofa in the evening but then I'm "boring" or "ducking out of family life". It's getting harder and harder to exist on so little sleep – especially as I get older. We've discussed moving to a local firm but we would never be able to have the lifestyle that working in the city gives us.'

These men would claim that they take their share of the responsibility, but, unlike hot meals on the table and collecting the children from swimming, their contribution is not so clearly visible.

MEN GET DEMORALIZED

Most men measure how much they're doing around the house and the amount of effort they're putting into raising a family against their father's contribution to their own childhood. Research from the Fatherhood Institute – an organization which lobbies on men's behalf – reported that by 1997 men were spending eight times longer with babies and young children than twenty years ago. So although today's fathers feel they are doing their bit, they often don't feel appreciated. The message they give me, time and again, is 'I'm doing all this and it's *still* not enough.' Although their wives hope that pointing out the responsibility deficit will make their partner see the light – and offer more – it often has the opposite effect. 'What's the point?' they say to themselves as they withdraw and do just enough to keep the peace but not enough to solve the problem.

Men are particularly likely to be demoralized if their partner is asking for help but refuses to cede control and therefore feels free to tell them what to do, over-supervise and criticize. The problem is compounded if their wife uses her 'expert' status to overrule him.

Returning to Natalie and Frank, whom we met earlier in this chapter, he would offer an opinion but found it was often ignored.

'At the first playgroup, I really liked the relaxed atmosphere but Natalie didn't think our son would be stretched enough so that was the end of the discussion. It's pointless explaining that he's only four, because, although it's not explicitly said but certainly implied, she knows him best.'

Meanwhile Natalie, who had given up a high-powered career, felt that raising their son was her domain. 'Sometimes, it feels like he's stepping on my toes. I've read all about how to stimulate children and how they learn best and he comes crashing in at the last minute into my project.'

'It's like you want me to rubber-stamp your choices,' Frank retorted.

There were stuck in a trap that I see quite often. Natalie was complaining that Frank was not involved enough, but then that he was interfering.

At the far end of this spectrum, Oliver, forty-two, was trying to save his marriage. In the middle of a argument where he had threatened to seek custody of their sons, aged eleven and eight, his wife Rosemary spat back that they were 'her' children.

Obviously, she felt hurt and rejected and she lashed out, but it made her husband feel completely demoralized.

'Didn't my efforts, all the hours at work to support the family, count for anything?' asked Oliver plaintively.

WOMEN'S EXPECTATIONS OF THEMSELVES

There is something about being human that makes us competitive. Men compete on who earns the most, who's best at sport (or supports the most successful team) and who has the most beautiful woman on his arm. When women compare themselves to others, it is more likely to be about their looks, how well the children are doing and what kind of home they live in. Obviously, their identity can also be tied up with their work, but not normally to the same extent as men. (I used to lead focus groups of male and female consumers talking about products for a market research company. When the men introduced themselves to the other participants, they would always mention their job but sometimes had to be prompted about their marital status and whether they had children. Conversely, women always started with how many children they had, followed by whether they were married, divorced or a single mum, but sometimes had to be prompted about work.)

With so much of a woman's identity tied up with being a great mum and having a beautiful home, it is not surprising that many women have higher standards and expectations of themselves.

'My home isn't just somewhere I live but an expression of who I am,' explains Cristabel, twenty-nine and the mother of two boys aged eight and five, 'so if the place is a tip, I also feel all over the place and can't relax until order is reinstated. I'm horrified when Toby invites someone round and the place looks like a bomb has hit it. What must they think?'

'They're dads too. They know what family life is like. They're more than used to stepping over toys,' replied her husband.

'I'd never invite another mum round without running the vacuum cleaner round the house first. Same if there are other children coming round for tea; I don't want them taking back tales that our house is a tip.'

'That's fine, we have different standards, but what makes me angry is that you expect me to care as much as you do if there's a coffee-cup ring on the table or the skirting boards are a bit dusty. It's important to you. I get it. It reflects on you. But it's dominating our lives. What about having some fun instead?'

In effect, some men aren't 'pulling their weight' not because they don't believe in doing their share, but because their partner has standards and expectations that they don't buy into.

Toby summed up a lot of their attitudes: 'I thought, If Cristabel wants to run herself ragged that's a pity, but don't expect me to do half. So I stepped back and let her get on with it.'

When I drill down into 'high standards', I often find something else that is particularly unsettling. Fortunately, by this stage in their counselling, I had built up a strong relationship with Cristabel and could probe deeply.

'So if things are not perfect, how do you feel?' I asked her.

'That the whole edifice that I've built around myself will be destroyed and they'll see what I really am.'

'What's that?' I asked, holding my breath.

'Worthless,' she replied. 'I'm not acceptable, and worse still, they might have a point. There is something wrong with me.'

'There is nothing between perfect and worthless?'

Cristabel nodded. No wonder the stakes were so high.

Time and again, I find perfectionism is a defence against shame (possibly the most destructive emotion, because it does not attack just our behaviour but our whole being).

There is one final problem with having sky-high expectations of yourself: it allows you to ask something similar of other people. And when they fail – for example, to clean the sink in the 'perfect' manner – to brand them as worthless too.

SOCIAL CHANGES

Both fathers and mothers are interacting more than ever before with their children. When the Centre for Time Use Research in Oxford asked parents to keep a diary of activities and compared them to a generation ago, the contact time had trebled. While previously children would have gone into the street or the park to play, there is much more adult-supervised play and education work. Even if this is not always being led by mothers or fathers, they have to drive their sons and daughters to the activities and collect them. Children are also spending more time in adult-orientated places like restaurants.

Meanwhile, despite the extra time pressures, we still cling on to all the activities that our parents did with us when we were kids.

'I never feel so right as a mother as when I'm doing things that my mother did with me. So I'll love baking cakes and making jam –

giving my daughter the spoon to lick and helping her write the labels for what fruit and what year,' explains Jocelyn, thirty-three. Except her mother had not worked three days a week, and had let Jocelyn and her sister wander in and out of their friends' houses in the street. 'Round here, it's very different to where I grew up. It's mostly younger couples without children and older couples.' So despite having more responsibility outside the house and less shared childcare with other local mums, Jocelyn still felt compelled to replicate her mother's mothering (and before having children had baked about one cake and never made jam).

There are two other social changes that are putting immense strain on parents. At one end, we're getting married later – around thirty – and having our children around ten years later than in the 1950s. At the same time, the peak career years – for promotion and laying down pension payments – have come forward. Take British prime ministers: they used to be older men and women with greying hair and grown-up children. In 2000, Tony Blair was the first leader in 150 years to have a child in Downing Street, and both his successors have had small children. While we used to spread our peak career and child-rearing years across three decades – so the responsibilities could be staggered – it's now focused down into one.

IT'S HARD TO STEP INTO THEIR PARTNER'S SHOES

For many women, running a home is more than a practical necessity; it's also an expression of their nurturing and love for their partner and children. So if they don't get any help, appreciation or anything back in return, it can feel like an insult or rejection. Meanwhile, for men, chores are chores are chores. Doing the weekly shop is something functional. Nothing more, nothing less. Therefore, chores have low status for a man and he would much rather employ a cleaner or get the shopping delivered. He shows his love by providing and is bemused that all his hard work is not enough.

When it comes to childcare, men really do want to be involved with their children but define the concept differently. They rate having a good emotional relationship and being able to talk to their sons and daughters over seeing them often. Women, conversely, value the sheer volume of time spent, as they feel closeness and connection comes from doing small tasks together – like supervising brushing teeth – because you cannot schedule intimacy.

When both partners work and share the load in childcare and chores, there is generally a good understanding of each other's burdens, but when the workload is split into home maker and provider, it can still be hard to step into each other's shoes – even though the gender differences have lessened over the last fifty years. Men no longer go straight from their mothers to their wives. They've had to cook, clean and iron their own shirts for ten-plus years. Similarly, women have earned their own money for a similar amount of time. They know the problems of keeping the bank account in the black and fears that the restructuring at work could spell redundancy and financial disaster. However, the arrival of children changes everything and a little knowledge of the other's stresses can be misleading.

'I don't think Nicholas understands the sheer volume of washing that three children and two adults generate,' said Naomi, thirty-eight, 'or what it's like to cook two meals, one for the kids at six and one for us at eight. It has to be washed up, cleared away, and all while you're being asked a million and one questions by the kids and juggling play dates to fill a gap in childcare and wondering who will come in and feed the dog while we're out on Sunday afternoon. Perhaps I'm being a bit harsh. He does have some idea, but when the going gets tough, he can opt out. He'll say, "I've got an important presentation in the morning, so I'll go downstairs and sleep on the sofa so I can guarantee at least six hours' sleep." That's fine. But I've also got a big day and lots to do and I can't just bow out.'

Not surprisingly, Nicholas, a company rep, saw the situation differently. 'I don't think Naomi understands what it's like to do a job that you don't really like. She always did fulfilling and creative work in TV production. If she didn't fancy a particular contract, we'd talk it through and maybe she'd wait for something better – as we could rely on my steady income. When there was a huge contraction in work – about five years ago – and she was getting bored, I was happy for her to "opt out" and become a full-time mum. We agreed it was best for our children. However, I think she sees work through rose-tinted glasses, it's all people in sharp suits being dynamic and having interesting conversations. She forgets the tedium of interminable meetings, office politics and the daily slog. Especially as new technology means my supervisor has a log of every call I make and can track everywhere I've been in the car. There's times when I dream of just throwing in the towel, retraining and doing something interesting – but who would pay for it? We're only ever two or three pay cheques away from disaster.'

Not only is it always easier to repeat our position in the responsibility gap than try and understand our partner's, but the media and online communities each gender consumes can act as an echo chamber, making our complaints seem even more right and our partner's failings starker.

■ ■ ■ ■ ■ ■

Building Bridges

It's hard to step into your partner's shoes if you're feeling angry, resentful or unappreciated. So to get an idea of the state of play, I ask couples to do an audit of the balance between positive and negative interactions over a good week and then a bad one. But first, let me explain the differences:

POSITIVE INTERACTIONS	NEGATIVE INTERACTIONS
Smiles	Nagging
Thank you	Ignoring
Eye contact	Raised eyes
Greetings	Sarcastic comments
Laughter	Coldness
Listening	Talking over someone
Sharing personal information	Holding back personal information
Casual touches	Turning your back
Cuddles	Shrugs
Kisses	Walking away
Small presents (like a bar of chocolate)	Complaints
Making a cup of tea	Holding grudges
Doing something for the other person	Long silences
Compliments	Criticism
Pet names	Name-calling

Write down how the contact between you divides in a good week, a bad week and perhaps the last seven days. Ask your partner to do the same and share the results.

INTERPRETING YOUR BALANCE

When researchers at Washington University looked at the balance between positive and negative interaction, they found couples heading for divorce were reporting an even split. Those who were in conflict – but maintaining their relationship – had five positives to one negative. However, for a good relationship, they recommend a ratio of twenty positives to one negative.

IMPROVING THE RATIO

Think about how you could be more positive. Often couples have warm or loving thoughts – for example, looking forward to getting home or being pleasantly surprised at some help they were offered – but instead of saying something keep it to themselves. Look at the list of possible positives and think about what you would like to offer your partner. It is not an exhaustive list, so perhaps you can think of other ideas too. For example, sending a nice text ('Can't wait to see you') or making explicit your gratitude ('Thank you for your help yesterday when we were expecting guests and I panicked'). Make a commitment to perform least one item off your list every day. At the end of the week, write down your ratios between positive and negative and share the results with each other.

■ ■ ■ ■ ■ ■

How to put your partner first

One of the key messages that I give my clients is: *If it's good enough for your kids, it's good enough for your partner too.* (See my Golden Rules at the back of the book.) It's not only children that thrive on praise. Adults need it as well. That's the reason that successful companies review their employees on a regular basis and give positive feedback. However, when it comes to our home life, we are slow to give compliments (and sometimes even a thank you). In fact, I would be a rich man if I'd been given a bonus every time I heard the words: 'I shouldn't have to thank my husband for . . . emptying the dishwasher/looking after his own kids/coming home when he said he would' (put in your own pet bugbear) or 'I shouldn't have to thank my wife for . . . a nice cuddle on the sofa/letting me go fishing/keeping the children quiet while I'm busy' (put in your own example). However, imagine for a moment how you would feel if, in your view, you have put yourself out to do something and not only was there no recognition but also there was a slight overtone of 'About time too' or 'Is that all?' My guess is that you wouldn't be rushing to repeat the job again. It's like a company telling its employees: 'At last, you've made your target.' How motivated would that workforce be?

One of the best ways of motivating your children is descriptive praise (praising what is right rather criticizing what is wrong). So how can you use this idea with your partner?

- We are often too busy going through our mental to-do list to register what our partner has done that is helpful, or to give positive feedback. So make a conscious effort to slow down or stop. It only takes a few seconds to offer descriptive praise.
- Instead of general comments – 'That was a great day out' – pick out a particular aspect and talk about that. You can never be too specific. (This is why the technique is called *descriptive* praise.) For example: 'You really handled our son well when he had a tantrum about the ice cream.'
- If you can't find anything recent to praise, look for something in the past that you'd like to happen again. Chose a quiet moment – like on a long car journey – and reminisce. For example, 'It was really nice when you came home half an hour early and we were able to have a cup of tea and talk over the day before I went out,' or 'I still remember that time you looked after the children for the weekend and I went off with my sister to a spa.'
- In same way that I've asked you to avoid over-the-top superlatives with your children, I'd like you to do the same with your partner. So drop 'You're a wonderful mother' or 'You're the best dad' and concentrate on the detail – remember the appraisal at work: they spell out what you're doing well to encourage more of the same.
- Look for any small step in the right direction and praise that. For example, if you need your partner back at a certain time but he or she is running late again, but does at least call with an update,

rather than biting his or her head off say: 'Thank you, it's helpful to know.' Alternatively, for looking after the children – even if it was with bad grace – 'It was so nice to come home to a quiet house and find you'd put them all to bed.'

- Explain *why* a particular behaviour was helpful. For example, 'It gave me a chance to alter my plans slightly' or 'It was really nice to have some time alone together.' After all, your partner is not a mind reader.

- Don't take change for granted. Notice and comment on improvements: 'You've made a real effort to . . . and I wanted to let you know how much I appreciate it' will encourage your partner to continue and offer more.

- If you feel that you don't get enough descriptive praise yourself, use descriptive praise to remedy the situation. For example, think back to a time when you were motivated by positive feedback, and tell your partner: 'When you noticed that I'd cleaned the bath, I thought, You *do* appreciate my efforts.' In this way, you are modelling the behaviour that you'd like back.

Summing Up

When you're trapped in a dispute about who does what about the house, it is easy to take your partner's behaviour personally or make blanket statements about men or women. However, parents are under more pressure than ever before – from society and each other's expectations. Deep down both men and women can feel a sense of injustice and easily get demotivated – that's why it is important to praise rather than criticize. Often it's not just how the responsibilities (for running the house, raising the children and earning money) are divided, but whether you feel you're taking too much of the burden. There is more in the next chapter about closing the responsibility gap and finding a middle way that will work for both of you.

Parenting as a Team

I hope that by exploring the pressures on parenting from society, ourselves and each other, I have made you feel more understood and less overwhelmed. It's only once you've been heard that you can begin to listen to your partner and the two of you can work as a team. Time and again, I find parents get trapped on either side of the housework and responsibility gap because they have rushed to find a solution before each partner feels truly understood.

There are three steps to resolving a problem together – rather than one person imposing a solution – and these are:

- Explore,
- Understand, and
- Action.

You can't get to the last without going through the first two. If your negotiations hit the buffers, my advice is always to go back to the beginning and explore again: 'Why is this issue so difficult?' or 'What's stopping us making progress?' or 'Why are we both upset?'

With the last chapter devoted to exploring and understanding the responsibility gap, we are ready to move to Action and find ways of closing it.

Drop the word 'should'

At the heart of most arguments over childcare and how best to bring up children, there is one small word that causes a lot of misery: 'should'. John and Marie, in their early thirties, came into counselling because he had fallen out of love with her, but I suspected that at the heart of their problems were parenting issues. They had two children, one aged seven and one aged three. Marie was a full-time mum and John spent a lot of time travelling because of his job. Although they claimed that they never argued – and only occasionally had arguments about how they argued – it did not take long to remember a niggle from the past few days. As I suspected, it was about parenting.

'We've decided that I'll get out more when John's home and can look after the kids,' explained Marie. 'But if I was going to go to the gym, I had to go right that very minute.'

'So I told you to get ready and I'd give them their tea,' said John.

'When I came down, the kids were eating and he was on his laptop – which just drives me wild.'

'They were happy, involved doing something, I just took a sneaky look.'

'But they hardly see you. I think when you're with the kids you *should* give them your undivided attention.'

I was not surprised that Marie didn't say anything at the time – she had to go off to the gym. However, she didn't say anything when she returned home or at any point over the next few days. With no argument, there was no opportunity either for Marie to let off steam or for John to challenge the idea that he *should* give his children his undivided attention. So I asked, John to address Marie's statement.

'I suppose Marie has a point. I don't see them very often. OK. I won't do it again.'

If John wasn't going to challenge the 'should', I needed to give him a nudge.

'What were you doing on the computer?'

'I just had a couple of emails to check. It only took a second.'

'But you *should* have waited until the children were in bed,' said Marie. There was that word again.

'We don't spend much time together either and I wanted to have all my work finished so we could watch a movie together – or something – when you got back.'

'But it meant that you didn't put the children to bed properly. When I came back, Charlie [their three-year-old son] got out of bed and he was complaining that he hadn't had his story.'

'We did a jigsaw together, I thought that would be enough to settle him down.'

'I have this tried and tested way of getting them off to sleep and I think you *should* stick with the plan.' Marie had tried to soften this 'should' with 'I think you should' – which is better than just a plain 'should' – but she was still laying down the law.

John just sat there looking miserable.

At this point, I remembered one of my own mother's sayings, which I suspect had been handed down from her mother too. Sometimes, I just go with my instincts and say them:

'There's more than one way to skin a rabbit.'

Finally, John seemed energized. 'They seemed happy enough eating while I replied to my emails. I got them washed, teeth brushed and our daughter in her pyjamas. It all went very smoothly.'

Marie seemed to have softened too. 'I had to go away for the weekend and I rather dreaded getting back because Gracie's teacher [their seven-year-old] had left one of those "parent" homework projects. She had to build Dracula's castle and I'd left everything for John but I sort of expected to come back, find the house in chaos and have to make the castle last thing on Sunday night.'

'I did things my way but everything ran really smoothly,' John chipped in.

'To your credit, you built the Dracula castle – not the way I would have done it, but you fulfilled the task.'

I loved the idea that there was possibly a right and wrong way to build a castle for a class project but let the subject drop.

It's not just 'should' that drives arguments and undermines team work but also 'must' and 'always' and 'never'. These words – however well meant – come across as domineering and shut down conversations.

What rather than Why

Lots of couples worry that these arguments seem petty and spoil the atmosphere, so swallow their differences, and the 'helper' parent bows to the 'in charge' parent's wishes. But what happens when these parenting niggles don't get expressed? There are two problems: nothing gets solved but, more worryingly, the unexpressed niggles can pollute the way you see your partner. In effect, you start concentrating on *what* your partner has done, without thinking about *why* – or, worse still, come up with your own 'why' (often something incredibly negative) which over time solidifies not into your opinion but a fact. So let's return to John and Marie's argument to see these twin problems in action.

'When I'm tired or stressed all these resentments come pouring out,' Marie explained.

'Normally when we're in bed and about to switch the lights out,' John interjected. 'I'm tired and want to go to sleep, so I suppose I have argument deficit disorder. I can be quite rational and calm for about five minutes but then I want to close it down. So I'll say something like "Got it."'

'Which really winds me up.'

Hence the argument about arguments. In effect, if you don't sort out the niggles – what I call pinches – you cash them in for a crunch. Indeed, John and Marie had described their week as very up and down.

So, moving on to the second problem of suppressing parenting niggles, *what* had John done that night that Marie could have been storing away for a future fight?

'He had been too busy on that laptop to look after his children and he hadn't put them to bed properly and left me to sort everything out when I got home,' she explained. 'No wonder I sometimes think it's far too much hassle to go to the gym.'

It was a pretty damning list – especially when you consider it was just one evening's worth of pinches. However, even with three issues (mealtimes, bedtimes and 'You only pay lip service to my me-time') it would be difficult to sort out the crunch (when it finally arrived) and especially late at night.

'Turning back to that evening,' I asked Marie, '*Why* did you think John behaved in this way?'

'Because he doesn't love me or the children enough to put himself out,' she replied – without hesitation.

This is an incredibly negative 'why' and one not really supported by the evidence. For example, in the counselling session, she had learnt that he checked his emails so he could give her his undivided attention when she returned home. He substituted a jigsaw for a story because he thought that would be a nice way to get their son to relax. (Marie had not known about the jigsaw until John told her about it during our dissection of the issues.) In other words, John's *why* had been reasonably benign. However, concentrating on *what* he had done had made Marie take her negative interpretation, treat it as the gospel truth and overlook hundreds of other explanations for John's behaviour.

If you're ever in any doubt about *why* your partner did something, don't assume, but stop and ask him or her.

Sorting out the niggles

Ultimately, there is no right or wrong way to give children their tea or put them to bed. In some cultures, children have separate meal-times and food and in others they eat with their parents and just have smaller portions. Some cultures have separate bedrooms and in others everybody sleeps in the same bed. Despite living in hundreds of dif-ferent environments and eating a wide variety of diets, humans con-tinue to thrive. There is no 'should' for bringing up children. However, the benefits of dropping 'should' are wider than just making child-rearing less contentious and the source of a million and one nig-gles. It gets round the trap of one partner (normally the mother) being in charge and the other (normally the father) feeling de-skilled and relegated to assistant.

In the case of John and Marie, she was indeed an expert – being the eldest of five and having helped her mother bring up her younger siblings.

'When I was sixteen, my parents went away for the weekend and left me in sole charge of a child of four and a baby of eighteen months old. So when it came to bringing up our own children, I knew what to do. In fact, John has never had been woken in the night by a baby crying because I had it all sorted.'

'She's right, but the downside was that I felt that my opinions didn't count, or not as much as hers – and her mother's. In fact, I wasn't just Marie's assistant but second assistant after her mother.'

Fortunately, John was gaining in confidence and started to give his opinion – whether it was asked for or not. In a subsequent counselling session, he reported the following conversation:

'Marie was arguing with Gracie about how to bring her maths book home. Gracie was being awkward and coming up with a reason why she couldn't do first one and then another thing,' said John.

'One of my younger brothers was just the same and Mum and I would try and solve the problem for him.'

'But you were getting more and more wound up and Gracie was enjoying the sport. I thought, Just tell her she needs to bring her maths book home tonight. She's seven and old enough to sort that out for herself.'

'I realized that he was right. She was deliberately winding me up. So I listened, stepped back, and Gracie brought back the book without her and me having a row about it.'

In effect, they had begun to turn into a team where each partner was allowed to give the other feedback – to the benefit of the smooth running of the household and the upbringing of their children. Even better, when you're a team deciding together, the tyranny of 'should' is no longer an issue because you've discovered there truly are endless ways to skin a rabbit.

■ ■ ■ ■ ■ ■

Resetting the Default

If there is a housework or responsibility gap in your relationship, instead of forever scrapping over particular tasks or having to ask for help, what would happen if you looked at how tasks are allocated and found a fairer formula? In this way your partner could take on responsibility for something as a matter of course rather than forever having to be asked, reminded or nagged. In my experience, the division works best where there are clear boundaries. For example, I had a couple where she was responsible for taking the children to the doctor and he was responsible for the dentist's appointments. What works worst is where everything is left woolly. For example, she does the laundry but if he sees the laundry basket is full, he is 'expected' to load the machine or empty the dryer. With this kind of arrangement, the person who cares most about there being enough clean clothes – normally the wife – is *de facto* in charge and the other is being nagged to 'help out'. So how can you reset the default settings in your relationship?

- Chose a good time when you're getting on well – rather than on the back of a row.
- Tell your partner what you appreciate him or her doing. If you can't think of anything around the house, talk about how hard he or she works to pay the bills or sort out everything to do with the car. (If your partner feels appreciated, he or she will not be so defensive and ready to listen.)
- Talk about how you've been feeling. You are the expert on your feelings so there cannot be a dispute on them. For example, 'I've been feeling really tired and irritable lately . . .'
- You might like to consider making a fulsome apology (see p. 88), as admitting to your mistakes will really get your partner's attention. (This is especially important if you've tried to have this conversation before but it ends up with a row and one of you getting defensive and the other blaming.)
- From here onwards, ask questions – rather than making statements ('It's not fair') or offering solutions ('You could do the ironing') – because questions build teamwork. For example, 'Could we look at how we divide the tasks around the house?' or 'What could you take over?' or 'How would that work?' In contrast, making statements can easily tip into describing the problem (which will be heard by your partner as more examples of what a poor parent he or she is) or offering solutions (before each party has had his or her say), and can lead to a power struggle.
- Look for specific jobs to divide ('If you cook, I'll clean up everything afterwards') or hand over ('I'll bathe the children in the evening and be responsible for keeping the bathroom clean').

- Agreements stick where there is something for both parties, so ask you partner what he or she would like from you in return. (In most cases, in my experience, the 'helper' partner does not ask to be relieved of a particular task. Normally he or she will ask: 'Can I have half an hour to unwind when I get home without being asked to do something?' or 'I'd like to go on the computer after ten without being made to feel guilty.')
- Once your partner is 'in charge' of an area, it is up to him or her to do the task in his or her way and to his or her timeframe. Please don't interfere, otherwise it perpetuates the 'in charge' and 'helping out' roles – or even worse 'master' and 'servant'. If after a few weeks it is not going well – for example, the ironing pile has reached the ceiling – you can have a review. Once again, ask questions rather than make statements: 'How do you think the arrangement has been going?', 'How could we make things better?'

Becoming a team

Time and again, female guilt and male stubbornness turn dividing up responsibility for running a house and raising children into a minefield that threatens to destroy relationships. However, when couples become a team, the men find the rewards of a closer relationship with their sons and daughters and the women are freed to think about their own needs more. So how do you reach this goal?

STOP WHAT DOESN'T WORK

If you're in a hole, the first thing to do is to stop digging. It seems such sensible advice, you'd think I wouldn't even need to give it. However, I find couples using the same failed strategy over and over again. Somehow they imagine that if they shout louder, pour out more feelings or make nastier personal comments, there will be a breakthrough. Their partner will see reason, be shocked into changing or admit, 'You're right and I'm wrong.' Except they've tried this behaviour one thousand times before and there is no reason to believe that using it once more will achieve anything – except make the situation worse. So look down my list of potential failed strategies and make a commitment to change; if changing the habit of a lifetime proves too difficult, monitor what happens and whether the hole does indeed get deeper.

- Festering in silence (just builds resentment, sarcastic comments and makes non-cooperation the norm in your relationship).
- 'It's not fair' (invites a long academic discussion or the Suffering Olympics, with each partner going for gold as most misunderstood).
- Nagging (puts your partner's back up and makes him or her believe that he or she is 'put upon' and therefore his or her intransigence is justified).
- Sulking (builds a wall between you and your partner).
- Walking away (freezes the problem – especially if this discussion is shelved rather than continued when both parties are calmer. It also makes your partner anxious and more likely to use a failed strategy in return).
- Criticism (puts your partner's back up and makes him or her defensive).
- Judging (puts you in 'expert' position and your partner as 'slave').

- Hovering (poisons the atmosphere in the house).
- Losing your temper (just puts you in the wrong and makes it easier for your partner to 'label' you as the problem).
- Pouring out your feelings (normally so much material comes out that your partner is overwhelmed by the avalanche and cannot properly respond to any one item).
- Making life unpleasant (your partner is unclear what in particular is wrong and is left guessing, or switches off and doesn't care).

Turn it around: Instead of arguments having the potential to sabotage your relationship at any moment, start a weekly planning meeting. This allows you to flag up any issues over the coming days (and head them off before they become a problem) and to calmly discuss any differences of opinion from the past few days. I find these planning meetings will lower the temperature because the partner who is aggrieved can let something drop during the week, as he or she knows there is a forum to sort it out. Chose a good slot (like Sunday evening) and a fixed amount of time – for example half an hour – and try to stick to it. Even if you don't think there's anything on the agenda, double-check with your partner that she or he has no issues stored up and get out your diaries to walk through your upcoming commitments. If you know, for example, your parents are staying on Sunday evening, shift the planning meeting to another day or time but don't skip it.

STOP DEFENDING YOUR POSITION

When we are not appreciated or feel misunderstood, the temptation is to stop listening to our partner and just repeat our position – over and over again. I ask my clients to imagine sitting on a see-saw: the more you push down on your side of the argument, the higher your partner will pop up on his or her end. So your partner pushes down on his or her side of the see-saw and it's your turn to fly up into the air. The only way to stop see-sawing up and down is for you both to move into a more central position in the argument.

Josie and Howard, in their early forties, were arguing about planning their new year's holiday for themselves and their daughter. It had been Josie's responsibility – along with the other mums in their circle of friends – to find a cottage. Unfortunately, one family hadn't been included and there had been a socially embarrassing conversation. Later, when Josie and Howard were alone, it turned into a nasty row.

'Josie had tried to smooth it over by making some polite but empty phrase like "I'm sure there would still be room somewhere close by" and I'd joked that was typical girl behaviour,' explained Howard, 'because boys would have just been more direct and explained there weren't enough bedrooms.'

'I don't like my behaviour being dismissed as "girly"– especially after I've done all the hard work organizing the holiday,' replied Josie.

'I can't even make a harmless joke without getting my head bitten off. Aren't I allowed an opinion?'

'Can't you see that my opinions being discarded because I'm a woman is insulting?' Josie fought back. 'What's the point? You'll never understand.'

While both Howard and Josie pushed up at their ends of the see-saw, gathering more evidence from other arguments to reinforce their points of view, the higher the other one went – along with the stakes too. In the end, Josie had stormed off after swearing at Howard and the row had not been referred to again. Not surprisingly, the issue was still live forty-eight hours later when they arrived in my counselling office, and replaying it took up half the session. Finally, I was able to intervene and ask them to imagine sitting on the other end of the see-saw.

'It can't be particularly nice,' said Howard.

'I've been wound up all day worrying about how this session would go,' explained Josie.

'I didn't realize it affected you so badly,' admitted Howard.

'I know it's stupid that I should let something like that get to me, but it does.'

Finally, they were beginning to come towards a middle position where Howard would try to give less offence and Josie would try to take less.

Turn it around: Ask yourself: how much of the problem is me? It is easy to see your partner's failings but harder to spot your own. After almost thirty years of listening to couples argue, I believe that problems are six of one and half a dozen of the other. If your contribution to a row is hard to spot – perhaps you were quietly getting on with something and were ambushed – widen the timeframe. What if you look back over the past twenty-four hours? From your partner's perspective, does this fall into a pattern, and therefore you might need to think even further back? If you still can't see your contribution, perhaps you need to look deeper. Perhaps you *do* want your partner to take a fairer share of the burden but, if you were truly honest with yourself, perhaps you *like*, for example, playing the martyr. It could make you feel important, or your mother played the martyr, and although the role is unpleasant, it's at least familiar. Once you're aware of your part in the problem, think about what you could do differently. We like to imagine that everything would be better if only our partner did . . . (fill in the gap with your particular wish), but we can't *make* our partner do anything. The only person's behaviour that we can change directly is our own. So what would you like to do differently?

STOP TURNING YOUR PARTNER INTO A CARICATURE

When we are angry, stressed or tired, it is easy to see everything in very black and white terms. This is particularly the case when it comes to our partner's behaviour or motivations. Instead of seeing them as complex and rounded people, we turn them into cartoon characters with one defining feature. For example, Wile E. Coyote is hungry (and therefore wants to catch the Road Runner), Pepe le Pew is amorous and Donald Duck has a short temper. What's worse, once we've exaggerated a particular characteristic out of all proportion, we get angry with our partner for behaving like that. It's like we're both counsel for the prosecution and judge.

Ryan and Anna, in their early thirties, had been married for ten years and had two young children. Ryan had been reluctant to start a family as he had still wanted to travel and see the world (and believed that children would make this harder). One Sunday, he had been surfing the Internet and come across a blog from a couple who had sold up everything and planned to visit every country in Europe in a camper van over the next two years.

'I just said something like "Wouldn't that be fun?" and I really got my head bitten off,' said Ryan. 'I was told that I wasn't pulling my weight, that I was thoughtless and irresponsible, and all I was doing was trying to read Anna a funny snippet from a blog!'

'It's like he's got gypsy blood in him and nothing will please him but the open road and somehow me and the kids are holding him back,' Anna came back.

'What makes you think I didn't want to take you and the children with me? I never said I wanted to sell up everything. I was thinking about taking a couple of weeks off, maybe three, and renting a camper van – perhaps travelling down through France to Spain.'

'OK, that's different, but you'd really like to pack up everything. What about the children's education? I don't want our daughters to be running around campsites with twigs in the hair in dirty vests.'

'It's just a fantasy, and I did say the people writing the blog were probably in their sixties, their children had grown up and they had no responsibilities.'

Meanwhile, Ryan had created a caricature of Anna where she was obsessed with order and cleanliness and getting on in the world. Once again, there was more than a crumb of truth. She did want promotion at the bank where she worked. She did value tidiness and being able to find things. She did want the children to wash their hands before meals. However, there was more to Anna than being sensible and responsible. In the same way, Ryan was not just about fun and freedom.

Turn it around: Once again, start with what you agree on, not what you disagree about. For example, Ryan and Anna could have talked about how they both wanted their children to experience different cultures and understand different ways of life. They both wanted their children to know and enjoy nature – not just watch it on the TV. They both wanted their daughters to do well at school – so that they had more choices in the future. By focusing on agreement, they were less likely to caricature each other and more likely to build agreement. What's more, in most circumstances, the middle way is always the best. Their daughters needed both to be able to enjoy themselves and to work hard at school.

RECRUIT OTHERS

The more adults who are regularly involved in your children's lives the better, as they thrive on adult attention. Look beyond the obvious members of the family – like grandparents – and ask brothers and sisters without children to do some babysitting. I have several clients who have confirmed their desire to start a family after having looking after their nieces and nephews for the weekend while the parents had some time alone together. Other possible recruits for childcare are godparents and close friends. Unfortunately, most people feel uncomfortable asking childless siblings or friends, for fear of imposing. Meanwhile, most childless adults never think of offering. On the rare occasions that I have looked after my nieces and nephews – either because I've offered or been asked – I've really enjoyed myself. It was great to see the world through a child's eyes and connect back to that sense of wonder, possibility and freshness (and to be able to give them back afterwards). For parents, it's great to have extended time together without your children (and to be reunited with them afterwards). It's a win-win situation.

The other pool of untapped energy that could fill the household chores gap is staring you straight in the eye: your children. Research conducted by the Children's Society found the majority of teenagers are *never* expected to do any jobs around the house. However, children as young as two can pick up their toys and a three-year-old can lay the table. Mothers of boys have a particular responsibility to make certain they do their fair share of chores, partly because their future daughters-in-law will thank them, but mainly because it's in their sons' interest not to be helpless and hopeless. I left home at eighteen having never used a washing machine or an iron and unable to cook anything beyond a boiled egg and beans on toast. I still can't sew on a button.

Turn it around: If you find the idea of asking for something from your parents, siblings or friends difficult, ask yourself why. Did nobody listen when you were a child, so you don't expect them to now? Were you told something like '"I want" doesn't get' or encouraged to suppress your needs: 'Can't you see I'm busy?' Remember being assertive – see Chapter Two: it's OK for you to ask and it's OK for the other person to say no. So choose someone who knows you well and you feel safe asking for something from. Be direct and get to the point, rather than dropping hints. Listen carefully to their response rather than jumping to a conclusion. If they say, 'I'd love to but not this time', it's fine to ask again, but after that I would take a second refusal as a polite way of saying no. (There's advice on asking your children to take on chores in Chapter Eight.)

AIM FOR 'GOOD ENOUGH'

When I challenge perfectionists, they seem to think the alternative is chaos. So it's either sparkling-clean surfaces or rats and disease. However, there is a middle way. We're back with 'good enough'.

'I have a guilty secret but I doubt I'm the only working mum who thinks the same way,' says Jane, forty-two. 'I always talk about "being organized" but, to be honest, you have to let things slide or you'd go mad. My husband doesn't mind a bit of mess and the children create most of it. Nobody cares if you lower your standards – except you.' Jane had her epiphany when she thought back to her grandmother's house. 'She lived in one of those terraced houses in Yorkshire where the homes opened straight on to the street. She had this stone – a donkey stone – that she used to rub against the front step. It would clean and colour at the same time – not that the effect would last long – and all the women in the street would be on their hands and knees scrubbing every week. It was supposed to be a sign that you ran a clean and respectable home. Even by the late sixties, when I was a girl, it was dying out. Nobody does it now. I doubt you'd even be able to buy a donkey stone. I stood in my kitchen thinking about all the energy my grandmother put into cleaning her front doorstep and suddenly it hit me. One day, they'll be laughing at some of the things *we* think essential.'

It's not just housework where you need to question whether you are aiming too high. Sometimes it's not a bad thing to lower our standards for our children too.

Marie, whom we met earlier, wanted her daughter to be a high achiever – even though she was only seven. So when it came to her dance exams, instead of letting her daughter just prance around, she insisted that she learnt a routine and made her practise until it was drilled into her memory.

'It was a lot of hard work but she was thrilled with getting a distinction and thanked me afterwards,' said Marie.

178

'But you put both yourself and your daughter under a lot of extra pressure,' I pointed out.

'You were really crabby and short-tempered with us and complaining that I wasn't pulling my weight,' added John.

'What would have happened if she had just pranced around and got a pass?' I asked. 'I doubt she wants to be a professional dancer.'

Marie smiled. 'It wouldn't have been the end of the world, and of course she's no idea what she wants to be when she's older.'

In effect, once she had stepped back and considered the bigger picture, Marie realized that she could aim for good enough for herself and her daughter.

Turn it around: Good enough looks different on the opposite side of the responsibility gap. If you're the partner who is holding more responsibility, it might feel frightening to relax your control – either because you're worried that your partner will not pick up the slack (and, for example, there will be no food in the house) or because your self-image is so tied up in the house or being 'in charge'. If this is the case, experiment for a week or a month. What would happen if you left something to your partner and he or she did it 'well enough'? What would happen if you lowered your standards and, for example, left the bedlinen on for a couple of extra days? Remember it is an experiment, not a commitment from now to eternity.

If you're the partner who is normally on the supporter side of the responsibility gap (perhaps you work full-time), it can seem daunting to fill the chores-and-childcare deficit. Lots of men in this position get depressed as they stare into the void and either become defensive ('I already do so much') or give up ('What's the point? She'll never be satisfied'). Instead, experiment with good enough. By this, I mean make a contribution towards closing the gap by taking on something. For example, the laundry or Saturday childcare. It might only be a gesture, but it shows willing.

Alternatively, your deficit can be made up in a different sphere, for example romance. Time and again, when I counsel couples with a wide responsibility gap, the wives are asking for a little more help but what they really want is to feel loved and cherished. So although, for example, being responsible for the children on Saturday or doing the laundry is a help, it will seem like something for the children or the household rather than her. However, bringing home some flowers (for no reason whatsoever), giving her a hug (beyond when you want sex), making an effort to notice when she's bought something new (and complimenting her) or using some imagination to fix a date together (rather than the same old restaurant and movie) will make her feel not only appreciated but also desirable. (There will be more on this subject in the next chapter.)

■ ■ ■ ■ ■ ■

King or Queen for the Day

This exercise gets round the 'He just doesn't get it' and 'She's turned into a control freak' trap. As the name suggests, you take it in turns to be in charge for the day and, like royal proclamations, your wishes are granted.

- During your day, you choose all the activities for the family. (Except for something that would terrify your partner or cause a major row.)
- You are in charge not only of what happens but how and when – starting with getting the children up and ending with putting them to bed.
- Your partner complies with good grace and follows your suggestions, requests and even instructions about managing the children without question.
- Don't talk about how things are going during the day or make snide remarks: 'See, it goes better like this' (which could start

an uprising from your subjects) or criticize from the wings: 'I told you so' (which could get you sent to the darkest dungeon!).

- Enjoy yourselves and be playful.
- Afterwards, when you've had time to digest, talk about what you've both learnt from the day.
- On another occasion, perhaps the next day or next weekend, the rules are reversed and the King or Queen becomes the loyal subject.
- The same rules apply, along with a debrief at the end of the day.
- Finally, look at what you've both learnt and what could be incorporated into your normal life together.

Let's look at this exercise in action. Rachel and David, whom we met in Chapter One, should have been cooperating. She wanted more help and he wanted to be more involved, but weekends were a battle zone.

'If I don't do it exactly as she says and when, she criticizes,' David complained.

'He has no idea how much work is involved in caring for a baby twenty-four/seven,' replied Rachel.

So I started them with David being King for the day: in complete charge and with everything he said treated as law. Rachel could choose to be around – but taking the back seat – or go off and pamper herself.

'I had to bite my tongue because I would have done things differently but I helped out as and when asked,' she explained. 'We went out for lunch in the restaurant in the park, fed the ducks and played on the swings and instead of micro-managing every moment I could relax and David seemed to bond better with our daughter.'

Meanwhile David admitted: 'I never really realized how much concentration it took because I would sort of zone out before.'

When it was Rachel's turn to be Queen for the day, David learnt a lot: 'Rather than resenting her systems, and getting moody, I went along with what she said and a lot of her ideas made sense.'

■ ■ ■ ■ ■

When the gap narrows

The more a couple can step into each other's shoes and understand the particular problems of running a home, managing childcare and being responsible for paying the bills, the less likely their relationship is to be undermined by having children. There are individual benefits too to being creative about how you divide up responsibilities. Men who are fully involved with their children, and prioritize the whole family's happiness rather than their professional status, don't miss out on the closeness that comes from casual everyday intimacy with their children. Women who keep at least one foot in the world of work, and share the economic burden of running a family, don't miss out on the intellectual stimulation and financial security of having a life beyond their children. Over the past thirty years that I've been counselling couples, there have been huge changes to the way we work. More people are their own bosses and can choose their working hours. Technology has allowed us to have an office at home and our twenty-four-hour society has meant less nine-to-five, Monday-to-Friday working, and that's brought more opportunities for parents to share childcare.

Jeremy, twenty-seven, had always played lip service to being a hands-on dad to his son, aged three, and his daughter, aged six.

'I worked hard and I didn't really see why I should keep working when I came home, so I would often pretend that I had lots of emails that needed to be done when it was really one, and I'd relax playing computer games,' he explained.

However, his work patterns changed. His job in the leisure industry meant that he could be away at the weekend but home on Monday and Tuesday. Meanwhile, his wife returned to work as a teaching assistant three days a week.

'I had the chance to do things with my son that I'd never done before, and the more you do, the more you see needs to be done. I did the weekly grocery shop and afterwards fancied a sit-down, so I had a coffee and my son had a cake and I told him we were going to have a "man talk". Previously, I would have just let him prattle on but I thought I'd give him my full attention and discovered he's really funny. Now he often asks me, "When are going to have another man talk?"'

On another occasion, his son had also brought him a broken toy.

'Previously I would have just said "What a pity" but done nothing about it. However, this time I asked, "Do you really want me to fix it?" He did, so I got out my toolbox and it only took about ten minutes. He ran round the house shouting, "I've got the best dad in the world." It was like a bolt of electricity going through my whole body: the more I put in, the more I get out.'

Ellie and Clive are both forty-one and have two sons who are five and three. Ellie originally returned to her job as an IT consultant for sixteen hours a week after her maternity leave ended. 'I wasn't getting the juicy or difficult projects. I wasn't feeling effective and felt my career had stalled. Meanwhile Clive was only seeing our children at weekends and felt he was missing out.'

Clive worked as a physiotherapist and struck a deal with his employers to work two and a half days, and Ellie went up to four short days a week.

'If I saw any more of my children, I'd strangle them because they can be really demanding – always asking to "do this with me" or "wrestle with me",' Ellie explained. 'I find work helps me relax and unwind as I like getting engrossed in problem-solving. The result is that I'm a better parent because when it's my turn, I'm refreshed and ready to see them. I'm also a hundred per cent confident in Clive's ability to give the kids a really great time. I came home yesterday and found them all wriggling on the floor and pretending to be pilchards – which really made me laugh. It takes so much pressure off me, knowing they're getting quality input from their dad.'

She also thinks the jobshare has helped their relationship as there is no unspoken resentment: 'We have insight into each other's lives and we're a team, not two isolated individuals. Although we do wish we had more time together. Sometimes, we'll have a passing cuddle in the kitchen and say, "See you tomorrow."'

How to put your partner first

Bringing up children, providing a roof over their head and running a home is a serious business. If you're not careful, all the fun and pleasure can drain out of your relationship and before long it seems that the two of you are just pay cheques, childminders and housekeepers. On the surface, your relationship might be ticking over and beyond a few rows about who does what (or more likely who has not done something) everything seems OK. However, it is a long way from what brought you together in the first place: you had fun in each other's company and you enjoyed doing things together. While you might have fun with the children – either individually or as a family – it is easy for your relationship as partners to become about chores and responsibilities. And here's the catch, which most couples don't understand: a happy relationship is not just defined by an absence of serious problems but by sharing a life together that is exciting and where you feel connected to each other.

At this point, in my therapy office, couples will either start to roll their eyes (when are they going to have time for fun?) or they'll sigh and think I'm talking about date nights (which require a lot of organizing, and that's another chore to add to the list). So what do I mean by having fun and enjoying each other's company?

- Smiles and laughter
- Pet names
- In-jokes and shared catchphrases (for example, references to your favourite sitcoms or films)
- Saving up jokes that you hear at work or funny things the children say to share
- Sending a nice text in the middle of the day
- Forwarding a link to a comedy sketch on YouTube
- General silliness and messing about together
- Leaving small presents (like chocolate on your partner's pillow) or a note on the dashboard of the car

As you can see, my ideas of fun don't require a lot of time or money but are more about how you interact on a daily basis. However, these gestures show that you're thinking about your partner and that he or she is more than a co-worker on the project of raising a family. Of course, there will be times when you need to talk, plan or have a business meeting, but have some team-building time too.

While I'm talking about fun and being silly, I think it is important to make one thing clear. It is only fun if both of you enjoy yourself. So if you partner does not like being teased, that does not fit my definition of fun. For me, fun is anything that builds connection. So even chores – like writing the Christmas cards – can be fun if they are done together.

Let's return to Blake and Emily from Chapter Two – who have two children under three – and reflect on the need for a rock-solid relationship: they both had demanding and absorbing jobs and little time for fun.

'We try and do nice things and make life easier for each other,' said

Emily, 'so the other morning, I said I'd take our eldest to nursery while Blake got the younger one ready for the childminder. In that way, he'd be able to start work a bit earlier.'

'I like to get up earlier and take my time, so I can, for example, play a little game with my daughter as she brushes her teeth,' said Blake, 'while Emily prefers to lie in and be more efficient with her time and just get on with it.'

'It works well because Blake can have the bathroom first and it's then free for me blitz through later,' replied Emily.

I was aware that they worked very well as a team but on separate tracks. Where was the connection? Where was the fun? The next week, they decided to work together rather than split the tasks.

'We decided to clean together, rather than me taking the kitchen and Emily doing the bathroom,' said Blake. They were also able to use his sense of fun. 'I put on some music I've been enjoying and wanted to introduce to Emily, and we talked about what we'd been doing over the week.' They also played a game where they had to come up with as many recording artists for different letters of the alphabet as possible.

In effect, they had made their connection with each other a priority rather than just ticking off their list of jobs.

Summing Up

You cannot find a solution until you have fully explored the problems and understood each other's feelings and thoughts. When you have been through the first two stages, you can move on to the final stage: Action. In most cases, the resolution is not so much aiming for a fifty:fifty split but understanding each other's contribution to the family and making certain you both feel loved rather than just a service provider. That's why fun and silliness are not just things for your children, but part of your everyday relationship with each other too. In fact, this idea is so important that it straddles two of my Golden Rules (see p. 289).

Being Mum and Dad
and Lovers Too

Every couple expects babies to have an impact on their sex life. The later stages of pregnancy can make love-making uncomfortable and it takes a mother time to recover from the pain and sometimes physical trauma of giving birth. Throw in the sleepless nights and the relentless demands of a newborn and it's not surprising that parents' love lives will be disrupted. However, there is a guilty secret that many couples do not tell anyone – not even their friends, health visitor, doctor and sometimes even their relationship counsellor. What's more, they are unlikely to discuss it with each other. So what is this secret? Although most couples resume making love again within the first few months after giving birth, the frequency of sex drops dramatically and for many it can happen less than ten times a year – which sex therapists categorise as a 'low-sex relationship'. If this is the first child, there is normally a boost to love-making as a couple try for a second baby, but once they have been successful, it is not uncommon for their sex life to fall off a cliff. In the worst cases, I have counselled couples who have been in a sexless marriage for years – beyond once or twice when they have made a special effort – despite both their children being old enough to be at primary school. Fortunately, the vast majority of couples do not fall into this category but most parents with two children under five have issues around the frequency and the quality of their love-making.

The impact of hormones on your sex life

Advances in neuroscience have given us a better idea about the biology of desire. When a woman gives birth, she produces more oxytocin – a hormone designed to encourage bonding, nurturing and nursing her child. This increased level of oxytocin will last for around two years and then it will start to wane and she will become more sexual again. In this manner, evolution has encouraged women to want a child about every two years. Dr Glyn Hudson-Allez, a psycho-sexual therapist and author of the training guide for counsellors *Sex and Sexuality* (Wiley-Blackwell), believes that once women have had as many children as they personally want, their overall sexual desire drops. 'Instead of being spontaneously horny, as they might have been before they had children, they become sexually responsive. In effect, their partner has to push the right buttons for them to be sexual. They are less likely be rushing around feeling up for it.' I know this sounds depressing, but I have plenty of advice to overcome this problem.

Unfortunately, the man whose body and lifestyle has not been through the same seismic shift can begin to think his wife does not fancy him any more. If he is unsure how to woo her from the everyday world of nappies, feeding routines and cleaning up after babies into the sensual world of making love, he can become angry and resentful. It goes without saying that this is a turn-off for most women and the chance of sex drops even lower.

'I love my youngest daughter but I really resent that she came along so quickly,' said Robert, thirty-nine. He already had a son, eighteen, from a previous marriage and a daughter, five, with his current partner. 'I agreed to a second child – even though I was happy with our family at the size it was – because I thought I'd get lots of sex, but she fell pregnant almost immediately.'

'I'm sorry but I just don't need to make love. I have two small children hanging off me half the day and I don't need to be groped by you too,' explained Claire, thirty, his wife.

Although I needed to look at how Robert initiated sex – which was clearly part of the problem – it seemed that the physical demands of childcare provided plenty of skin-to-skin closeness that satisfied most of Claire's needs for intimacy (which Robert, who was out at work all day, did not get).

Dr Hudson-Allez sees another difference between men and women: 'When men have sex with a long-term partner, it is part of showing their love. So when women say "I don't want it", men feel personally rejected because it is their love that has been turned down.' This is possibly because, as scientists have discovered, ejaculation is the only time when men produce oxytocin. 'For women, sex becomes an optional extra as they are showing their love with all the other things they're doing in the relationship,' explains Dr Hudson-Allez.

Whether you have two children under five (and your hormone levels had only just returned to normal before the next child came along), your children are older (but your love life has still not recovered) or you just want to improve the frequency or quality of your sex life (so it is a resource to keep you lovers rather than just parents), it is important to understand what promotes desire and what kills it.

Three barriers to desire

In my experience, turns-offs have their roots in our attitudes, the things we have done and the things we have left undone. Here are the three most common reasons for couples falling into the low-sex or no-sex trap.

UNREALISTIC EXPECTATIONS

If I could change just one preconception about relationships, it would be that *love happens naturally*, because it does more damage than anything else. With this myth, what matters is the 'connection', because the strength of the chemistry between a couple will overcome all obstacles. As I've explained, with this expectation you feel you don't need to feed your relationship – or prioritize each other – because your partner loves you and your relationship is naturally self-sustaining. So once you are married the work of courting and seducing each other is complete and you can relax and put your feet up. Worse still, it is only a hop, skip and a jump from 'love happens naturally' to 'sex happens naturally', and that somehow good love-making should happen spontaneously.

Returning to Claire and Robert: 'I don't want to plan to have sex,' explained Claire. 'What if I'm not in the mood? It all seems a bit calculating and . . .' Her voice petered away.

'Dirty?' I wanted to add, but I kept quiet and instead asked about her sex education. I wasn't surprised to discover that her mother had very puritanical views.

'She warned me that "boys were only after one thing" and "they can't be trusted". If there was any what she called "lovely-dovey" on the telly she would start bristling or go very quiet and sometimes it was easier, and less embarrassing, to change channels.'

'It sounds like sex is OK as long as you're carried away by a wave of passion, but to actually ask for it makes you into what?' I asked.

Claire thought for a second: 'Not a nice girl?'

'And probably a whole lot worse.'

She nodded.

'No wonder you believe in spontaneous sex,' I continued. 'But what about when you were trying for a baby? I bet you took your temperature to know when you were ovulating and counted how many days from your last period to maximize your chances of conceiving.'

Claire laughed: 'I suppose I would say that's different.'

Of course, there is nothing wrong with spontaneous sex. I'm all for it. However, in my experience, the only time when parents have enough time to unwind from everyday responsibilities and are in each other's company enough to synchronize their desire is when they are on holiday, and that's not enough to sustain a good sex life.

A related unrealistic expectation that harms our sex lives is *my partner should fill in the blanks in me and fulfil me.* You have only to listen to popular music to realize how deeply this idea is ingrained into us. Whether it's 'You lift me up' or 'I believe I can fly' or 'lost without your love', the belief is that love will transform or rescue you. It's also at the heart of one of the most popular fairy tales: 'Cinderella'. This story structure has been used a million times in movies and books like *Pretty Woman, Cocktail* ('Cinderella' in reverse, with a man being saved by a woman) and *Jane Eyre* (where they 'save' each other). Of course, love does feel good and someone finding us attractive does make us feel worthwhile. However, it is a big jump from this to making your partner responsible for your well-being.

During their counselling, Robert had complained about his job as a salesman and how hard he found it to keep positive. 'There is a lot of rejection. You have to pick yourself up after a potential customer has said no. Of course, it's the product that they're not buying, but it's easy to take it personally. However, if I've had sex with Claire that buoys me up. I have a spring in my step. I feel funnier, nicer, a better man. I can shrug off any setbacks. But if I haven't had sex and I fail to get the order, I can really plummet down.'

Claire was also expecting Robert to fill in the blanks in her life. 'Sometimes I'm almost counting the minutes until Robert arrives home. It gets really boring being home alone all day and starved of adult company. However, he can be stressed and wants to unwind and I want to unload everything that's happened.'

Of course, our partner should be kind and offer help, but he or she is *not* responsible for our happiness and self-esteem or for making sense of our life. If Claire and Robert had taken charge of their own lives, rather than expecting each other to fill in the blanks, she could have arranged to meet other mums during the day (so she was not starved of adult conversation) and he could have asked his boss to send him on a sales course (so he had new selling techniques). In that way, when Claire offered sex or Robert provided a listening ear immediately after arriving home, it would be as a gift, not a duty.

The most dangerous expectation is that *a couple does not need to have sex but they can still have a good marriage*. Traditionally, it has been women who have bought into this myth that somehow if their husband loves them and the children that this will be enough. However, I have counselled lots of relationships where men have a low libido and the women feel unwanted. Whichever way round, it is equally harmful for the relationship. Of course, nobody should be forced to have sex they don't want. However, equally, nobody should have to go without the sex they *do* want.

Turn it around: When couples cannot talk about something, each partner's expectations of the other remain unspoken and therefore un-challenged. Unfortunately, sex is notoriously difficult to discuss. If you said to your partner, 'Can we talk about our summer holidays?', you'd order brochures or do an Internet search about possible destinations. If you said to your partner, 'Can we talk about our sex life?', he or she would probably reply, 'What's wrong with it?' or, worse, 'Are you having an affair?' So how can you bring up the subject without one or both of you becoming defensive?

I recommend using Appreciative Enquiry – an idea that comes from management consultancy. Traditionally, workers identified a problem, tried to understand what went wrong and then looked for a solution. However, staff would fight their corner, opt out and not bring any creativity or imagination to finding a solution. So they turned their working process on its head and focused on what *was* working, and asked: 'How can we build on that?'

There are four stages to Appreciative Enquiry: Discover what works. Dream. Design. Deliver. So start by discussing the good times: 'When do we have good sex?', 'What do you enjoy?' Remember a particularly good occasion and try and give as much detail as possible. Not only will this make your partner feel appreciated but will provide material for the next stages. Second, Dream about how you would both like things to be: 'What sort of sex would you like?' Third, in Design, you work together to make your dream into a reality: 'How could we make this happen?' and 'What would each of us have to do differently?' Finally, in Deliver, you discuss how to sustain the changes.

PESTERING

There are many different styles of pestering for sex. There is dropping hints – normally incredibly unsubtle ones: reminding your partner how long it is since you last made love – and making blue jokes or sarcastic comments. There's also sulking, and being in a bad mood that is only lightened when you're given sex.

In the same way that people who nag know it doesn't work (but builds resentment, undermines their relationship and only gets partial results), deep down, people who pester for sex know it is similarly destructive. Just like nagging, pestering is an equal-opportunity failing (although there tend to be more men pestering for sex and more women nagging for chores). Both naggers and pesterers find it hard to stop because they can't think of any other strategy.

'I don't like to keep asking,' says Timothy, a forty-one-year-father of two teenagers, 'but if I didn't push for it, we'd never have sex.'

'How do you know you'd *never* have sex?' I asked. '"Never" is a long time.'

'OK. I *fear* we'd never have sex.'

'I don't mind you asking, it's what happens if I'm not in the mood,' explained his partner, Charlotte, thirty-eight. 'You let out a deep sigh or get angry or turn your back on me. I feel horrible. If I try and reach out to you, you inch further away. It takes ages before I can fall asleep.'

'It's not great for me either,' replied Timothy.

The situation had got so bad that Charlotte was going to bed early, so she was asleep by the time Timothy came up. She had also started to avoid all casual physical contact. 'I don't come and sit with him on the sofa when we're watching TV in case I send out the wrong signals.'

Not only did pestering put up a wall between Timothy and Charlotte – making it harder for him to initiate sex and increasing the chances of being rejected – but when they did have sex, it was not particularly satisfying.

'It feels like her heart isn't in it, like she's going through the motions,' said Timothy. 'So although I've had an orgasm, it's frustrating because the gap between us is wider than ever.'

'Have you ever thought why that might be?' replied Charlotte.

Not surprisingly, Timothy was beginning to doubt whether Charlotte found him attractive. And that brings me to the biggest problem with pestering. You partner is responding to your desire rather than feeling sexual and initiating sex him- or herself.

Alan Riley is a professor of sexual health at the University of Lancashire and he's been tracking a large number of people and their levels of desire. He has plotted graphs from those with the lowest levels of arousal to the highest. The majority of us lie somewhere in the middle. However, Professor Riley has found that, in general, women tend to fall somewhere on the lower end of the scale and men on the higher. Therefore a typical woman in a relationship with a typical man will want to have sex less often than him. If he starts to pressurize and she starts to give in to keep him quiet, there is a danger that she will never feel totally aroused and sex becomes something for him rather than a shared pleasure.

Turn it around: If you're frightened that if you don't pester for sex you'll never, or more probably hardly ever, have sex, the solution might be hard to accept. So what is it? Wait for your partner to initiate. It will probably take a while. Your partner will need to let go of some of his or her resentment and to begin to feel in the mood again but, trust me, he or she will want sex – probably much sooner than you expect. And what's even better, if your partner initiates, you will feel desired rather than placated. When Timothy agreed to wait for Charlotte to approach him, it took about twelve days – whereas normally they had had sex about once a week – but afterwards they lay in each other's arms and felt truly close for the first time in years.

It is important to stress that this strategy needs setting up properly – rather than just saying nothing and waiting. First, you need to make a fulsome apology (see p. 88) where you take responsibility for your half of what's gone wrong and identify the impact on your partner. For example, 'I'm sorry I've pestered for sex, it must have made you feel pressurized and fed up.' Next make a commitment to change: 'I'm going to wait until you feel ready and ask me.' Finally, discuss casual touching and whether it has become a minefield (because your partner is worried that 'one thing will lead to another'). If this is the case, recommit to waiting for your partner to initiate, so in the meantime a cuddle can be just a cuddle rather than an overture for sex and the two of you can experience the joy of stress-free intimacy. It will be hard to hold back – and keep the touching sensual rather than sexual – until your partner either gives the green light for sex or decides just to cuddle. However, the effort and self-control will be repaid by a dramatic increase in your loving connection to each other.

RESENTMENT

I have placed this chapter about sex after the ones on chores and child-care because there is often a link. It happens in two ways. First, if the person who is responsible for running the house and managing the children's lives feels unappreciated and resentful, it often seeps out somewhere else – most frequently in the bedroom. Second, it is far harder for this partner to switch off (because what needs to be done is right under her or his eyes) than for the partner who is the principal breadwinner (who can at least close the door to the office and go home). If your mind is forever running down a to-do list or you cannot relax until all the chores are complete, it is going to be hard to find enough psychological space to feel sexual. So one of the first tasks for improving a couple's sex life is to find a more equitable split over chores and childcare, as this has an immediate impact in the bedroom. Similarly, goodwill created by a happier sex life makes it easier to close the responsibility gap in the rest of a couple's life.

Timothy used to really enjoy sex in the mornings but his wife would often have to get up early and take his eighteen-year-old son off to catch the bus to college: 'There's no reason why you can't come back to bed afterwards and have a nice long cuddle before it's time for us to get up.'

'But once I've dressed and put my make-up on, I don't really want to,' Charlotte replied.

With the link between childcare responsibilities and a lack of opportunity to make love presented so starkly, it was really easy to persuade Timothy to experiment with making a change. Next week, he reported back on the arrangement.

'If I get up and take my son to the bus, it's a real win-win situation. We get a chance to have a chat together and on the way back I'm looking forward to slipping into a warm bed and cuddling up to Charlotte.'

'I've really enjoyed the occasional lie-in,' replied Charlotte and then teasingly added, 'I don't even mind your cold feet.'

I was not surprised to discover that they often ended up having sex too.

The chores-and-childcare gap is, of course, not the only source of resentment. There is pestering for sex, and annoying habits that make one partner feel unappreciated or second-class – for example, forever checking your emails on your phone, or not delivering on a promise.

Turn it around: Don't ignore your resentment, irritation or outright anger as it will either seep out through your body language and snide comments, or explode in a row. Fortunately, there is a middle way. I call it Reporting Your Feelings, and it works best when you use this formula:

I feel . . . when you . . . because . . .

If you name your feeling, it removes any possibility of a misunderstanding (for example, your partner thinking you are angry when you're only frustrated) and releases a small part of the pent-up feelings. If you qualify the specifics – with 'when you' – your partner is reminded that you're not permanently frustrated but under specific circumstances. Finally, by using 'because', you are explaining the reasons and stopping your partner from jumping to the wrong conclusions. I *feel* lonely when you are working late *because* I want some time alone with you.

■ ■ ■ ■ ■ ■

Myths about Sex

Look at the following list of statements and decide which are true and which are false. (The answers follow afterwards.) When you've finished and checked your answers, go back through the list and identify the myths that you believed or would probably have believed before reading this book, or still half believe. What impact have these myths had on your relationship? In the light of these myths being exploded (or half exploded), what would you like to change about your behaviour? If you're working through this book with your partner, compare your answers and discuss the implications for your sex life.

1. The sexual revolution of the 1960s and '70s threw off our Victorian inhibitions about sex and our prudishness.
2. All touching is sexual or should lead to sex.
3. A man can have an orgasm even if he doesn't have an erection.
4. Nice girls are not as interested in sex as men.
5. It's a man's job to make the earth move for his partner, or at the very least leave her begging for more.
6. Sex should involve intercourse and anything else is preparation for the main course.
7. Woman with better bodies enjoy sex more.
8. Good sex involves being selfish sometimes and concentrating on your own sensations.
9. If someone wants to use sex toys, it means they're dissatisfied with their love life.
10. Men who use pornography are comparing the models to their wives.
11. There's something wrong with a woman if she can't reach orgasm through intercourse.
12. A man has to have an erection for sex to take place.
13. Women don't enjoy pornography.
14. Men should know all about sex.
15. Sex should be spontaneous, without planning or talking about it.
16. Women have a G-spot which, if their partner finds it, will make her multi-orgasmic.
17. If you do not feel turned on, there's no point even starting down the road to sex.

18. You cannot teach an old dog new tricks.
19. My partner ought to know what I like without me explaining.
20. Sex should finish with an orgasm for both people.

ANSWERS

1. False. (We have made great strides but the majority of people are still uncomfortable talking about sex, even with their partner – especially their partner! When I'm interviewed on the radio or write articles for daily newspapers about sex, I'm often asked to avoid using the words 'penis', 'vagina' or 'intercourse', and for some reason any discussion about masturbation – beyond euphemistic references – is banned.)

2. False. (It is important that couples connect physically on a daily basis – as he guides her through a door or she strokes his neck while he's watching TV – so they do not fall into the 'all or nothing' trap where it is sex or separate sides of the bed.)

3. True. (A flaccid penis is still sensitive and it is possible for a man to masturbate and ejaculate without having an erection.)

4. False. (Although, in the playground, girls who were interested in sex or had experimented with several boys were called sluts, in the real world, a woman who is interested in sex is a real asset for keeping a couple's love life passionate and plentiful.)

5. False. (A good sex life is a shared responsibility and each partner has to speak up and explain what makes them feel good.)

6. False. (There are lots of ways to have sex beyond intercourse. If you're talking dirty to each other on the phone or Skyping and masturbating at the same time, you don't even have to be in the same country.)

7. False. (Ultimately what counts is feeling comfortable in your own skin and accepting yourself as you are – rather than at some mythical point in the future when you're lost more weight or had a surgical procedure.)

8. True. (Although good sex is about communication and sharing

pleasure, there are points – especially when heading towards orgasm – where it is necessary to focus on receiving rather than giving.)

9. False. (Sex toys provide variety and opportunities for creative play together, they are not a replacement for a partner.)

10. False. (Men use pornography to escape from their everyday life and to unwind.)

11. False. (While men are more likely to orgasm when sex includes vaginal intercourse, women are more likely to orgasm when a variety of acts like masturbation and oral sex are included. The clitoris has more nerve endings than any-where else in the human body but rarely gets stimulated through intercourse. Sometimes the penis entering and with-drawing from the vagina pulls on the hood of the clitoris and indirectly stimulates it. Sometimes rubbing against a man's pelvis can provide an orgasm, but the woman needs to be on top and leaning forward enough, which makes it hard to main-tain the right degree of contact.)

12. False. (Men also have a tongue and fingers and for many women this is a surer way of providing an orgasm. In addition, erections come and go – even for young men – so if a man concentrates on giving pleasure rather than worrying about how turned on he is, his erection will most probably return.)

13. False. (I have counselled women who enjoy a wide range of pornography. Meanwhile, some agencies who help people whose porn use has got out of control report than as many as one in three of their clients are women.)

14. False. (This myth causes a lot of unhappiness and I regularly get letters from men who are virgins, terrified of being found out and their partner discovering they lack some 'essential knowledge' about how to satisfy a woman.)

15. False. (If parents did not arrange quality time together or for the children to be out of the way, they would seldom if ever

have sex, and how can this be arranged without planning and discussing?)

16. Neither true nor false. (Certainly there are some parts of the vagina that are more responsive, but experts are divided on whether the G-spot is a true separate anatomical structure like the clitoris or nipple.)

17. False. (You could easily get into the mood, and the sensual pleasure of being touched can be transformed into a desire for sex.)

18. False. (It is never too late to learn new skills or brush up on forgotten ones, but often it is easier to believe this myth and avoid the anxiety induced by trying something different.)

19. False. (You're changing all the time, your partner might know what turned you on when you first met, but are you still that same person? In addition, explaining your desires to your partner will help you become more aware of them.)

20. False. (This myth stops us starting down the road to sex as we're frightened of not delivering, but it's fine to be in the mood just to be held and help your partner to orgasm through masturbation, or for both of you to just drift off to sleep in each other's arms without either of you climaxing. Sex is what you want it to be and therefore does not always have to involve an orgasm.)

■ ■ ■ ■ ■ ■

Three bridges to desire

When a couple are first courting – and limerence has crystallized – they don't have to think about how to cross over from the everyday into the sensual world. They are spending as much time together as possible, and if they are apart they're texting, leaving funny messages or sighing and thinking about each other, and when they're finally reunited lust means they can't keep their hands off each other. With sex at the beginning being so easy, few couples are aware of what builds or sustains desire. However, if you have been together for years and have children together, you cannot rely on lust alone, and you've got lots of other things on your mind beyond how cute he looks in a pair of jeans or how her face lights up when she smiles. Therefore, once I have removed the barriers to desire, I help couples find alternative bridges from their everyday reality into being sexual together. There are three bridges that parents find particularly useful:

PLAY

When we were children, play was at the centre of our lives. It is how we learned to interact with our siblings and friends, tried out new skills and developed our imagination. It was also a way of releasing excess energy or motivating us when we were feeling sluggish or bored (and therefore provided us with the first clues about how to regulate our emotions for ourselves). Most importantly, play was fun. However, somewhere around puberty, lots of children put play behind them. Although some teenagers continue to play sport, a musical instrument or perform in the school show, most people give up these activities by the time they leave university or full-time education. Certainly, by the time we are adults and committed to the serious business of raising a family, play has been relegated to something we used to do or a guilty pleasure (e.g. a round of golf on a Sunday afternoon). Of course we play, with our children or as a personal hobby, but seldom or ever with our partner. No wonder, our partner feels that feel that we put him or her last.

Why it is important: Play is anything that has no purpose beyond giving pleasure and having fun. It is about throwing off constraints, about novelty, being open to new ideas, living in the moment (rather than planning for the future or worrying about the past) and building bonds – exactly what you need for keeping your sex life passionate and interesting.

Why we find it so hard: Lots of people received mixed messages as children. We watched our parents work all hours and learnt that work is a virtue and the ultimate validation. Some parents even explicitly tell their sons or daughters that play is a waste of time, that winning or excelling is everything, or that we are clumsy, have two left feet or are not as talented as our brother or sister. As adults, we are frightened of making mistakes (although it's part of the learning process) or looking silly (because we have low self-esteem and would not survive the shame). Some couples are also competitive or see the world through 'right' or 'wrong' lenses. With this mindset, you *shouldn't* need to play dressing up (for example in lingerie) to feel desire or you *shouldn't* behave like children in public and push each other on the swings in the park.

Turn it around: Think about what activities you have previously enjoyed together and provided fun, positive feelings and a sense of connection. To what extent do you do any of those things now? What new activities or interactions have you tried lately?

■ ■ ■ ■ ■ ■

How to Play

It is important to stress that these activities should be for just the two of you – adult play – rather than something child-friendly and therefore family play. Look down the list of the types of play and think which ones you would enjoy.

- Cultural play: be a tourist in your own area, go to a comedy performance, the theatre, a concert or a lecture.

- Entertainment play: go out and sing karaoke together, go danc-ing, visit an antiques or craft fair, go bowling or watch a sporting event together (not one where your children are playing).
- Great outdoors: go to the seaside and skim stones over the waves, go for a long ramble, go canoeing or bike trekking, play tennis, go bird-watching or spend a weekend in a tent together.
- Learn something new together: take a stand-up comedy class, try snowboarding, climbing, scuba diving or wind surfing, or enrol your dog in agility classes.

Make up a list of three things that you would like to do – perhaps from the list or ideas of your own – and ask your partner to choose one. Look at his or her list and chose one that you'd like to do. Just like fun, it is only play if both partners are getting pleasure from the activity.

■ ■ ■ ■ ■ ■

ROMANCE

When we are courting, we are naturally romantic. We lean across the table, we show enthusiasm for each other's interests, we make good eye contact and find lots of little ways to say: 'You're special.' Unfor-tunately, when we have won our beloved and finally feel sure of his or her love, we think we can relax and forget romance.

Why it is important: Some men are confused about how to be romantic. They know it involves flowers, chocolates and candlelit dinners, but what else? So let me explain. Romance is anything above and beyond the everyday that shows your partner that you appreciate him or her. So picking up your beloved from the railway station is part of what it means to be partners. However, if you have a bottle of cham-pagne in a bucket of ice in the back of the car and a card saying 'I love you', that's romantic. Cooking your partner his or her supper is not romantic – because it's a regular event and we need to eat – but if you make a special trip to the butcher for rump steak or cook a complex recipe and dress up to serve it, that goes beyond the utilitarian and demonstrates that you have really thought about your beloved. Raking up the leaves when your partner asks is a kind gesture, but it is not romantic. Going for a walk in the woods, holding hands and kicking leaves together is romantic because you're not just getting from A to B but enjoying each other's company and indulging your senses. Although I have stressed the importance of romance for romance's sake, it does have a purpose. Romance helps build sexual energy, and the planning involved shows that your partner is on your mind, even when you're apart. So when one of you decides to initiate love-making, romance has already got the engine running rather than trying to start from cold.

Why we find it so hard: Romance has been turned into big business and we've been sold the idea that it involves large and expensive gestures. So it is a cruise round the Mediterranean, a trip on the Orient Express and a box at the opera. No wonder couples tell me they don't have the time or money. Of course, these big surprises are great but it costs next to nothing to leave a trail of Post-it notes around the house giving clues to where you've hidden a bar of chocolate. When it comes to showing you care, twelve individual roses on twelve separate occasions is more powerful than having a dozen delivered at once.

Sometimes men complain: 'I'm not the romantic type.' If I question them further, they can't see the point. So I try to repackage romance by explaining that even in action-adventure movies, James Bond or Spiderman does not scale burning buildings to serve his country or save the world but to win the girl. Romance is just one of the tools in a bigger adventure: keeping your sex life passionate and plentiful. It is about being chivalrous, idealizing your beloved and love being not just about sex but strong affection too.

The final reason why men find romance difficult is because it's seen as something for women. When a man says something along these lines, I always ask him: 'Don't you want to feel special and desired?' Obviously, the answer is yes, because everybody wants to be appreciated.

Turn it around: Use the power of three to translate romantic energy into sexual connection. For example, don't share the bathroom while getting ready to go out (so there's an element of surprise because you don't know what each other will be wearing); warm the car up so it's not freezing when your beloved steps inside; and then drive past your usual place because you've booked somewhere special. A second example of the power of three to change kind but normal gestures into something romantic would be wrapping a birthday present inside progressively larger boxes (to build intrigue and excitement as your partner goes through layer after layer); sticking the birthday card to the steering wheel of the car; and getting flowers delivered to work. Doing things threefold underlines just how much you care. Another tip is to store away small bits of information about your partner and look for ways to translate them into romantic gestures. If he likes the music of a particular rock star, you could buy the new biography that you saw reviewed in the paper. If she has fond memories of being taken, as a small child, to the ballet to see *The Nutcracker* at Christmas, you can book tickets when it's staged in your town. Ultimately, what will turn your partner on is the amount of thought put into something, as much as the act itself.

■ ■ ■ ■ ■ ■

How to Be Romantic

Romance is about showing your partner that you care, but its power is increased by novelty (so it's forever being performed in different ways) and therefore has an element of surprise. So look through the list for new ideas.

- Be sensual: have a bath together, wash each other's hair, give each other a massage, build a campfire and stare into the flames, light a scented candle, read a poem out loud.

- Add a new dimension to the ordinary: take your partner out for breakfast, meet for lunch, leave a chocolate on your partner's pillow, dress up and look nice even though you're staying in.
- Bring back memories: watch a romantic movie that you both enjoyed when first dating, look at your wedding photos or video together, put on a favourite song and dance in the living room. Go somewhere with special associations.
- Give small presents: buy flowers, novelty gifts (like a cuddly toy), a piece of jewellery or music you know your partner will enjoy. Express gratitude for something that could easily be taken for granted.

■ ■ ■ ■ ■ ■

FLIRTING

When I talk to couples about the bridges from the everyday world of raising children into the sensual world of making love, it's always a relief when I find that they are still flirting with each other. It normally means their sex life is alive and well. Unfortunately, this is another activity that is standard when we are courting but is either forgotten or considered unnecessary once we're married. Sadly, only 20 per cent of the couples that I counsel are still flirting. Think back: when was the last time you flirted?

Why it is important: Flirting is giving your partner a bundle of sexual energy and seeing if he or she sends it back – hopefully with interest. It says, 'I'm still attracted to you', reveals something about your heart, builds romance and boosts your partner's self-esteem. However, it is important to stress that flirting is playful and fun, rather than a demand for sex.

Why we find it so hard: Flirting is not just in your intent but in how your partner receives it. For example, a husband might think surprising his wife by coming up behind her and fondling her breasts is fun and demonstrates his desire for her. However, if she interprets it as pressurizing her for sex or a form of harassment, then it's not flirting. Lots of couples find flirting such a minefield that it seems safer to step around the area altogether. Unfortunately, they are likely to slip into the role of co-parents, friends, or brother and sister rather than staying lovers. If you find the idea of flirting difficult, don't despair. Your skills might be rusty but there's nothing stopping you from either brushing them up or relearning them.

Turn it around: I have placed flirting as the last bridge to desire because it can be difficult – especially if there is a wall of distrust or anger between you. However, if you can play and be romantic together, there will be a more positive atmosphere. So even if your flirting is too strong (and needs to be toned down slightly), your partner will be able to tell you and you should be able to take feedback as a gift (to help you be better next time) rather than as simply criticism (and therefore rejection). Start by taking a general audit of how you and your partner communicate. Are you in the same room, or do you shout up and down the stairs to save time? Do you put down what you're doing when your partner is talking? What is your eye contact like? (A lot of flirting is in the eyes.) Make a commitment to stop practices that almost guarantee misunderstanding and undermine connection.

How to Flirt

The secret of flirting is to start small (at the non-sexual end of the spectrum) and build slowly (checking out the reaction from your partner) into something a little more explicit and only later making sexually charged overtures.

- At a distance: leave a sweet message somewhere only he or she will find it, send a saucy text, tell your partner what you're going to do to him or her when he or she gets home.

- Casual touch: rub your leg against theirs in a restaurant, gently touch your partner's face, stroke their hair.
- Teasing: play peek-a-boo (look from behind the menu in a restaurant and then hide your eyes). Show him that you're wearing something naughty – like a garter – under your dress. Show her you've bought a small present but don't let her open it until later. Tickle your partner.
- Kisses: Give an extra-long kiss when your partner comes home, kiss with your eyes open, kiss him or her somewhere unexpected, vary your kisses (try lots of light butterfly kisses on the neck followed by blowing a raspberry on the stomach).

■ ■ ■ ■ ■ ■

Have better sex

Although a lot of my work is in helping couples improve the frequency of their love-making, it is equally important that when you do have sex it is satisfying and anxiety-free (and therefore builds a virtuous circle where you want more sex and it becomes easier to initiate). In the same way that there are three blocks to parents having sex and three bridges to desire, I have three strategies for improving technique.

SLOW DOWN

In general, it takes the average wife longer to become turned on than for the average husband. Fortunately, most couples are aware of this discrepancy and make allowances. However, once a wife has children, she will also need to shift out of mother mode into sexual-woman mode. Unfortunately, once you have children, time is short. There's always the fear that the baby or children will wake up. You're tired, there's another long day ahead tomorrow and you want to go to sleep. All these factors make it more likely for a couple to rush their love-making, just when they need to slow down more in order to ensure that the woman is fully engaged and ready for sex.

'I don't really feel that sexy,' explains Zoe, twenty-nine. 'Since I had my daughter I've not been able to lose the weight I put on while pregnant.'

'I still fancy her but she has a hard time believing it,' added her husband, Ben.

'My mind is full of what needs to be done tomorrow, what I need to remember and what I've forgotten,' she explained.

'Sometimes it feels that you're not with me when we do make love,' explained Ben, 'like you're mentally running down that list. It can feel very lonely.'

'To be honest, it's sometimes "Just get on with it" – which I know sounds cruel – but once I do get into the mood, I do enjoy myself.'

'How long does that take?' I asked.

'I don't know.' Zoe replied.

But I sensed she was being diplomatic because the truth could hurt Ben. 'Is it sometimes too late for you get any real satisfaction out of your love-making?' I asked.

Zoe nodded.

Turn it around: Extend your foreplay. First, allow at least fifteen minutes for sensual touching – by this I mean stroking, fondling and kissing each other but avoiding touching breasts and genitals. You can take it turns to pleasure each other or do it both at the same time but make certain that you explore every inch of your partner's body (beyond breasts and genitals). Don't let each other know what's coming next. In this way, sex is not predictable and possibly boring. Change direction, speed, intensity of touch (lightly skimming to firm massage) and alternate between fingers and mouth. Look for new places that might be sensitive and elicit pleasure for your partner. Make certain that you communicate (let out a sigh if something feels good), listen to your partner's breathing (does it sound heavy and turned on?) and check that your partner is not tensing up (which suggests that you're doing something wrong).

Secondly, after fifteen minutes of sensual touching, you can move on to exploring breasts and genital areas with your fingers or tongue. Once again, vary your approach – stop, wait, start again – so that you keep an element of surprise. Allow at least ten minutes of this sexual touching, either taking it in turns to give pleasure or pleasuring each other at the same time, before finally moving to intercourse (or deciding to make oral sex or masturbation the main course of your love-making).

BE LESS PENIS-FOCUSED

One of the most pernicious myths about sex – which I have hopefully challenged earlier in this chapter – is that there needs to be an erect penis for sex to take place. You might imagine that men are most concerned about the strength and sustainability of their erections but I'm afraid that women are just as obsessed.

'I don't really like to say anything,' said Zoe, checking with Ben, 'but if we want things to change, we've got to be honest.'

'What she's trying to say is that sometimes I lose my erection,' he explained.

'It's not that often but . . .' her voice trailed away.

'I do fancy you,' he tried to reassure her.

'You never used to go soft.'

'So if he fancied you, he'd have a rod of steel,' I interjected, hoping to add a little humour into the situation and lighten the atmosphere. 'Except the quality of a man's erection is not just about how turned-on he feels. It's possible for men to have erections in the morning – when a full bladder is pressing on the prostate gland – when they don't feel remotely sexy. Equally, a man can be really excited but nervous or anxious and that stops him getting an erection. There is no straight-forward connection between desire and erection.'

'I do worry about being overheard or whether our daughter will wake up and want to come into our bedroom, so the slightest noise or click from the central heating can break the mood,' said Ben.

'Men are not sex machines, we're fallible human beings,' I ex-plained, 'but what happens if you're not giving Zoe a reassuring round of applause with your rampant penis?'

'I see the look on her face and I get angry with myself. The more I worry, the worse it gets.'

'So you retreat to separate sides of the bed and love-making stops?' I asked.

This time, they both nodded.

'And so when you do have an erection, you want to – excuse me for being so direct – get on with it. So perhaps it's not surprising that Zoe hasn't had enough time to relax, unwind and join in your love-making, because you're rushing towards the finishing line.'

It had become a vicious circle. Ben was focusing on his penis rather than communicating his love. Zoe was not fully engaged and therefore not giving him any sexual feedback or encouragement, so he was feel-ing less turned on and more likely to lose his erection and want to rush sex.

Turn it around: Erections come and go. Contrary to popular myth, even teenage boys don't walk around with constant erections. So instead of worrying, focus on something else. For example, the man could give his wife oral sex or masturbate her, or the couple could return to the sensual touching and cuddling part of foreplay. On most occasions, the man's erection will return. However, it could be that he's tired or had too much to drink and a cuddle is enough. Contrary to another common myth, sex does not have to end in an orgasm for both parties. What counts is that both parties feel close, sharing intimacy and a sense of being connected. It's also fine for one partner to masturbate him- or herself while the other partner kisses him or her or whispers encouragement.

Having a variety of possible outcomes to sex helped to turn round Zoe and Ben's love-making. Instead of being focused on his penis, their love-making could be anything from simple sensual touching, through to getting sexual gratification from masturbation (either by themselves or pleasuring each other), both of them climaxing (from masturbation or oral sex), or having full intercourse.

MAKE SEX A SHARED RESPONSIBILITY

When a woman feels responsible for running the house and the children's welfare, she can easily feel unappreciated and resentful. Equally, when a man feels responsible for initiating sex the vast majority of the time, he can easily worry that his wife doesn't fancy him, that she's only doing sex for him (which is a turn-off) and that there's no real sexual connection. In just the same way that I want to close the responsibility gap for housework and childcare, I'd like to close the responsibility gap for sex too.

In many cases, men are not just responsible for initiating sex but for turning their woman on and giving her an orgasm too. (We're back to our myths about sex again – see earlier in this chapter – this time that it's a man's job to make the earth move for his partner.) Returning to Zoe and Ben, it was Ben who was responsible for initiating sex.

'Except in the early days when we first got together, I suppose it must be ninety-five per cent-plus that I make the first move,' said Ben.

'I've never really thought about it, but you're probably right,' said Zoe. 'Certainly you've kept track of how often we've made love, and once when we went through a dry spell told me that we hadn't had sex for five months. I'd been aware that it wasn't recently but not that long!'

'Once he has initiated, whose job is it to pull you out of mummy mode so that you can feel truly sexual?' I asked.

Zoe looked puzzled for a moment: 'I suppose I want him to seduce me,' she replied.

'That's fine, and that's part of being a loving couple, but what I'm asking is for you to take equal responsibility. After all, it's *you* that's going down your list of mummy jobs. Sure, he can take his time, so you have a chance to close down that part of your brain. However, ultimately it's up to you to tell yourself: "Enough of this mummy stuff. There's more to me than just being a mother. Let it drop." So you're *equally* responsible for turning yourself on.'

Unfortunately, what can happen is that women – often unconsciously – give their husband the responsibility for love-making and then become resentful when they fail to deliver, which makes sex harder to initiate and less satisfying for both partners.

However, men don't help themselves either. In the same way that some women complain about carrying the burden of chores and childcare (but hold on with both hands to being in charge), men find it equally hard to share responsibility for sex.

'I get my pleasure from giving pleasure to Zoe,' explained Ben.

'So how do you feel if Zoe pleasures herself to achieve an orgasm or if, for example, you try a position for intercourse where she is on top and therefore setting the speed and depth of your penetration? If she's giving you pleasure rather than just receiving it.'

He looked uncomfortable for a moment but finally he replied, very quietly and looking down at the floor: 'That I'm somehow less of a man.'

Deep down, men know this is nonsense. However, when couples don't talk about sex and confront the myths, they hold on to outdated ideas that spoil not only their own pleasure but that of their partner too.

Turn it around: Negotiate about when to have sex. Instead of sex being an unmentionable subject – so you send semaphore signals about your willingness or unwillingness to make love – I'd like you to be able to talk to each other. I know this sounds a daunting task but remember assertiveness. In a nutshell: 'I have the right to ask (in this case, for sex), you have the right to say no and then we can negotiate.' This strategy works best if you have already extended your foreplay. In this way, the person who says no to sex can offer a cuddle and extended sensual touch as an alternative. The other possibility would be to use another bridge to desire: planning. I'm particularly keen on planning because it makes initiating a shared responsibility. So, for example, the person who says no could offer to make love the next day or on Saturday morning. This is followed by a discussion where both partners decide if this option is practical and how to turn it into a reality. Obviously, this is not a cast-iron guarantee of sex. If one of you is ill, your parents drop round or the boiler has broken down, you might need to negotiate a new time.

■ ■ ■ ■ ■ ■

The Pros and Cons of Switching off

Talking about sex, taking responsibility for your own pleasure and dealing with your hang-ups is hard, really hard. It is much easier to put the children first, reassure yourself that all parents' sex lives take a knocking and switch off. So I wouldn't be surprised if you're thinking, Yes, but . . . 'Yes, I should do something about our sex life, *but* my husband loves me and the kids' or 'Yes, I should bring up my unhappiness about our sex life, *but* my work is really stressful at the moment' or 'Yes, *but* it'll be easier when the kids are older.' That's fine, but before you move on to the next chapter, I'd like you to complete this cost/benefit analysis of switching off:

PROS	CONS

If you're finding it difficult to come up with costs and benefits, I've gathered together some of the responses from my clients:

PROS	CONS
No anxiety about whether I please my partner.	Missing out on the possibility of a better sex life.
No embarrassing discussions about sex.	Poor cooperation in other areas.
I can hang on to my viewpoint and feel right.	No romance and courting.
I win an argument.	Fewer orgasms.
Sex is a bargaining tool for getting what I want.	I don't feel close or connected.
I don't have to confront a problem.	More rows.
Revenge.	Infidelity.

How to put your partner first

Every couple would agree that they should be lovers as well as Mum and Dad. Unfortunately, they send out signals that say 'Our children's needs are more important than our couple needs' and sex drops down their list of priorities.

Stella, forty-one, and Graham, forty, had two children, ten and eight; they both enjoyed sex – when it happened – but they found it difficult to find the time. Fortunately, they were comfortable with the idea of planning sex so we were able to discuss when was the best time.

'Around about nine o'clock would be good for me,' said Stella. 'Any later and I'm too tired.'

'Except that's around the time that we finish putting the children to bed,' said Graham. 'If they go to bed too early, I don't see them when I come home, but they can dawdle getting to bed and want an extra story.'

'Some nights we could be more focused and switch their lights off by eight-thirty and come to bed,' said Stella.

'But then you've got to prepare for the next morning, sort out their games equipment and books,' said Graham, 'so that's not always possible.'

They sank into silence.

'Let me get this straight,' I interjected. 'Preparing your children for school the next day is more important than finding time to make love to each other. Something you both enjoy. What message are you sending each other?'

They looked even more miserable.

'What would happen if the children prepared their own kit for school? After all, they are ten and eight. The responsibility would be good for them.'

'I never thought of that,' said Stella. 'We could introduce it for next term.'

Another example is Julie and Max, both in their early fifties. I had given them homework which involved setting aside half an hour to do sensual touch exercises. They had decided to have an early night together but at the last minute their fourteen-year-old daughter announced she needed five pages of typing for her exam the next day. Max was angry because instead of arriving in the bedroom relaxed and ready to be intimate, Julie was stressed and unreceptive. When I questioned her, she admitted that she found it almost impossible to say no to her child. Almost immediately, Max interrupted: 'But she can say no to me.'

One of the best ways of staying lovers – and sending a clear message that couple time is important – is to go on a date together (from time to time). Unfortunately this is another idea that couples might happily sign up for in theory but find difficult in practice. So what goes wrong?

- Indecision leads to no decision: the husband does not take the lead and the woman does not say what she would enjoy.
- Planning becomes another wifely chore: basically, if a woman arranges everything it's domestic, if a man does the planning it's romantic. (This also extends to planning childcare. I can't tell you how often men tell me they don't know any babysitters and I ask, 'Does your wife hide this information from you?')
- Talking about your relationship: this is a chance to enjoy yourselves together. If something difficult comes up, make an appointment to discuss it at another time.
- Mobile phones, social networking, etc.: turn off all electronic equipment. If you take messages from work or check your Facebook page while your partner goes to the bar, you are saying, 'You don't hold my attention' or 'I'd rather be somewhere else.'
- Too much drinking: this increases the chance of rows or one

partner feeling 'You can only touch me when you're off your face.'

Now let's look at what makes a successful date:

- Admit that you don't know everything about your partner. Ask questions: 'What would you do if you won the lottery?' or 'If you could live anywhere in the world, where would you be?' or 'What are your top ten favourite albums of all time?'
- Share an activity together. Instead of just talking over a meal, do something fun.
- Be fully present. Look into your partner's eyes, notice something attractive about him or her and touch each other from time to time.
- Make an effort. We are committed to entertaining our children but not each other. Turn this around by storing up interesting stories, gossip or snippets from the news to share on your date.

(There's more information about being lovers rather than parents in my books *Make Love Like a Prairie Vole: Six Steps to Passionate, Plentiful and Monogamous Sex* (UK) and *Have the Sex You Want: A Couple's Guide to Getting Back the Spark* (US).)

Summing Up

If you were to take only one idea from this chapter, it would be that sex does not only have to be spontaneous. After the birth of a baby, it takes longer for a woman to become physiologically turned on. As you can no longer rely on lust to bridge from the everyday world into the sensual world, you need to find other ways – like having fun, being romantic, flirting and playing together. In this way, sex becomes something to feed not just your relationship but yourself too, so you do not become trapped in the role of parents (giving out energy) but are lovers (receiving energy) too. Whatever happens, it is important to talk about sex rather than just hoping things will improve at some unspecified date in the future.

Red-Carpet Kids

Throughout time, our ancestors have sought to improve the lot of their children, to give them the best possible start and watch them thrive. To our grandparents, almost any sacrifice was worth it to give our parents the opportunities they didn't have. In turn, our parents strived to pass on to us the advantages that they enjoyed. Now it's up to us to pass the baton on to the next generation.

Up to this point in the book, I've been stressing the importance of prioritizing your marriage – because unless you invest in your relationship, it will wither and die, and that's not good for your children – but now I'm going to shift my focus. I accept that everybody wants the best for their children – it's part of human nature – but I question whether making them the centre of the universe is good for their welfare or prepares them properly for the world they will inherit. I'm concerned that we're creating a generation of 'red-carpet kids'.

So what do I mean by this term? Basically, I've combined two very different ideas: ancient Buddhist teaching and the modern cult of celebrity. Buddha advised that if we have to walk across rough and thorny terrain it's impossible to cover it in leather (or carpet), but we can cover our feet in shoes. In effect, he was saying that we can't change the world (and eliminate unwelcome events) but we can change ourselves (and our reaction to those events). Unfortunately, modern parents want to make everything safe and welcoming for their children, but sometimes it's like trying to flatten out the rough ground, uproot the thorns and carpet the world. Meanwhile, the red carpet is the apex of the celebrity world: just walking down it triggers off banks of flashing cameras and fashion spreads in glossy magazines. Nobody remembers the film whose première these princes and princesses were attending because the red carpet is the true event and being on it has become an end in itself. Today's parents – often to boost their children's confidence – offer unquestioning adulation and, in effect, are forever rolling out the red carpet for their sons and daughters.

A lot of the ideas in this chapter will be challenging, but I think that's good. Hopefully I will make you think about some of the modern myths about mother- and fatherhood and question not only whether they are good for your children but whether some of the energy currently devoted to parenting would be better channelled elsewhere – like maintaining your marriage and your sexual connection with each other.

Why are we raising a red-carpet generation?

Babies and toddlers need a lot doing for them. They are small and vulnerable. So it's not surprising that we pour so much energy into looking after them. However, toddlers turn into children who need us less, but for some reason we find new ways to serve – even to the point of exhausting ourselves and our marriages. So what makes us go over the top and risk spoiling our children?

SMALLER FAMILIES

My family is just one example of this trend. My grandfather was one of eight, my mother was one of four and my sister has two children. But how does this impact on parenting? At the most basic level, if you've lots of children, it's impossible to roll out the red carpet for the older children because you're too busy breastfeeding the youngest and possibly still changing the nappy of the second-youngest. However, it goes deeper. If you have fewer children, each one of them becomes even more precious.

'I worry about my son going to nursery and being out of my sight for four and a half, almost five hours a day: what if another child wants a certain thing? He'll be one of the youngest. What if he gets bullied?' says Archana, who is thirty and has just one child. 'He currently goes to a playgroup for two hours but that just gives me enough time to come home and clean rather than fretting, but what about when he goes to big school?' In a bigger family, there is always safety in numbers – with older children looking out for younger ones – but behind our modern tendency to be overprotective there is an unspoken fear: our whole family could be wiped out by one fatal mistake. 'My son is so precious and irreplaceable – and being an only child just emphasizes that,' says Archana.

This trend is exacerbated if you wanted a larger family but had to settle for a smaller one. I did some research into family sizes with babycentre.co.uk and found that 38 per cent of UK mothers would like more children but were worried about the costs and whether they could give their existing children enough attention. Twenty-eight per cent of mothers said they would like one more and 10 per cent wanted two or more further children. When these mothers were children themselves, only 4 per cent dreamt of having just one baby; however this is the reality today for almost one in three mothers in my survey. With all these missing babies that we wanted but did not have, it's not surprising that we make the children we do have the centre of our lives.

WE WANT TO BE LIKED

At work, there are flatter hierarchies and we are more likely to socialize with our supervisors and employers. We are less deferential to people who would previously have been figures of authority – for example, we will use our doctor's first name and he or she will use ours in return. We also have less respect for institutions like the House of Commons, the BBC and the monarchy. No wonder we find it diffi-cult to be an authority figure to children and would much prefer to be 'mates'.

'I was very young when I had my daughter,' says Katie, who is now forty and her daughter Nicole eighteen, 'so we sort of grew up to-gether. We are incredibly alike to the point of being telepathic, and I'd definitely say we were friends. Once when she was really upset about a boy, we talked for two hours over a whole bottle of Bailey's. We borrow each other's clothes, although she has a black skirt that she thinks is too tight on me and says that people stare if I wear it.'

It's not just the risk of squabbling with your children – like two siblings – but also that of losing your parental authority. 'Generally we get on well but if I get cross – she's not studying enough for her exams – and I start shouting at her, I fear that I haven't acted as her friend,' explained Katie. 'I've laid into her and told her she was useless. I panic and worry that our relationship will suffer because I got so heavy; that she won't confide in me and I won't be there when she needs me. I'm so frightened of losing her friendship that I end up backtracking and giving in.'

There will be more from Katie and Nicole in a moment.

IT'S EASIER

When you're stressed and busy, it's much easier to give in to your children and let them have what they want. If your daughter is making a scene in the supermarket, you can avoid a prolonged tantrum by buying the chocolate biscuits. If you're trying to get out of the door in the morning, it's quicker to dress your six-year-old son and tie his shoelaces rather than insist that he does it himself. Parents think that giving in makes their children feel loved, but they often get a different message.

'I'm the youngest of five and my eldest brother is twenty years older than me,' explains Keith, thirty-three. 'By the time I came along I think my mother was fed up with babies. She'd just started a business and my pram was parked round the back of the shop and the staff used to take it in turns to check on me. Meanwhile, it was a family joke that our father missed out on our childhood because he travelled a lot for work and never came home before nine in the evening. They tried to compensate with the latest toys or gadgets – my brothers and sisters thought I was spoilt – but it felt like I could have anything except their attention.

'I went to a school where "gold stars" were a big thing. Once everybody in the class had one, we got an afternoon off. At that point in the term, everybody had one except me. In my hurry to finish my French classwork and get my gold star, I wrote *le port* [for bridge] rather than *le pont*. Obviously, it was wrong and I was marked down and, once again, let the class down. So I went back to my desk and changed the R to an N and told the teacher that he'd got it wrong. Obviously, he wasn't a fool and told me to sit down again. However I reported him to my mother, who phoned the headmaster and got the teacher reprimanded. I was awarded the gold star and the class got the afternoon off.'

'Did you feel that she had attended to your needs?' I asked.

'Not at all.'

'Why?' I asked, slightly surprised – after all, he'd got what he wanted.

'She didn't stop and ask. Would an experienced teacher make such a mistake? She didn't take time to get to the bottom of the problem or ask why I felt compelled to cheat. No. She did the easy thing.'

GUILT

There are hundreds of reasons for modern parents to feel guilty: not spending enough time with their children, not being able to afford everything their children want or need, losing their temper and not feeling 'good enough'. Children have an unerring knack for sniffing out parental guilt and exploiting it, because when we feel guilty, we'll do almost anything to compensate.

Amanda, forty-one, from Chapter One, feels that she has let her daughter down by not providing her with a brother or sister. To as-suage her guilt, she has rolled out the red carpet: 'If my husband and I are out and discussing whether we should go home and cook or go to a restaurant, we'll ask our daughter – even though she's three.

'Unless I accept that she's going to be an only child – and that's not a bad thing – I'm at risk of turning her into a very unpleasant person because she will expect to always be the centre of attention.'

■ ■ ■ ■ ■ ■

Saying No to Your Children

Everybody likes to be liked, and saying yes is normally the quickest way to being popular. Of course, we know that we need say no too. And we say it reasonably regularly. Except we don't want to upset our children, so we say no one minute and change our minds the next.

So how do you say no and mean it?

AUDIT YOUR NO RECORD

Over the next few days, keep a mental record of how often you say no and the reaction of your children. Here are a couple of things, in particular, to keep an eye open for. Do you have to say no several times and possibly shout or lose your temper before your children listen? Are you training them to tune out because if something is truly important you'll raise the roof? Do you follow through on your 'no' or do you back down ('OK, please yourself') or bribe them ('Have an ice cream') or simply give in because they're causing a scene? Could your children assume that you don't really mean no? Are you, in effect, training them to wheedle, manipulate or throw a tantrum to get their own way?

FOR FUTURE EVENTS

Children have a habit of asking something when you're least able to think through the implications – like cooking the tea or walking out of the door. They're not stupid, they know they're increasing their chances of a yes if they catch you off-guard. However, you don't have to answer straight away! It sounds obvious when I spell it out but in the same way we've been trained to drop everything and answer the phone, we've also been trained to respond imme-diately to a question. So don't fall into your children's trap. Buy yourself time: 'I will need to think about that' or, even better, 'I'll have to talk about that with your mother/father.' Another good ploy would be to train your children to ask at a better time: 'That's a good question. Ask me another time when I'm not so busy.' When they ask a second time, reinforce the good behaviour with some descriptive praise: 'You've waited until I was sitting down and had time to think and answer questions, that's really thoughtful.'

FOR SOMETHING HAPPENING NOW

Sometimes the children are asking to do something straight away (like eat a biscuit) or have already started to do something forbidden (taking down your grandmother's china animals to play with) and effectively asking in retrospect. In these situations, it is necessary to say no immediately and mean it. If you're not in the same room – and your child's request is shouted up the stairs – go to your son or daughter rather than shouting back. Be calm and firm. Stay close rather than walking away, as your presence will reinforce the required behaviour. Use descriptive praise to recognize any step – however small – in the right direction, for example: 'You've stopped playing with the china dog, that shows you're listening.' Keep praising good behaviour rather than complaining about bad. If necessary, give two acceptable options: 'Shall I put the biscuit tin back in the cupboard or will you?' (This allows your child to feel that he or she still has a choices in how they behave.)

ACKNOWLEDGE THE UPSET

If your child is angry, upset or frustrated by 'no', rather than feeling guilty, reframe the event as a great opportunity to help him or her regulate his or her emotions. Start by acknowledging the feelings: 'You're frustrated that you're not old enough to play safely with Grandma's china animals' or 'It's hard not being able to have your own way.' Follow up with descriptive praise – even if it is the absence of something. For example, 'You didn't roll your eyes at me, that's polite' or 'You've stopped crying and you're listening.'

INVITE THEM TO UNDERSTAND 'NO'

There is a good reason why you've said no. Of course, once your child has calmed down, you could explain your response to him or her. However, he or she is more likely to accept your explanation and buy into your rules and values if he or she says them out loud.

So ask your child: 'Why do you think you can't have a biscuit?' If he or she claims not to know or refuses to come up with an answer, ask him or her to have a guess. If it is something rude ('Because you're mean' or 'You never let me have anything'), don't rise to the bait but keep descriptively praising: 'You're beginning to think about the reasons, that's good; now have another guess.' If your child is par-ticularly stubborn and walks away, don't go after him or her. Wait until your child comes and asks for something or needs your help. 'That's a good question and I'll answer it, but only after you tell me why we don't eat biscuits between meals.' In this way, you'll show that you will follow through, no matter what. When your child has identified the right answer – or something close enough – use descriptive praise again: 'You've come up with the right answer, you've really thought this through.'

NEGOTIATE

Sometimes, you're saying no when it is a cut and dried case – end of discussion. However, often the situation is more complex. For example, you don't feel your children are old enough to go camping but under different circumstances – putting up the tent in the back garden – you might say yes. In these cases, you can use the ABC of communication: A for Address the issue: 'You can't go to a music festival', B for bridge: 'But . . .' or 'However . . .' and C for Communication: 'I'm happy to drive you to a local concert and collect you afterwards.'

STICK TO YOUR GUNS

Slowly but surely, your children will feel more comfortable with 'no' – which is useful because the larger world is full of 'no'. Believe me, it will get easier. If you find yourself weakening, remind yourself: 'If I say no and follow it with yes, I'm training my children to keep asking until they get the answer they want.'

GIVE YOURSELF A PAT ON THE BACK

You've taken your children's feelings seriously and taught them that it's OK to be disappointed, upset or frustrated; we have to tolerate these upsetting emotions and get over them. This is an important step towards helping your children to self-regulate.

■ ■ ■ ■ ■ ■

What is the impact of the red carpet on children?

Fortunes have been made peddling the idea of princesses to girls, and one of the latest fads for children's parties and high-school proms is to have a red carpet outside and fake paparazzi taking photographs. Is this just harmless fun that makes our children feel special, or could it be dangerous? On a day-to-day level, is doing so much for your children and picking up after them a demonstration of your love, or do you risk becoming their unpaid servant? Let's look at the effect on your son or daughter of being at the centre of your world.

STRESSED CHILDREN

If you prioritize your child's football practice over anything else, or spend the summer taking him or her round tennis competitions, you are going to be particularly invested in whether he or she wins. If you do the vast majority of the chores round the house, so your child can concentrate on doing his or her homework, you are sending an unconscious message: 'Your grades trump everything else.' Under these circumstances, sport is not just a bit of fun and a source of exercise but tied up with your children's self-esteem and identity. Meanwhile, passing exams and gaining qualifications becomes the key to a successful and fulfilled life (whereas it is only part of the picture). Even slipping behind in subjects that your children don't like or have little aptitude for will feel like a disaster. No wonder today's young people are stressed and anxious.

Equally, giving your children a pivotal role in the family can easily unbalance and stress them. By deferring to her daughter over where to eat, Amanda was making her effectively 'head of the household'. I know I'm exaggerating – but from where her daughter was standing that's effectively what they were doing. Unfortunately, at three, her daughter could not understand all the options and implications of her decisions. No wonder she had problems fitting in with her peers and older friends. She would have been far happier knowing her true place in the family hierarchy and deferring to members who had the knowledge and ability to see the whole picture. In fact, Amanda admitted: 'I scare myself when I think about how much power we've inadvertently handed over to our daughter.'

Katie also found that her daughter, Nicole, would overstep the mark. 'If I don't tidy the kitchen, I'm told off for not putting things in the dishwasher. I find myself saying, "Don't reprimand me as if you're an equal – I'm your mother."'

The constant switches in status, and not knowing where she stood, was also a problem and a source of stress for Nicole. 'I get really cross when Mummy sides with Daddy and I feel betrayed. One moment we are really, really close it's ridiculous, and the next she's my father's ally. I feel so alone. I have to realize that he's her husband and he's my father. I can't have all her attention. It's equally difficult when Mummy and I argue – it's like she's two different people. One of them I can talk to about anything and the other's nagging me about my homework. I never know which one I'm going to get. For example, I came home once at four a.m. – after a party – and instead of covering for me, I met both parents in their dressing gowns and was summoned into the lounge.'

PROBLEMS GROWING UP

For previous generations, growing older meant more privileges and more freedom. But what are the benefits to today's red-carpet children, who already have everything and expect all their needs to be met?

Nicole, who is now eighteen, is considering the next step in her education: 'I want to commute daily to university and although Mummy doesn't want me to, I really want to stay at home. People don't understand and I've had arguments with my teachers. They say, "Nicole, you've got to be independent." I tell them I don't want to be independent yet – I'm OK at home.'

No wonder there is a growth in adults watching children's entertainment, reading books aimed at teenagers and a booming 'kidult' market, because retreating into childhood is so appealing.

TOUGHER TO REGULATE THEMSELVES

When we are small, we need our parents to help us identify our feelings, deal with the painful ones and soothe us. Slowly, as we get older and go off to school and spend more and more time apart from our parents, we take over this role and begin to regulate ourselves. However, what happens to red-carpet children who only have to click their fingers and every whim is fulfilled?

Returning to Keith, whom we met earlier in the chapter, he had no idea how to soothe himself. He would either expect his wife to make him feel better after a row or self-medicate his unhappiness away with the attention of other women. (He had come into counselling after his wife discovered a string of infidelities.) One week early in the couple's work with me, they had a row in the car on the way to my office. The atmosphere when they walked into my room was overpowering. It was like Keith was a cartoon figure with a dark cloud hanging over his head. If I'd had to guess how old he felt inside, I would have said four.

So like a parent with a small child, I used a lot of descriptive praise: 'It's really good that you've still come, well done.' (On a previous time when they'd had a row in the car, they had turned round and gone home.) I also acknowledged his feelings: 'It's really difficult when you've got so much pain inside.' When he was calmer, I could find out what exactly had happened. It turned out that his wife, Elizabeth, had stood up for herself in the argument rather than backing down and placating Keith. I finished the session with looking at ways that Keith could soothe himself, rather than expecting others to do the job for him. It became a real turning point in his counselling.

The next week, it was like meeting a different Keith. So what had happened?

'When we fell out over something, I decided to go for a run and sweat out my frustrations and anger – whereas previously I would have boosted my self-esteem by flirting with other women. I've also been doing a lot of thinking. If there was a problem, it was always someone else's fault that I felt terrible, but I've started to step into other people's shoes.'

'Returning to your story about the French teacher, what must it have been like for him to be reprimanded by the headmaster and forced to give his class the afternoon off?' I asked.

'I've never really thought about it. I suppose if I had, I'd have said "It served him right for humiliating me." In a way, I've been doing the same with Elizabeth. I told myself I "deserved" those flings after what "she'd done to me", but of course nobody "deserves" to be lied to and cheated on.'

However, Keith would never have reached this level of insight unless he had learnt to tolerate the upset, self-soothe and regulate his feelings. Finally at thirty-three he was acquiring the skills his parents should have taught him when he was a child.

IMMEDIATE GRATIFICATION

One of the most influential long-term studies into how childhood behaviour impacts on adult outcomes was conducted in the late 1960s and 1970s at the nursery of Stanford University. Walter Mischel sat six-year-olds at a table with a marshmallow and a bell on it. He explained that he was going to leave the room and if they could wait until he returned, he would give them two marshmallows. If they couldn't wait, they could ring the bell and eat the marshmallow immediately. About ten years later, he contacted the children's parents again and asked them to score how well they were doing both academically and socially. He returned to his subjects when they were adults and looked at weight problems, drug issues and whether they had been divorced. He discovered that the children who could wait at six (and had enjoyed two marshmallows) had the best school marks as teenagers and were least likely to have weight, drug or marital problems as adults. Why should this be? It is all about *delayed* gratification. If you can weigh up the advantages of waiting and getting another sweet at six, you will also be able to balance the desire to go out and play against the need to study as a teenager, and when you're an adult, the importance of not throwing away your marriage tomorrow for a moment of pleasure today.

So what's this got to do with red-carpet children? If we want to be friends with our children, take the easy option or assuage our guilt about their upset, we are more likely to buy them off or take away their upset with a treat, thereby reinforcing their natural desire for immediate gratification – because who likes to wait – rather than helping them develop the resources to delay gratification for a greater reward later.

What is the impact of the red carpet on your relationship?

If your children are the centre of attention in your family, it is easy to overlook the state of your marriage and any individual problems with which you or your partner are struggling. Returning to Muriel and Neil, who went halfway across London to buy a Thomas the Tank Engine costume before turning back, they were very focused on their three-year-old son.

'I'm worried because he seems more sensitive than other children his age,' said Neil. 'I've tried to toughen him up by taking away his ball and encouraging him to come and get it off me.'

'But that just makes him cry,' said Muriel angrily. 'He thinks Daddy is teasing him.'

I wanted to reassure them that some children are just more sensitive than others and that it's better to acknowledge their emotions and find out what is behind the upset. However, my focus is my client's relationships with themselves and each other.

'So why is it is so important to "toughen him up"?' I asked.

There was a long pause and I could see that Neil was fighting back a tear.

'I suppose that's what was done to me. I was a sensitive child too.'

It turned out that Neil's parents had divorced when he was a small boy and he was encouraged to 'be a man' and 'look after his mother', and not just be 'less sensitive' but to completely bury his emotions.

'What about you?' I turned to Muriel.

'My parents came from Eastern Europe where it is bitterly cold for half of the year and life can be extremely tough. You just have to put your head down and get on with it. Yes, I was a sensitive child too, but my parents did their best to beat it out of me,' she replied sadly.

As you can imagine, Neil and Muriel's anxiety about their son, their different backgrounds and clashing opinions on how best to raise him had been causing rows. Fortunately, they had enough insight to recognize that they had a marital problem and sought my advice. Understanding that their worries about their son being 'sensitive' were really about them was a breakthrough in their counselling. As they worried less, got on better and started to work as a team, their son began to thrive too.

Sadly, a lot of people are so focused on their children that they are almost blind to everything else. So when their son or daughter starts 'acting out' any unhappiness (because they often don't have the words to express it, or have but are not heard) and misbehave at school, develop an eating disorder, or experiment with sex too young, etc., they are rushed off to an expert. I work closely with a family therapist who treats such problems, and he is always amazed at how resistant parents are to looking at the whole family (and how the general dynamic or their behaviour might be contributing to the specific problem) and would much rather he concentrated on their son or daughter.

Returning to my metaphor of red-carpet kids: we are so busy taking photographs and applauding as our children walk down the carpet that we not only forget about our own problems but, if something goes wrong, it is easy to assume it's about them.

Hopefully, if any of this sounds familiar, you're beginning to consider making some changes to the way your family is run. I expect you're also feeling a bit overwhelmed and don't know where to start. Don't worry, I'm going to break it down into small steps. The following exercise is the first one.

■ ■ ■ ■ ■ ■

New Rules

I'm a great believer in change. Just because something has been done one way in the past doesn't mean that it has to be like that in the future. Children are always growing and have different needs at different life stages, and this makes 'New Rules' not only a natural part of parenting but a very powerful tool too. So how do you set up change in your family?

1. *Discuss the issue with your partner:* It is important that you both agree on any new rule – otherwise your children will divide and conquer. Take time to listen to any concerns from your partner – not just to humour him or her – but because two heads are better than one in spotting potential pitfalls or inconsistencies. Keep talking until you have ironed out any problems and both signed off on the rules.

2. *Admit your mistakes to your children:* If you haven't been doing something particularly well – perhaps you've been letting them stay up too late – tell them about it: 'Mummy and Daddy have been thinking about bedtimes and we think it's a mistake to let you stay up so late.' First, nothing gets your children's attention better than admitting your mistakes, so you can be sure they will be *really* listening to what comes next. Second, you're modelling behaviour you'd like from them and giving them permission not to be perfect (and thereby taking away a lot of unspoken pressure). After all, mistakes happen. They can be rectified and the world doesn't end – which is a valuable lesson for life.

3. *Set a start date.* Change is easier when we have some time to mentally prepare. If we have something sprung on us – especially retrospectively – it seems not only unfair but that the world is full of chaos (which is frightening). For example, you could set up the

change by saying: 'When you go back to school next week, we're going to have a new bedtime.'

4. *Explain the rule:* Although this is the main part of the communication, it only comes at the middle of your discussion. It takes time to set up a new rule and to make certain it sticks. If you have tried to make new rules in the past, but failed, you will probably have skipped the preliminary or later stages. Do not justify the rule, just put it as simply as possible: 'You will be going to bed half an hour earlier.'

5. *Acknowledge and name your children's feelings:* They are unlikely to welcome the new rule with open arms. So acknowledge their reaction: 'I can see that you're feeling . . .' and name the feeling: 'upset' or 'angry' or 'that I don't love you'. Don't worry if you get it wrong because they will soon correct you. However, you have shown that you're interested in their feelings and that it's OK to be disappointed (or whatever negative feeling they are experiencing).

6. *Help them to own the rule:* Once again, instead of explaining why you've decided to make a new rule: ask *them* to think why, and tell you. If they come up with something negative ('You're horrible') don't get defensive; praise them for starting to think but ask them to look again for a positive reason ('You love me and want the best for me'). For example: 'You want me to be properly rested so I'm ready for school in the morning', 'I've been cranky in the evening and you hate to end the day with a row','It will make it easier for me to get up in the morning.' If you're asking them to do more chores, the reasons for change could be 'to make us more self-reliant' or 'We're becoming older and can take on more responsibility' or 'Everybody does their fair share in this house.' When they get the answer right, descriptively praise.

7. *Deal with any questions:* This is a positive sign as they are beginning to think ahead. So give some more descriptive praise: 'I can see that you're thinking about how this rule will work – that's very sensible/grown-up/responsible' (or whatever seems most

appropriate for your children). Hopefully you will have talked through any possible problems with your partner and be ready with an answer. 'Of course, you can keep the same bedtime on a non-school night.' If they come up with a good point that you hadn't anticipated, you can always praise and buy yourself time: 'That's a good question, thanks for raising it. I'll have a think and discuss it with Mummy/Daddy and let you know what we decide.'

8. *It applies to everybody:* This will not always be the case but children have an innate sense of fairness, so it helps to make the change something for everybody. For example: 'We're going to go to bed slightly earlier too, so we can get up earlier and be less in a rush in the morning' or 'It's not just you and your brother but nobody is going to leave the table without asking permission.' (So you will ask your partner before wandering off to answer the phone or get something from the fridge in the middle of the meal and vice versa.)

9. *Help the rule along:* At the end of your conversation, ask your children to put the new rule into their own words. Once again, this will help them to own it and allow you to check that they've properly understood. If they are rude or sulky, still use descriptive praise ('Well done, you've remembered the rule') but ask for it again without the sarcasm, rolled eyes or whatever. If they are still resistant, acknowledge and name the feeling but still ask again. Praise any step in the right direction: 'You looked at me this time when you spoke, that's really polite.'

10. *Reinforce:* A couple of days before the new rule starts, ask your children about the new rule (rather than tell them). And help them to think ahead about what needs to be done: 'I will need to have my bath half an hour earlier/switch off the computer and lay out my pyjamas.'

11. *Follow up:* On the start day, perhaps in the car going to school, think ahead to what will happen tonight. When you're getting into the zone of the change, make certain that you're in the room. It

will help focus your child on the preparatory steps and show you mean what you say.

12. *Descriptively praise:* Hopefully, if you have taken the time to set up the new rule, everything will go like clockwork, but don't forget the praise: 'You are in bed at the new time – that's really cooperative.' If they are slow or uncooperative, find something minor to praise: 'You've stopped typing on the keyboard, that's a step in the right direction' and offer choices (where both options are acceptable to you): 'Would you like to brush your teeth first or put your dirty clothes in the laundry basket?'

■ ■ ■ ■ ■ ■

How to roll up the red carpet

If you have started to say no and introduced new rules, you will already have two useful tools to start redressing the balance. Here are some more ideas.

DEAL WITH YOUR OWN STUFF

If you're rolling out the red carpet to assuage your guilt or trying to overcompensate for some personal failing, it stands to reason that it is better to go to the root of the problem. Returning to Archana, who we met earlier in the chapter, instead of just managing her anxiety by keeping her son under close scrutiny all the time, I asked her to think back to her own childhood.

'My father died when I was about eight. He had cancer but my mother thought it was best to hide this information from us,' she explained.

'So one minute he was there and the next he was gone,' I commented.

'She didn't think we should go to the funeral either.'

'So you had no chance to process or deal with the information.'

'And it remained a closed subject because my brother and I didn't want to upset her.'

'No wonder you're anxious.'

So I helped Archana to work on her own anxiety – with simple breathing meditations – and to accept that although her feelings made sense because of her history, her coping strategies today could have a negative influence on how her son saw the world.

I know it is going to sound strange to leap from childcare to dog-training, but there are useful parallels. When I went to puppy classes with both my first dog, Flash, and my second one, Pumpkin, the instructor gave the same message: 'Your anxiety goes down the lead.' We would be concerned that our puppies would lunge to play with another puppy or let us down (possibly with good reason). However, the more wound up or even angry we'd get, the more anxious or excitable our dogs would become. In just the same way, your feelings and fears are transmitted to your son or daughter – through your body language and tone of voice. Staying with dogs, my morning walk often coincides with parents taking their children to school. Even when Pumpkin is on the lead and walking to heel, a parent will occasionally shrink away and pull their son or daughter behind them. Invariably they tell me: 'Sorry, he's frightened of dogs.'

I smile, but inwardly I think: I wonder why that should be!

Make it a reality: Small children live in the moment. It's a great frustration when we're trying to get them out of the door because they don't understand that we have a long list of things to do and places to be. However, it also means they don't bear grudges about ordinary day-to-day things. They also think the way your family is organized is the right way – after all, until they go off to school, they don't really have enough experience of the outside world to judge. So if, for example, you work and they go to Grandma on Thursday and a childminder on Friday, that's just the way it is. You don't have to compensate. If you find yourself feeling guilty, of course check there is not a good reason and your child isn't truly suffering, but tell yourself: This is about me. If you're calm and relaxed about something, the odds are that your children will feel the same.

REPLACE FRIENDSHIP WITH RESPECT AND TRUST

It's fine to be friends with your adult son or daughter – after all it's a relationship of two equals who are both responsible for their own lives. However, the relationship between a parent and a child is not one of equals, because you are legally responsible for them. You also have more experience of the world, the ability to see the bigger picture and an understanding of the impact on the future of decisions made today. So there are times that you need to step in and take charge. If you're a friend one minute and a parent the next, that's not only confusing but it makes it harder to trust you. After all, which hat have you got on: friend or parent? For example, one minute Nicole's mother was hiding her late nights, and the next she was disciplining her. No matter how close Katie might have been to her daughter, she still remained the responsible adult.

Because pretending an unequal relationship is an equal one creates problems, it is much better to have a relationship based on respect (for your opinions and experience) and trust (that you want the best for your children).

Make it a reality: Look for examples when your children are respectful – for example, listening and taking on board what you're saying – and make certain that you descriptively praise. For example: 'You didn't walk away even though you were upset, that is very respectful' or 'You asked to get down from the table and you followed our new rule, that was very respectful.' Even though it might seem easier to let your children get away with sarcastic tones, heavy sighs and other passive-aggressive behaviour, it's letting them get away with being disrespectful. Instead bring the unexpressed emotions up to the surface: 'What did that sigh mean?' Or when they say, 'Whatever', stop them and ask: 'What would you really like to say?' Follow up their answer with descriptive praise: 'That was really grown-up and respectful to tell me your concerns and feelings rather than trying to hide them. Now we can talk about them.' As for trust, that normally follows on naturally from respect – as long as you are consistent in your decisions and follow through.

ENSURE THAT AGE BRINGS BENEFITS

This strategy further underlines the idea of respect by giving precedence to people who are older and have more experience (like grandparents and teachers) but also gives an incentive for growing up and taking responsibility (rather than seeking to always be a child). So what do I mean by 'age brings benefits'?

Let's start with your oldest child. He or she had the benefit of your undivided attention when he or she was small. Therefore, when your next child arrived, he or she could easily have felt sidelined. When I talk to my clients about their childhood, youngest children will often reminisce about the benefits of being the 'baby of the family'. Meanwhile, older children will sometimes complain that they had all the battles with their parents – for independence, privileges and self-autonomy – but their younger siblings got a 'free ride' on the back of their efforts. You can get round this problem in the future and ensure less squabbling between your children today by giving a few extra privileges to your oldest child. The most obvious example would be a later bedtime – even if it's only fifteen minutes. As they get older, remember the milestones and by and large stick to them. So, for example, if your oldest was not allowed to stay out to midnight until he or she was sixteen, don't let the youngest have that privilege at fourteen. Children like consistency and fairness within the family. In a big, scary and confusing world, it helps them feel safe and makes it easier to start regulating their own feelings.

Moving on to grandparents, you can encourage your children to give precedence to older people by insisting they open the car door for their grandmother or take a cup of tea to their grandfather. Make certain your children don't talk over older people at family gatherings and listen to what they have to say. You can also set a good example too.

Excuse me for stating the obvious, but one day we'll all be the eldest in the room. So by giving precedence to the older and wiser, we are laying the foundations for respect for ourselves in the future. In this way, we all have a stake in 'age brings benefits'. By contrast, giving precedence to the youngest means our best days are behind us and we can never achieve that pre-eminence again (and it can also be overwhelming for the golden child who does not really understand the world or their power in it and is forever anxious about losing his or her shine.)

Make it a reality: Formal meals – like Sunday lunch and Christmas – provide a simple but powerful way to ensure age brings benefits. Serve the oldest person first and the youngest last. (I've been the guest at several families where the children were served first – to keep them quiet – and they'd almost finished by the time the last person had food and everybody else started eating. Obviously this does nothing to teach the children about delayed gratification.) If the mealtime does not fit in with your baby's feeding routine, give him or her something to eat separately before everybody else sits down and then a little something to chew on while everybody else is eating. The baby can also have dessert with the family but is still served last – at his or her place in the family hierarchy.

GAIN COOPERATION

Nagging your children is not only exhausting, time-consuming and puts a barrier between you and them, but it is also training them to ignore you the first time – in the hope that you'll give up or do the task for them. By contrast, gaining their cooperation makes you a team (for example, to get out of the door in the morning) rather than your children's personal assistant running after them on the red carpet (for example, putting on their coat and remembering to bring their games kit). You are probably thinking that sounds wonderful but impractical. However, if you've been implementing the ideas in this book, you'll already have a lot of the necessary skills in place. You could use New Rules to set up a new way of getting ready in the morning and back it up with lots of 'think ahead' so that they not only know what is expected of them but, by repeating back the new rules, they also own their tasks.

The next item for your toolkit is called 'Stop repeating yourself'. It is pointless shouting up the stairs, so go to your child. It is pointless talking to his or her back or when he or she is immersed in something else – you need his or her full attention because you're aiming to ask once and therefore you need to make it count. So stand and wait until your child stops what he or she is doing. Your presence alone, quiet, determined and calm, will make him or her look up at you. When he or she does, use descriptive praise: 'You stopped what you were doing and gave me your full attention, that was very respectful.' If your children are doing something really immersive – computer games, TV etc. – your presence alone in the room may not be enough. If necessary, ask your children to turn down the volume and look at you. Notice every step towards this goal and reinforce with descriptive praise. Now you are now ready to ask *once*: 'We're leaving for Granny and Grandpa's at ten, make sure you're ready.'

You might need to set up 'Stop repeating yourself' as a new rule

('I've decided not to keep going on at you and therefore I'm going to tell you once, rather than keep reminding') but it is important to stick to your guns. So if, for example, the rule is that they have to be ready at a certain time to go to football practice, with all the correct gear, you will *not* keep reminding them as the time arrives. At zero hour, if they're still on the computer, you just get on with something you want to do and say nothing. Wait till they suddenly realize the mistake; at this point you can either arrive late or decide it's not worth going. If they forget an important piece of equipment, they have to live with the consequences. I know this is tough and really hard-hearted but I'm going to say it anyway: You are not their social secretary or their servant.

Make it a reality: It might seem cruel to let your children fail, and they could easily get upset or critical. Stay calm and don't lose your temper or tell them 'I told you so.' Fortunately, you have just the tools for dealing with this situation. Acknowledge and name the feelings: 'You're feeling angry and annoyed.' Follow up by asking why they think you've done this. Use descriptive praise when they give the correct answer: 'I'm old enough to take responsibility for being on time/remembering my kit myself.' If you're still finding this hard, tell yourself that self-reliance increases confidence and there is a big difference between what your children *want* (you running after them) and what they *need* (to learn to take responsibility for their own actions). Fortunately, children quickly learn that you will not ask twice and will listen carefully the first time.

DO LESS ABOUT THE HOUSE

Even small children can learn to tidy up after themselves, look after their belongings and do small chores (for example laying the table and carrying their dirty plates to the sink). Before deciding on their responsibilities, it is important to agree with your partner so you can present a united front. If your children are used to being waited on, it is important to acknowledge and name their upset – especially as it could feel that by removing a small part of your care that you are withdrawing your love. You can overcome this problem by staying with them the first few times, so you are giving your support and encouragement (but not doing it for them). Obviously, the chores will also have to be set up using New Rules.

A good rule for tidying up is that toys have to be put away straight away after your children have finished with them. Not only does regular tidying up keep everything under control and the mess seems less of a mountain to climb, but it can be presented as a positive: 'You'll know where they are next time you play with them.' You can also have a penalty. For example, once a day you will remove anything left lying around or not in your children's rooms, but they can earn it back by doing an extra chore.

If there are several tasks that perhaps need to be done on different days, you can help your children buy into and remember the plan by getting them to create a wallchart – they can design it themselves and draw pictures for particular jobs. You might also consider having stars for tasks completed. (I will cover rewards in a moment.)

Make it a reality: Teamwork can make a dreaded chore seem easier. For example, you could help clean your child's room (especially if the mess has got out of control). Descriptively praise all efforts but explain you're just helping out so he or she has to put away the majority of items.

It also helps if there is a regular time to do chores – like after your evening meal – and for everybody, not just children, to do something useful around the house. You can also give your children a choice between two chores: Do you want to clean out the guinea pigs or scrub the pots? From time to time, swap chores around so nobody is left with something they hate.

INSTIL DISCIPLINE

This is a really difficult topic because, while everybody is fervently against child abuse, they're equally keen on discipline. Sometimes, it can be a fine line. Few of my clients are comfortable criticizing their parents and very few will admit to anything abusive. However, if I ask, 'How did your parents discipline you?', they will happily relate tales of being hit (with a metal rod), locked under the stairs, sent to their room without food, thrown out of the house at sixteen and, in one case, not being spoken to for three months. Sadly being tired or at the end of their tether means that some parents will lash out and sometimes strike their children. Remember, children learn from us, and if you do succumb to physical punishment it will encourage them to hit their younger siblings or smaller classmates.

I've left discipline almost to the end of the chapter because there are lots of tools to avoid reaching this point (which I hope I've started to explain), and I wanted to stress that most children misbehave because they are full of negative emotions and don't know how to cope. (Fortunately, you have learnt to help them by acknowledging and naming feelings.)

Sometimes all the new skills and understanding will not be enough. You will need to stop your child misbehaving, but he or she is too wound up to be able to listen, so what should you do? This is when I recommend 'time out'. (It's a variation on what I use for adults who have passed the point of having a reasonable dialogue and risk becoming verbally or physically abusive.) So how does it work?

The child has to sit in one place and with their freedom curtailed. Some people call it 'the naughty step' – but I'm not keen on this term as it can sound like your child is naughty (their whole character) rather than having done something naughty (their behaviour). I'd like your place to be somewhere close by and easy to monitor so there's no sneaking off to play. If your child is very agitated and acting out their anger, you might need to stay close. However, there should be no chatting or scolding, just descriptive praise: 'You've stopped hitting your brother, that's good' or 'You've stopped fidgeting' or 'You've sat silently for a whole minute, that's very cooperative.' As a guideline, I would suggest one minute's time out for each year of your child's age, but you know them best.

Afterwards, ask them to repeat why they needed time out and why their behaviour was wrong and descriptively praise when they give the right answer: 'That was right, well done.' In this way, you end the disciplining on a positive note.

Make it a reality: You can often avoid disobedience and stop your child from doing a forbidden behaviour or gain their cooperation by using a countdown. Remember, children live in the moment and it takes them a while to get their brain in gear; they might also be testing if you really mean it. So tell them: 'I'm going to give you a countdown from ten and when I reach one I want you to . . .' However if you do threaten time out or some other penalty, it is vital to follow through – even if your children are upset and throwing a tantrum – or they will neither respect nor take you seriously.

Reward rather than indulge

You don't want your children to behave because they are frightened of the consequences but because they have understood the reasoning behind a rule and accepted it as right for them, your family and the wider community. There is a second reason why I put the emphasis on rewarding good rather than punishing bad behaviour, and that's because threatening some dire punishment will make your child angry, rebellious and less likely to cooperate. For example, some parents threaten to take things away from their children (like their bicycle) in the hope that it will make them reflect on their bad behaviour, but it just causes outrage. This is because when these parents gave the treasured possessions they never said keeping it was conditional on good behaviour – just 'Happy Christmas' or 'Happy birthday' or 'Well done for passing your exams.' So what's the alternative? This is where rewarding rather than indulging your children comes into play. We love our children and therefore want to indulge them, but too much giving, without any strings attached, encourages a feeling of entitlement. In contrast, if you reward good behaviour, your children will not only feel that they have earned the treat but will feel good about themselves too.

There is also a benefit to your marriage in stopping indulging and starting to reward. While few parents will agree to the right level of indulgence – with what is OK and what is harmful a fertile source of running arguments – most couples can come up with a reward structure on which they can agree.

WHAT MAKES A GOOD REWARD?

You want a simple and immediate connection between the good behaviour and the reward (rather than 'Be good for a month and we'll get a dog'). That's why the best rewards are small, easy to arrange or do, and either free or inexpensive (so money and love are not linked in your child's mind). In this way, your rewards can almost be immediate. One note of caution: I would also avoid using food as a reward – particularly sugary, high-fat and salty snacks – as not only are these bad for your children's health but can set up an unfortunate link between love and food (which is bad for their long-term relationship with food). So what's the alternative?

- Try on your jewellery.
- Go to the park for a kick-around with a ball.
- Painting on the kitchen table.
- An extra story at bedtime.
- Helping to bake a cake.
- Extra pocket money.
- Choosing what to cook for tea (from your normal range of meals).
- Screen time (by which I meantime in front of the computer, tablet, video games, TV etc.).

Screen time is a very useful currency. It is in your children's interest to limit their exposure as paediatricians recommend just one to two hours a day (and *no* screen time for children under two years old). They warn that going over this limit increases the chance of a child being less physically active, more aggressive and harder to put to bed, and increases attention problems, anxiety and depression. However, a survey published in *Pediatrics* magazine in the US which monitored 7,400 children aged between nine and fifteen found that one in four kids had more than the daily recommended limit (this did not include screen time for older children to complete homework).

Setting up Screen Time as the Currency in Your Household

If this sounds like a good idea for your children, you've already got the necessary skills to set up a New Rule. So here is a recap, adapted for the specifics of screen time:

1. Introduce a date for starting this new rule, so your children have a chance to get used to the idea. For example: 'On Monday, we're going to be introducing a new rule . . .'

2. Explain the rule.
3. Your children will be upset but instead of sweeping their feelings under the carpet, be certain to identify acknowledge and name them. For example: 'You're feeling hard done by/angry/worried about how it will work.'
4. Ask them to guess why the rule is being introduced.
5. Use descriptive praise for any sensible answers and ask for others.
6. Show your love. One of the reasons for less screen time is so that you can do more together as a family. (If they don't come up with this answer, please share it with them.) Ultimately, what your children want, more than anything, is your attention and interest in them.
7. Explain that they can also earn extra screen time for doing certain chores around the house (for example feeding the cat or tidying their room).
8. Answer any questions.
9. When the new rule is introduced and they complain about the screen being switched off, identify the feelings and sympathize ('New rules are always difficult at the beginning') and compensate with some extra attention. For example, dancing round the room together to music (for small children) or playing a board game or cards (for older children).
10. Be sensitive about your own screen time. If you have buried yourself behind the computer when they are around, it is sensible to limit your own consumption in the initial phases. Remember that children have an innate sense of fairness and it could be that you're having more screen time than is good for you too.

ALTERNATIVE IDEAS IN ACTION

John and Marie, whom we met in Chapter Six, had two issues: how to reward rather than indulge, and how to be consistent (as each had the children while the other worked). They solved both problems with an app that they downloaded and synced to their phones.

'The children get points for completing certain tasks (like getting dressed themselves and being ready to leave for school on time) and for general good behaviour. They could also have them taken away if they're naughty or uncooperative. The points can be cashed in for a small treat or saved up for a bigger one,' explained Marie.

'It's worked really well because we have a standard system that we both agree on,' said John, 'and if someone like Marie's mother is looking after them we put the system onto her phone and she can add or subtract points too.'

'I overheard the kids in the bath discussing whether they should pool their points and buy a toy they'd both play with,' added Marie, 'so it's teaching them how to cooperate. It's also allowed John and me to discuss how we parent – without it getting too heated. I could show John how he'd been giving lots of points whereas I'd been the one having to take them away. I doubt we could have tackled this subject otherwise.'

'What's best of all, I can keep track of how the kids have been behaving – even when I'm working away. Before I talk to them in the evening, I can have a quick look at my phone and know what they've been up to. It helps me feel more involved.'

How to put your partner first

I once counselled a mother who was prouder of getting her two daughters into Cambridge University than going there herself – perhaps because she had sacrificed her own career to concentrate on her children. Unfortunately, our children's failure is our failure, and their pain is our pain too. No wonder we want to smooth their way. It is almost as if our sons and daughters are princes and princesses and we want to run ahead to ensure a red carpet has been rolled out in front of them. Meanwhile we're on the sidelines cheering and taking photographs. With so much pressure to raise kids the 'right' way and guilt about being a working mum, many parents turn themselves into unpaid flunkeys too.

So when my client's daughter was making a one-minute video to support her application to a BBC graduate trainee scheme, her mother spent half the weekend running around sourcing material and acting as a second pair of eyes (meanwhile she had made no progress on relaunching her own career or sorting out her post-divorce life). Unfortunately, red-carpet parenting was her default mode and she found it hard to know when to let go and when her help was truly needed.

In the past, when men were less involved with parenting, there was an unspoken acceptance that the children would be closer to their mother and that somehow they 'belonged' to her. Today with equal parenting (or as near that goal as possible), I see an unspoken rivalry between parents – especially if their relationship is under stress – to be the 'most loved' parent. One partner will rubbish the other's contribution to raising the children or look to one or other child for 'emotional support' – which nearly always involves special privileges for that child, confiding secrets and creating sub-alliances (so they will stand up for that partner in arguments with their spouse).

It is only human nature to want to be popular or to show your exasperation with your partner when your children are around. However, making your child your ally will do neither him or her nor your marriage any favours. Ultimately, children 'belong' to nobody. They are their own people and although you are responsible for them while they are minors, they are just passing through your relationship and one day they will leave home, get married and start their own families.

So how do you stop competing with your partner and start cooperating?

- It is OK to listen to your children when they complain about your partner, but don't agree with any criticism (however justified it might be) or run your partner down. If there are mitigating circumstances or something your children have misunderstood, please feel free to defend him or her. However, it is best to encourage your children to take the problem up directly with their father or mother.
- If you disagree with your partner about something fundamental, discuss it together behind closed doors.
- Always support your partner on matters of child-rearing policy in public.
- Set aside enough private time together to talk through any disagreements and present a united front. It will make your partner feel his or her views are respected and therefore make him or her feel valued.
- If this is hard, resolve to keep talking, listening and debating.
- No couple think exactly alike, the problems arise when people give up trying to communicate.

Summing Up

However much you love your children, it's not possible to carpet the whole world. They are going to fall in love and get their hearts broken. They will go for promotion but someone else will get the job. Their football team is going to be relegated. That's why they need to learn to be resilient, cope with setbacks and become self-reliant. This will also help your relationship, because the time saved servicing your children can be channelled into nurturing each other. At first, it might be hard getting your children off the red carpet, and developing new habits takes time, but it will bring great benefits in the long term and reduce your stress levels. Even better, with your eyes no longer fixed on the red carpet, you will notice each other again, let go of your end and be free to dance together.

What Will Your Children
Tell Their Therapist?

We are the first generation to have fully taken on board the ideas of Freud and the founding fathers of psychology. We accept the profound impact of childhood on shaping the adult we become. The result is that today's parents face anxieties that never crossed the minds of their mothers, fathers or grandparents. What if we make the wrong choice about breastfeeding or toilet training? What if our attention slips for a moment and some harm happens to our children that has a lasting impact on their mental well-being? What passed for a socially acceptable joke in previous generations – like 'Hitting my children might not do them any good, but it makes me feel better' – will now bring conversations to a juddering halt. With our knowledge of the unconscious, we no longer take at face value remarks like 'It never did me any harm.' We are fully aware of the responsibility of being a parent, and I have to say this is a great step forward.

At the same time, there has been a parallel revolution in our attitudes to therapy. When I first started working with couples in the mid-1980s, there was a sense of shame about admitting that you had a problem. Today we have a much more straightforward attitude: if you need help, it's best to put your hand up and ask for it. The result is that seeing a therapist, counsellor, psychologist or psychiatrist is a much more mainstream activity, and, whereas thirty years ago I was surprised when clients had had counselling before, today I'm surprised if I'm the first person they've seen. Once again, I think this is positive.

Unfortunately, these advances are not without problems and today's middle-class educated parents have a new fear to add to their list: 'What will our children tell their therapist?' That's why I've decided to devote a chapter to offering some reassurance and addressing the underlining concerns. Most importantly, I will explain the difference between a passing trifle (which will soon be forgotten) and what really could cause serious long-term harm (and potentially be recounted in heartbreaking detail thirty years later).

Despite our greater exposure to therapy, there are still some misconceptions. Chiefly, that 'it is all about complaining about your mother'. I wish it was that easy! I have heard literally thousands of people talking about their childhood and very few are critical of their mothers. (Although it *is* easier for clients to complain about their fathers.) We are protective of our mothers because we idealize them and long for their love and their approval. My job is to help my clients have a balanced picture and accept that one or both their parents were not perfect. I'm not seeking to *blame* – far from it – but by accepting our parents' flaws, we can begin to accept our own. In the words of the German philosopher Immanuel Kant (1724–1804): 'From the crooked timber of humanity, no straight thing was ever made.' In a nutshell, *We are human, we make mistakes, it comes with the territory.* This is much better than trying to live as an 'ideal' person loved by an 'ideal' parent (and helped by an 'ideal' therapist).

The majority of my clients present a balanced picture of their parents' strengths *and* weaknesses. Even people who are critical are quick to explain the circumstances which caused their parents to fail. In the same way that we love our children no matter what, we love our parents despite their shortcomings.

Having offered the reassurance that your children are unlikely to assassinate your character, it is important to be aware of the behaviour that most damaged my clients when they were children, so you can avoid falling into the same traps. It goes without saying that these behaviours will not be doing you or your relationship any favours either. Therefore I will also cover the impact on these aspects of your life, as well as on your children, and offer advice on how to turn things around for everybody.

Expecting your children to regulate you

How often have you been in the street or the supermarket and heard a parent turn to a small child and tell him or her off: 'Don't make me mad' or 'Don't make me lose my temper'? It is so common that it goes almost goes without notice. We might even smile sympathetically because we've all felt the same way at some point. However, in a small way, this encapsulates a problem that, unchecked, causes huge long-term problems. Returning to the ideas in Chapter Four, it is a parent's job to regulate their children's emotions – not the other way round. So if your children are playing up, it is much better to acknowledge and name their feelings and discover what is causing the upset. In stark contrast, the stressed adult in the street or supermarket is asking their child to ignore his or her own feelings and tune in to those of his or her parent. (Obviously, if your children are doing something antisocial – like pulling packets off the shelf – you need to stop them. However, it is much more powerful to ask them why their behaviour is wrong – thereby getting them to own the reason for stopping – rather than just shouting at them. In the first scenario, they under-stand that they are making extra work for someone else or damaging something that doesn't belong to them. In the second, they are stopping because they are trying to appease you, i.e. regulate your moods.)

Unfortunately, there are lots of ways that we don't take children's emotions seriously – because it makes us feel uncomfortable. If they're crying, we tell them, 'Don't be a cry-baby' like we were told by our parents. Anger is even more difficult to deal with, and some people will go to great lengths to avoid it (by swallowing it or rationalizing it away). So instead of acknowledging and naming our children's anger, the temptation is to trivialize or dismiss it: 'What have you got to be so upset about?' or 'Don't be so stupid.' Once again, we are asking our children to regulate our emotions – and so avoid having to face our own demons.

WHAT IS THE IMPACT ON YOUR CHILDREN?

These relatively trivial examples are unlikely to be the source of tearful stories to therapists in the future but they explain the patterns and what can happen if a child is more interested in reading their parents' moods than their own (and therefore slam on the brakes every time a strong emotion comes up) or does not trust their own reactions to the world around them.

'I never knew what to expect when I got home from school,' explained Stacey, thirty-two, who sought help because she was anxious and found it hard to make long-term relationships. 'Sometimes, my mother could be wonderful and be the best friend ever: we'd clear the kitchen table and make things out of old cardboard boxes, newspapers and glue. Other times she would be withdrawn and sullen and I would tiptoe round the house trying to become invisible so as to avoid upsetting her. She could also fly off the handle over something that didn't really make sense – like I wanted blue wallpaper on the doll's house we were making – and that showed that I was "selfish" or "ungrateful". I was always trying to read the signs and to get it right.' In many ways, matters got worse when Stacey got older and was more likely to have an opinion of her own. She was thrown out of the house when she was sixteen, and again at nineteen over some dispute that Stacey could no longer remember. As an adult of thirty-two, Stacey could recognize that her mother had undiagnosed mental-health issues, but as a child, she thought the tantrums were caused by something that *she* was doing wrong. And that's the big problem: children are completely egocentric (because their brains are not fully developed and they haven't had enough experience of the world) and will turn themselves upside-down and inside-out to be accepted and try and fit into even a topsy-turvy family.

In all my years as a therapist, I have only come across two clients who consciously knew – before the age of seven – that their parents were 'dangerous'. One woman recognized that her father was an abusive bully and, aged six, set herself up as her mother's protector (even though she could not understand the complexity of an adult relationship and the part sex played in her parents making up after a row). One man realized that his mother was 'an emotional vampire', around the same age, and would 'suck you in, manipulate and push you away', and decided to distance himself. I can't begin to imagine how frightening those realizations must have been to a small child who is utterly dependent on their parents for food, shelter and money and because they have the legal right to make decisions about their life (like schooling and a million and one other important issues). No wonder small children would much rather believe the fault is theirs – because it gives the illusion of being in control by trying harder, appeasing more, disappearing into the background – than face reality.

WHAT IS THE IMPACT ON YOU AND YOUR RELATIONSHIP?

If you expect someone else to regulate you, you are always going to feel vulnerable and anxious (because they can always let you down by ignoring you, getting angry or downplaying your feelings). You are also going to crave your children's love and, if you fear love is a scarce resource, more likely to compete with your partner to be 'most loved'.

Turn it around: You can't be aware of your children's emotions – and take them seriously – without being aware of your own. So think back to your childhood. What were the forbidden feelings? Sometimes they are expressly suppressed – 'Don't make a scene' or 'If you don't calm down there'll be tears before bedtime' – and sometimes they are so much part of how the family operated that nobody needed to say anything. If you can't come up with anything, think back to your last extended-family gathering. What is acceptable behaviour and what would cause shock and consternation? Now you have probably identified what is forbidden. (There is more help in the exercise section later in this chapter.)

Doing the switch

Children need consistency – because how can you make sense of the world and your place in it if it is forever changing in unpredictable ways? Unfortunately, some parents switch between two unhelpful – but not particularly damaging – styles to create one toxic pattern that will keep their children's future therapists very busy. So what are those two styles and why is the combination so harmful?

The first is called Intrusive (or over-involved): these are parents who make their children the centre of their lives and therefore nothing is too much trouble. I know it sounds great to have someone so completely attuned to your needs, but it comes at a cost.

Gary had to go into hospital for a back operation and despite being thirty-five years old his mother did not just visit every day but brought a camp bed and moved into the hospital with him for ten days! Apparently, she was worried: 'What if he needs something during the night and the nurses are busy elsewhere?' When questioned about whether it was truly necessary, she replied: 'But that's what mothers do.' Can you imagine how marginalized his wife felt?

I had another client whose father died when he was just six years old and his mother not only didn't remarry but never had any boyfriends. 'Her life revolved around me and my brother, we were a tight-knit little unit,' explained Curtis. As the oldest, he became almost a surrogate partner for his mother – something that was rein-forced by well-meaning relatives, who told him: 'You're the man of the family now.' Curtis's mother treated him as the golden child who could do no wrong. Once again, the relationship between his wife and his mother was extremely fraught – because nobody would have been good enough for him (except her) – but worse still, Curtis found it extremely hard to imagine how other people might be feeling or how his remarks or behaviour might impact on anybody else. After all, he'd spent his formative years being always right and his needs, wants and beliefs were paramount (and therefore everybody else's of little or no consequence).

The second unhelpful style is called Disinterested (or neglectful). In these cases, the parents are too wound up in their own lives or have just too many children (and the younger ones are left to fend for themselves). Sometimes it can be an all-consuming job, or addiction, mental-health issues or divorce that has made the parents disinter-ested. In other cases, my clients' parents thought they were doing the right thing or had no other choice, and sent their children off to boarding school at seven (because they lived in remote places with no normal schools) or to live with their grandparents or another relative (because they had to earn a living). Distances, poor transport links and cost meant some of these children would only see their parents once a year. It sounds terrible but the impact is not as catastrophic as you might imagine.

Returning to Gary, who had an Intrusive mother: his wife Patricia had been put into care by her mother when she was five years old and had a succession of foster-families.

'Some were better than others, but most were more interested in the money than being parents,' she explained.

'You must have felt very alone,' I tried to sympathize.

'I had one foster-sister that I'm still close to but I'm not in touch with anybody else. I just focused on getting through my exams and getting on with it.'

This strategy had proved extremely successful. She had been to a top university and had worked for an international bank.

In most cases of Disinterested parents, children find support, interest and help from other parties – grandparents, teachers, older siblings or neighbours who see the void and step in.

Having described the two unfortunate – but not disastrous – parenting styles, let's examine what happens when they collide and why the combination can be toxic. Unfortunately, many children have to deal with parents who are intrusive one moment (and then become exhausted and overwhelmed) and neglectful the next ('After all I've done for my children, don't I deserve some me-time?'). It is almost impossible to maintain this level of over-involved parenting – in fact I rather admire the tenacity of Gary's and Curtis's mothers – and that's why many parents will collapse and become Disinterested, feel guilty and then redouble their efforts and become even more Intrusive, until the next time it becomes too much, and so on. The result is that they will switch back and forth between two unhelpful ways of parenting, confuse their children and make their lives significantly more difficult.

WHAT IS THE IMPACT ON YOUR CHILDREN?

With Intrusive parenting – meeting the child's every whim – the danger is that children grow up to view other people as simply a means to an end. In addition, every feeling has to be acted on without regard to the impact on other people. With Disinterested parenting – where the mother or father is switched off – children are forced to regulate their own feelings by, for example, crying themselves to the point of exhaustion. On the surface these children seem calm, but under the surface their feelings are skyrocketing. They find it hard to trust, and when they grow up can have difficulties making long-term relationships. With parents that switch between Intrusive and Disinterested, who are sometimes concerned and sometimes switched off, children are forced to exaggerate their feelings in a bid for parental attention. These children grow up to become overly aware of their emotions, so that small setbacks seem like the end of the world. Worse still, they still haven't learnt to self-regulate and expect their partner or even their children to soothe them instead.

WHAT IS THE IMPACT ON YOU AND YOUR RELATIONSHIP?

Intrusive parents run the risk of getting all their identity and self-worth from being a mother or father and that's fine when their children are small – but what happens when they grow up and start leaving home? I often counsel parents – particularly mothers – who hit crisis point when their youngest child is about to go off to university and ask: 'Who am I?' and 'What is my purpose in life?' If you are switching between Intrusive and Disinterested, it will have a damaging effect on your marriage too, as your partner will not to know what to expect when he or she returns home. As one male client put it to me: 'I can cope with hostility [because in his wife's opinion he'd not done enough] or being ignored [because she was preoccupied with the kids] but what I dread most is the unknown.'

Turn it around: I doubt that you will fall into the Disinterested trap, as the simple act of buying this book and reading this far proves the opposite. My concerns are about being Intrusive, because you love your children so much. In most cases this happens because a parent overidentifies with their child, so his or her successes become their successes and their sole source of personal validation. Under these circumstances, there is a danger of pushing our interests on to our children or hoping they can fulfil our unfulfilled ambitions. You can avoid this trap by stepping back and leaving enough space for your children to develop their own interests and find their own path. If your children are getting older and you're facing an empty nest, it is important to find new interests and reasons for getting up in the morning. It is also an ideal time to start focusing on your marriage again.

Labelling

When I ask my clients about their childhood, I draw up a family tree so I can keep track of the number of siblings, birth order, parents' divorces, etc. Particularly with a larger family, I often ask them to describe their brothers and sisters. It is amazing how quickly they come up with a label: 'He was the oldest' or 'She was the baby of the family' or 'He was the clever one' or 'the naughty one' or 'the rebellious one'. Sometimes, it is even more pernicious: 'She was Mummy's favourite' or 'the black sheep of the family'. I doubt their parents ever described their children in this way, but the unspoken messages, body language and the way they treated them made the label clear to everyone in the family. Similarly, I sometimes ask my clients who are parents to describe their children, and once again I discover labels. For example, 'She's a daddy's girl' or 'He's really sensitive' or 'We're really alike and that's makes for a volatile relationship.'

When I did this exercise with Heather, forty-eight, I discovered she was the youngest of six. She had four older sisters: 'The eldest is responsible, the next "the rebel" and the one after that "the carer" and my next eldest sister was ill and she died when she was only thirteen years old and was never mentioned again.' Next in the family tree came her only brother. 'He was the favourite because it was all about the boy.' When I asked Heather about her place in the family, she replied, 'I was the baby and the mistake.'

'How did you work that out?' I asked.

'My parents really wanted a boy so they kept going until they had one . . . and then came me.'

'What was it like being the baby?'

'Everybody is there to look out for you.'

On one hand that sounds really nice, but it comes at a cost: it can make you rather helpless. When her marriage hit a rough patch, she had neither the skills to sort it out nor the ability to ask for help. 'Looking back, there were so many of us that help always just arrived. So I suppose I kept my head down and hoped for the best, which is probably the worst thing I could have done.'

WHAT IS THE IMPACT ON YOUR CHILDREN?

Once we hang a label round someone's neck, we remember evidence that supports it and ignore anything that disrupts it. Not only does a label encourage someone to live up to their reputation but it often says more about the person giving the label. For example, a 'sensitive' child could equally be described as 'in touch with his or her feelings' – depending on how comfortable you feel about expressing your emotions yourself. Worse still, these labels stick and even years later our choices, interests and behaviour can still be governed by the labels our parents gave us or even the ones they gave our siblings – because if your brother was, for example, 'the academic one' it makes you 'less academic' or maybe even 'stupid'.

It is best to try and avoid labelling your children – even with positive labels. Over the past ten years, I've started to see more and more adults who were the 'golden child' in their parents' eyes because they were 'gifted' or 'extremely clever'. Indeed, they did do well at school, went on to top universities and held down good jobs, or have risen to the top of their chosen career.

There are two problems with being a golden child. First, your parents' love can seem conditional on doing well and even an A can seem like not only failure but being unlovable. Second, it can come as a horrible shock when things go wrong and other people – like your husband or wife or new boss – do not find you quite so golden. What would seem like a setback to mere mortals can quickly seem like the end of the world to a golden child.

WHAT IS THE IMPACT ON YOUR RELATIONSHIP?

You are also likely to label yourselves and each other as 'mother' and 'father'. Some couples even call each other that after they have children – as you can imagine, seeing your partner purely as a parent is not very sexy and does little to improve your love life. Getting stuck in one particular role – rather than getting your identity from a variety of sources – can also increase the likelihood of a mid-life crisis.

Turn it around: Labelling is part of human behaviour. We do it with whole nations and public figures, because it makes a complicated world seem simpler. So please don't beat yourself up if you've already labelled your children, as it's not too late to change. Awareness is the key. Look for evidence that contradicts your assessment – particularly the labels 'He's just like me' or 'He's like his father.' It is also better to look for multiple characteristics. So a child is not just 'pretty', but 'kind' or 'brave' too. Ultimately, though, it is up to your children to discover their own identity – rather than have it thrust upon them. After all, it doesn't matter which path through life your son or daughter chooses as long as it is the right one for them.

If you are beginning to question your own life path, don't panic. It is natural to wonder, 'Who am I?' from time to time, and 'What do I want from life?' – especially in the wake of one of your parents dying. The problems arise when we try and suppress these questions and get stuck with an out-of-date label round our necks. If your partner is beginning to wonder about his or her identity, this can be really scary as we find change difficult. However, it is better to listen and offer support (and therefore be seen as our partner's ally) than try to squash his or her concerns (and become the enemy).

Warring parents

All couples fall out from time to time. It's fine to disagree or argue in front of your children, as long as you can also listen, respect each other's viewpoint and find a compromise or negotiate a settlement. This shows that it is possible to disagree and fall out and still love each other. These are skills your children will need with their siblings, friends and partners when they're older. Unfortunately, some parents can't contain their conflict and model the opposite approach – shouting, making personal remarks or trying to punish each other. Unfortunately, even divorce does not necessarily solve the problem. Instead of fighting in the kitchen, they are fighting over the phone, in texts and emails and through the children. The problems are often compounded by new partners, financial disputes and unresolved pain. I've had clients whose parents divorced over thirty years ago but still couldn't be in the same room – for a wedding, christening or other extended family event – because they would cause a scene or still be fighting over who caused the break-up.

WHAT IS THE IMPACT ON YOUR CHILDREN?
Although we like to imagine that children take divorce in their stride – because it is much more commonplace – the long-term impact is substantial. Judith Wallerstein PhD (1921–2012) was a senior lecturer in the School of Social Welfare at University of California, Berkeley. She studied sixty middle-class families and 131 children over twenty-five years after divorce and discovered that only one in ten children experienced any relief when their parents' marriage ended; eighteen months later, the majority were still trying to make sense of what happened, and five years on, most children still secretly hoped their parents would reconcile – even if one of them had subsequently remarried.

WHAT IS THE IMPACT ON YOUR RELATIONSHIP?

Family breakdown can make parents fall into *all* the unhelpful traps. They can be so upset by the behaviour of their ex that their children feel the need to manage their feelings (and thereby attempt to regulate their parents). Divorcing parents can be so consumed with their own problems that they appear Disinterested to their children and then feel guilty and swing to Intrusive to compensate. Divorce also encourages labelling and black-and-white thinking, as each parent blames the other. For example, he is 'bad' for 'going off with another woman' or she is 'vengeful' for 'making it difficult to see the children'.

Turn it around: The main message of this book is that you should put your partner before your children and not neglect your own interests. However, relationship breakdown is the one exception to this rule and I would ask you to put the children first – above your own pain or what seems best for your relationship. I have seen lots of couples who say, 'We're splitting up while we're still friends so the children don't have to hear us arguing.' It sounds rational but my experience is that marriage (and trying to rub along together despite everything) forms a protective layer around a relationship. In general, we interpret our partner's behaviour in a reasonably favourable light. If she doesn't phone, it's because she is busy. If he can't look after the children on Tuesday night, it's because his exercise class is really important and helps keep him sane. Unfortunately, family breakdown rips away the protection and we interpret the same behaviour in the worst possible light: 'She didn't phone because she's angry with me' or 'He's chosen exercise over his children because he's trying to punish me.'

Couples break up because they have poor communication skills, but divorce calls for exceptionally good ones. Therefore, if you have any goodwill left in your relationship use it to resolve your marriage problems and seek professional help. Even if you fail, you could learn to talk and listen to each other. Having really tried will also help the partner who is less keen on splitting up to recover better. It will also help you to cooperate over reducing the impact on your children.

Forbidden topics

As I've already discussed, humans are made of 'crooked timber' and parents make mistakes. Ultimately, it doesn't matter if from time to time you expect your children to regulate your mood, switch from Intrusive to Disinterested, or label them. Similarly, it's not the end of the world if you get divorced. Children are more resilient than you think. The problems occur if it is impossible to discuss something – especially *your* failings.

If a child can talk about his or her relationship with you and ask, 'Why were you mad at me?' and you can tell him or her, 'I wasn't mad at you, I was just tired and short-tempered. You haven't done anything wrong. I'm sorry', then your slip-up has provided an opportunity to strengthen your relationship. It has also taught your child an important lesson: if he or she is upset, this is a sign that something is wrong and needs attention. It's when a subject is unmentionable that it becomes particularly pernicious.

'I went to see my first diet doctor aged eight,' explained Teresa, who is now fifty-eight. 'My mother was always making "helpful" remarks like "Your new haircut makes your face look thinner". At mealtimes, she would carefully watch what everybody else was eating but never ate very much herself. On Sunday nights, we would go out to a restaurant and if I would choose one of the delicious items on the menu like roast duck and gravy – considered fattening – she would give me one of her looks and say, "The poached fish looks very nice, I think I'll have that. Why don't you have the poached fish too, Teresa?" and I would give in and go along with her. At the same time as all this was going on, my mother would be eating alone in the living room while my brother and I were asleep. I would sometimes wake up and smell something delicious like pizza being cooked. She also had secret places where she'd hide sweets and chocolates, and I'd sometimes go and take just one – desperately hoping she wouldn't notice.'

Despite Teresa's mother's weight only ever being slightly above or below what would have been considered healthy for her height, she obviously had issues about her weight and transferred a lot of her anxiety on to her daughter – who spent the next fifty years gaining and losing weight. However, it was impossible for her to talk to her mother about her attitudes to food or even to debate whether being fixated on one's body image was a good or bad idea.

WHAT IS THE IMPACT ON YOUR CHILDREN?

Instead of listening to their emotions and acting on them, your children are being taught to ignore painful and difficult feelings and hope that they will go away. Sometimes, for minor setbacks, this can be OK because sometimes little problems do right themselves. However, for big subjects, and it's normally the big ones that families ignore, pretending the problems don't exist does not resolve them but makes them worse.

WHAT IS THE IMPACT ON YOUR RELATIONSHIP?

If you cannot deal with difficult subjects, there are only two options. First, to suppress them (which leads to depression and anxiety). Second, to run away (either by closing down, exploding or leaving the relationship). Neither option provides a long-term solution to unhappiness.

Turn it around: Therapy is all about making people aware of the unspoken messages and allowing the unmentionable to be talked about. After all, talking about something is the first step to doing something about it. Therefore, if you take what your children say seriously – even if it seems a bit strange because they come to difficult topics via routes that don't seem logical to us – they are unlikely to need a therapist when they grow up because all the important things have already been aired.

■ ■ ■ ■ ■ ■

Understanding Your Own Feelings

It is difficult to regulate your children's emotions if you ignore your own. You are also more likely to label someone else – like your children or your partner. Similarly, if you can't talk about some-thing like anger or sadness, your children are going to find it equally hard. All this self-awareness might sound like a tall order – especially if your parents were not emotionally literate – however, you've already started to learn some of the necessary skills:

- *Acknowledge and name:* When your children are upset or irritable, you have been acknowledging rather than ignoring the feeling, and naming it. In the same way, I want you to take your own emotions seriously rather than ignoring them, pretending they don't exist or talking yourself out of them. So ask yourself: What am I feeling? Why?
- *Keep a feeling diary:* Whenever you have a quiet moment, stop and jot down the most recent feelings and what promoted them, for example, pleasure at a frosty morning or joy when your baby smiled, or frustration when you couldn't get the lid off the jar. Keep the diary for at least seven days. When I do this exercise with my clients, I discover two important things: people under-record the good stuff, and no feeling lasts for ever but is quickly replaced with another. This is contrary to our fears that if we allow ourselves to be, for example, angry, we will be stuck there for ever.

- *Accept the feelings but challenge the thoughts:* Even the feelings that get a bad press have their advantages. For example, anger provides energy and a sense that something must be done. So please accept your feelings – no matter what. However, I would like you to challenge the thought that might underpin them. For example, your underlying thoughts might turn righteous anger – or sadness, disappointment, etc. – from something proportionate into something overwhelming. (For example, Tracey's husband had left her for another woman. She not only felt rejected but angry about there being less money and having to go out to work rather than staying at home with their eighteen-month-old daughter. These are understandable and natural feelings. However, some of her thinking and language was turning this into levels of rage and resentment that made her consider trying to stop her daughter seeing her father. 'I'm going to lose my daughter,' she sobbed uncontrollably. I accepted her anger but challenged the thoughts. 'You're not going to lose your daughter. That sounds like social services taking her into care. She's going to a nursery and you'll see less of her, which is upsetting, but you're not "losing her".')
- *Report your feelings:* If your partner or your children do something to upset you, don't swallow or act out your feelings (by slamming doors, sighing or rolling your eyes). Report it using the formula from Chapter Seven: I feel . . . when you . . . because . . . For example, '*I feel* angry *when you* don't wipe your feet *because* it makes more work for me.' In this way, everybody is clear what you feel (it's anger, not rage) and what the causes are.
- *Self-soothe:* Instead of expecting your children, your partner or your boss to calm you down or flying off the handle (and offloading on to other people), take responsibility yourself. Acknowledging, naming and reporting your feelings will help. Other ways of soothing include exercise (like running), unwinding (like having a hot bath or a cup of tea), giving yourself a treat

(like half an hour with a book), meditating or doing breathing exercises, and sharing (like speaking to a friend). Be wary of things that seek to remove the feelings – like alcohol or sugary foods – which I call self-medicating.

- *Address the problem:* Remember, feelings are clues to help you navigate through life – not something awkward that need to be avoided. So what is the feeling telling you? When you're calmer, you can then talk to your children or partner about their unhelpful behaviour or, if it's really about you, address the problem yourself.
- *Remember be to be assertive:* You can ask. Your partner can say no, and you can negotiate.

■ ■ ■ ■ ■ ■

How to put your partner first

One of the themes of this book is that if you're offering a courtesy to your children, you should consider doing the same to your partner. So if you're not going to label your son or daughter (because of the damage it does them), I'd like you to refrain from labelling your partner too. Unfortunately, it is all too easy to interpret other people's behaviour in a negative light and create a filter through which you see everything. For example: 'He's selfish' or 'She wants to control me.' In effect, this is labelling your partner as 'lazy' or 'bossy' and finding more evidence to back it up. Before too long, you have a caricature of him or her in your head which makes you exaggerate your upset ('This just proves how I'm taken advantage of' or 'I can't even breathe right') and simultaneously discount your partner's opinions ('What right has he got to complain after all I do?' or 'She would say that, wouldn't she?'). So how do you challenge your internal label of your partner?

- Instead of assuming the reasons for your partner's actions, try asking him or her what they are.

- Avoid leading questions. For example: 'Did you fail to pick up our daughter because you couldn't be bothered?' (This is slightly better than simply making an accusation, but only just! It will immediately get your partner's back up and triggers an argument rather than an explanation.) If you're in any doubt whether it's a leading question, these are ones that invite a 'yes' or 'no' answer.

- Find an open question. These start with: 'How?', 'Why?', 'What?', 'When?' For example, 'Why didn't you pick up our daughter?' Or 'What happened?' (These type of questions also suggest that you are genuinely interested in the answer and will give your partner a fair hearing.)

- Listen to the explanation with an open mind. If you find yourself slipping into black-and-white thinking (i.e. good/bad or right/ wrong) remind yourself that life is more complex. There are many shades of grey.

- Focus on the matter in hand. Thinking about past behaviour or worrying about the long-term implications will raise the stakes and encourage labelling.

- Ask follow-up questions. This will help you to truly stand in your partner's shoes and understand the complexity of his or her feelings on the subject.

- Look at your own motivations for something that's controversial between you. What makes you behave in this way? What are your conflicting urges? In most cases, you will find several layers of reasons for your actions, not just one fixed motivation. If you are complex, your partner is probably just the same.

Equally important as not labelling your children is letting them be true to themselves – rather than following interests or careers that you feel are right for them. Once again, I'd like you to extend this same idea to your partner and let him or her be their own person – not just a reflection of how you'd like him or her to be. I know this sounds difficult, and possibly even threatening, but let me give an example of what this means in practice.

Philip, aged thirty-two, had been almost talented enough to pursue a career as a golfer but became a car salesman to pay the bills. Although he had long since given up any ambitions of turning professional, he still looked forward to his weekend round. 'Obviously, I don't live for golf because my wife and children are the most important thing in my life, but I can take all my frustrations out on hacking round the course. I'm out in the fresh air and I can forget everything just concentrating on the getting the ball into the hole. I would go as far as saying golf keeps me sane.'

By contrast, his wife Kitty had her two children, her recently widowed mother and Philip at the centre of her life. 'I thought when we had children that he'd put golf to one side. I'm not suggesting that he gives up altogether, but not every weekend. He's up early on Saturday morning and not back until a late lunch and that's not the end of it. Sometimes he wants to go away on weekends for a team match and the odd Sunday. He's got responsibilities and it shouldn't be me always looking after the boys.'

'The problem is that Kitty doesn't have any outside interests. I'm perfectly happy to look after the children while she goes out,' replied Philip.

'I do go out. I'll have coffee with my girlfriends and I watch my soaps, but I don't let them interfere with family time.'

In many relationships, there is a pressure to be and think alike – in the hope that this will help a couple step round any conflicts. However, as I've explained, it is important to let your partner be his or her own person and not see being different as a problem but an asset. Let me explain how this works in practice.

As Philip and Kitty demonstrate, there is a conflict at the heart of many relationships where one partner pushes for couple time and one campaigns for time apart. However, good relationships need both we-time (so the relationship doesn't wither and die) and me-time (so you don't lose a sense of yourself as an individual). The problems happen when you get stuck on one side of the argument and start to perceive your partner as the enemy.

So what should you do if the thought of letting your partner be his or her own person, or speaking up for your own needs and thereby being different from each other, seems inherently threatening? Once again, if you've been trying out the ideas in this book, you'll have the necessary skills to hand. I'm talking about assertiveness, which I first discussed in Chapter Two. With assertiveness, you can ask for something and your partner can say no; you can discuss your differences, negotiate and find a compromise.

Returning to the subject of labelling, it is important not to think you know your partner's motivations. For example, Kitty assumed that Philip spent too much time on the golf course because 'he didn't love me and the boys enough' – whereas it helped him deal with the pressures of a job he didn't particularly like. Meanwhile, Philip assumed that Kitty wanted him 'to hang up my clubs' – whereas she wanted more time as a family and more attention for the boys. Once they had stopped assuming and started talking and listening, they were able to compromise. Philip came home straight after the game rather than drinking with his golf partners; he also started taking their eldest child (who was sporty) up to the club too. Meanwhile, Kitty started having some me-time and Philip committed to being home early to look after the boys one night a week.

Finally, if you can stop labelling your partner as a 'husband' or a 'wife' and a 'father' or a 'mother' and see them as a person too, you can probably extend the same generosity to yourself. In which case, you will allow yourself interests outside your relationship and family, and find hobbies and activities to help you relax, unwind and self-soothe.

The child-rearing years last for a surprisingly short time, and having multiple identities and seeing each other as complex, and therefore interesting, people will help smooth the transition back to just the two of you when the time comes.

Summing Up

The best way to avoid your children needing a therapist is to provide security and consistency, so they grow up knowing through both expectation and experience that you will protect them when they are sick, injured or simply feeling bad rather than not noticing, not caring or misunderstanding. Nearly every self-defeating strategy – like picking fights, withdrawing into oneself or pestering for reassurance – is to avoid anxiety or depression and to feel safe (if only for a few moments and no matter what the long-term cost).

At the core of my work as a therapist is providing security, so that my clients feel accepted, heard and no longer out of control. Hardly any of my clients question whether their parents loved them, but sadly that love feels conditional or unreliable.

If you're going to take just one idea from this chapter, it would be this: if your son or daughter has a problem or is acting out, it could be in response to you. Although this knowledge will make you feel uncomfortable, there is a silver lining. While it is really hard to get someone else to change their behaviour, it is relatively easy to change your own.

Conclusion

Why You Should Put Your Partner First

At the beginning of this book, I introduced a controversial idea: children should come second. I didn't expect you to accept it but I asked for your indulgence to make my case that putting your partner first is not only in the best interests of your relationship but of your children too. If you put all your energy into raising the next generation, you will not only exhaust yourself and your marriage but risk identifying so closely with your children that their success is your success and their failure is your failure, and this will put them under unnecessary pressure.

Unfortunately much of the modern debate about parenting swings between being 'perfect' or being 'neglectful' – with basically nothing in between. That's why I reintroduced the idea of 'good enough': the parent who is there to pick up a child when it falls over but stands back enough to allow him or her to make mistakes and discover the world for him- or herself.

I would not be surprised if, at the beginning of the book, putting your partner first seemed like another demand to add to an already long to-do list. I hope that the idea doesn't seem quite so onerous or impossible now and, most importantly, you accept that *it won't harm your kids*.

To recap, here are the central ways of putting your partner first:

- Greet your partner first.
- Don't let your children interrupt when you are talking to each other.
- Put a lock on the bedroom door.
- Even when your children are babies, dress up and go out together.
- Put your partner's interests over those of your parents and back him or her in any battle with his or her parents.
- Accept your partner's feelings (because from where he or she is standing they make sense), listen, discuss and don't jump to conclusions.
- Give positive feedback about what is working for you and use descriptive praise to encourage more of the same behaviour.
- Don't assume your partner knows what's going on in your head: tell him or her.
- Parent as a team and don't make unilateral decisions or compete to be most loved.
- Don't discuss adult stuff with your children, use them as go-betweens or create sub-alliances.
- Have fun together as a couple, not just as a family.
- Prioritize sex.
- Make children responsible for tasks around the house so that there is more time to be partners rather than servants.
- Let your partner be his or her own person.

Before I return to the exercise in the first chapter about priorities, and see if working through the book has brought any changes, I need to discuss two issues: work and self.

What about work?

When I do the 'What Are Your Priorities?' exercise from Chapter One, a lot of people complain that their partner puts work first – above the children and certainly above the relationship.

Work is an incredibly complex subject (and probably worth a book in its own right). On one level, our job brings us money to pay bills, provide for our children and save for the future. However, it is much, much more. It is part of our identity. It is also where we make friends and get a sense of belonging. In uncertain times, working hard provides the illusion of security. Finally, the feedback from senior staff and the respect of more junior staff can make us feel competent, worthwhile and valued. No wonder success at work is closely tied to our self-esteem.

When one partner accuses the other of being obsessed with work – or putting it first – I always hear the same defences: 'You like the holidays, house and lifestyle it brings' or 'I'm doing it for the family' or 'I thought it was the right thing to do.' I always ask people to reflect on other reasons why they might work so hard too. How much of the long-hours culture is financial need? How much personal satisfaction? How much old messages from our parents to 'work hard and achieve'? And how much simple habit?

If the amount of time spent at work (and on work at home) is an issue in your relationship, why not try this exercise: imagine that your job is a cake, and divide up the reasons for working so hard. What percentage would you give to my four categories: financial need, personal satisfaction, messages from parents (or society in general) and habit? (If there are other important reasons add them to the list.) Next, ask your partner why he or she thinks you work so hard, and to complete the same exercise. Afterwards, compare your results and discuss them. I would be surprised if you don't have very different conclusions.

While you may think you're working hard for the family, your partner will imagine you're doing it for yourself. If you truly believe that you're working for the benefit of the family, do you find it hard to ask for things for yourself? Does work provide you with a ready-made excuse for time alone or to get out of tasks that you don't particularly like and still feel a 'good' person? In the same way that some parents fuse their personal interests with those of the children, are you fusing your personal and work interests? It's always worth stopping and questioning the central importance of work. There are other ways of finding meaning for your life, a close circle of friends or self-esteem than from your job.

Finally, in the same way that children are just passing through but marriage should be for ever, a job is just something on your CV, and even the most successful career ends in retirement (or the business is sold or passed on to the next generation).

If you're guilty of overprioritizing your work, how can you make your partner feel that he or she isn't forgotten? Here are a few ideas:

- Switch off mobile devices during mealtimes.
- Set a time at night after which you will not take calls or respond to emails.
- Devote weekends to family time. If you need to do some work, flag it up with your partner beforehand, set a time limit and stick to it.
- Do not take work on holiday. If you must, negotiate a limit – for example, one hour a day – and discuss with your partner when it should be.
- Make a greater effort to attend your children's special events – concerts, sports matches, parents' evenings etc.
- Take time off to cover an occasional childcare emergency.
- Send texts, leave cards and make other small gestures that show that although you might not be there, you're thinking of your beloved.

What about self?

It is always hard to find a balance between being considerate to others and not neglecting your own needs. If you do swallow your needs, there is a danger of becoming passive (going along with what other people want) rather than being assertive (asking for what you want, listening to your partner and negotiating if your needs are incompatible). Conversely, if you're determined to get your own way, you risk becoming domineering or manipulative. In the short term, or over minor matters, most relationships can accommodate both passive and domineering behaviour, but over time and especially over major events, these patterns build resentment and anger.

So where should you put yourself in your list of priorities? Once again, there is no simple answer. It depends on the circumstances and what's at stake. However, if I had to come up with an aspiration (which won't always be possible), I think it is still best to put your partner first. So why do I say that? We live in a consumer society that's always stressing self-gratification. We worship strong people who get their own way and make things happen. Nothing wrong with that, *but* – and it's a big 'but' – we can become self-centred and not consider the impact on other people of our behaviour. After all, we know how *we're* feeling, but it's much harder to listen to others or take what they say seriously. If you're in any doubt about a particular course of action, ask yourself the following questions:

- Is this something I *want* rather than something I *need*? Double-check your answer as it's easy to dress up wants as needs. For example, I would question someone saying: 'I *need* this holiday in the Maldives.' I accept that they may need to relax and recharge their batteries but there are other ways of de-stressing and self-soothing – like going for a run or having a long weekend break. True needs are tied up with what makes our life meaningful – for

285

example, a musician has to make music, a writer has to write, etc.

- Why does this activity or item mean so much to me?
- Have I explained properly to my partner, or assumed he or she will somehow know?

If your partner is asking for something that seems unreasonable or impossible, ask yourself these questions:

- What is it about my partner's upbringing and life experiences that makes this request particularly significant?
- Is it a need or a want?
- How could I put myself in my partner's shoes to understand more?
- How could we find a compromise that would be acceptable to both of us?

■ ■ ■ ■ ■ ■

Returning to 'What Are Your Priorities?'

Get out the cards that you made up for the exercise at the beginning of the book and lay them out in the original order. Thinking about what you've learnt and your experiences doing the exercises, do you want to change your priorities in any way?

Self	Partner	Children
Work	Friends	Parents
Siblings	Hobbies	Fitness/Health
Fun	Home	Pets
Status	Personal development	
Sex	Intellectual nourishment	

Explain your thinking to your partner and listen (without comment) to their decisions. After you've both finished talking, discuss the reasons for your changes or staying the same. If you're going to make changes, how are you going to turn words into actions?

■ ■ ■ ■ ■ ■

What if I still want to put my children first?

There is no right or wrong answer to balancing the needs of your children and your partner. After all, you know your relationship and your children best. Perhaps you find the idea of priorities annoying or too general, or you dislike ranking. Whatever the reasons for disagreeing, I hope that my arguments have provided a way of discussing parenting with your partner, helped you understand each other better and removed some of the pressure to be perfect.

Alternatively, you might have altered your priorities but your partner has not budged on his or hers. In these circumstances, I would suggest approaching the subject in another manner. Take the top three or four areas (or however many are truly important to you) and imagine that your time and emotional energy are a cake (just like the exercise about work). Before reading this book, how much time and energy would have been devoted to your children and how much to your relationship and the other significant areas? Now, having finished, and thinking about my arguments, would you slice the cake any differently? I know about the pressures on parents and the natural desire to do the best for your children, but I hope that the chapters on what children really need, the pitfalls of being a red-carpet kid and what your children will tell their therapist have provided some food for thought. Your children might still take up the biggest slice of your life, but could you make it slightly smaller? What could be cut from the things you do for your children to provide more time for your relationship? How could you make this aspiration into a reality? To help you with these decisions, I have gathered all the key ideas in the 'Ten Golden Rules' at the back of the book.

Summing Up

Juggling priorities is really hard, especially with so many demands on your time. Don't worry if you and your partner don't always agree on how to prioritize work, satisfy your own needs and bring up the children. Nobody gets the balance right all of the time. However, if you have learnt good communication skills you are halfway to finding a solution that will lead to happy children, a happy marriage and feeling personally fulfilled.

The Ten Golden Rules

1. Don't neglect your marriage: it is the glue that keeps the family together.

2. Being a parent and a perfectionist don't sit easily together. Instead, aim for good enough.

3. The main job of a parent is to take your children's feelings seriously, but this doesn't mean giving in to every whim, rather explaining why something is not possible or sensible.

4. Happy relationships need good communication skills as well as love and connection.

5. When it comes to disputes about how to raise your children, there are no right or wrong answers. Listen to each other, be assertive and negotiate.

6. Don't draw children into adult issues or let them take sides.

7. Encourage your children to be self-sufficient and don't become their servant. In this way, you will have more time to invest in your relationship.

8. You need to feel loved by your partner and not just a service provider. To this end it is important to be romantic, have fun together and make sex a priority.

9. When there's a problem, try not to label your partner or the children as the cause; look at your own contribution.

10. If something is good enough for your children, it is probably good enough for your partner too.

Further Reading

BY THE AUTHOR

Make Love Like a Prairie Vole: Six Steps to Passionate, Plentiful and Monogamous Sex (Bloomsbury) – looks at how love-making changes over time in long-term relationship; how to talk about sex and keep the spark alive.

Learn to Love Yourself Enough: Seven Steps to Improving Your Self-esteem and Your Relationships (Bloomsbury) – how your childhood affects how you feel about yourself; how to make a fresh start with your parents and deal with your inner critic.

Resolve Your Differences: Seven Steps to Dealing with Conflict in Your Relationship (Bloomsbury) – more about assertiveness and how to deal with anger and relationships where you don't argue enough.

I Love You But I'm Not In Love With You: Seven Steps to Saving Your Relationship (Bloomsbury) – how suppressing issues might seem the best way to keep the peace but just stores up problems for the future.

BY OTHER WRITERS

Sue Gerhardt, *Why Love Matters: How Affection Shapes a Baby's Brain* (Routledge) – the science behind why regulating your baby's emotions is so important.

Noël Janis-Norton, *Calmer, Easier, Happier Parenting* (Hodder & Stoughton) – more advice on how to get cooperation from children aged three to thirteen.

Robert Schwarz and Elaine Braff, *We're No Fun Any More: Helping Couples Cultivate Joyful Marriages Through the Power of Play* (Routledge) – written for therapists but full of ideas for increasing the fun in your relationship.

Bernie Zilbergeld, *The New Male Sexuality: The Truth about Men, Sex and Pleasure* (Bantam) – classic guide to understanding men and sex, but my female clients also find it really useful for getting inside their husbands' heads.

Acknowledgements

Fiona MacDonald Smith and Sarah Maber (two journalists at *The Times*) took me out to lunch and during a discussion about what I might write next jumped on the idea of children and the impact on marriages. By saying, 'I'd like to read that book,' they gave me the courage to press ahead.

I would also like to thank Liz Gough and Cindy Chan at Macmillan, who commissioned and edited this book; and my agent Rachel Calder and my book group Gail Louv, Chris Taylor and Jamie MacKay, who all offered their personal experiences and made countless useful suggestions. I'm also grateful to Clare Christian at Marshall Method Publishing for introducing me to Liz Gough, and my team of associate therapists, Debby Edwards, Claudio Esposito and Sally Fifield.

My research into the topic was informed by Kate Figes (*Life After Birth*), Gaby Hinsliff (*Half a Wife: The Working Family's Guide to Getting a Life Back*), Rebecca Asher (*Modern Motherhood and the Myth of Equality*) and Nina Grunfeld (who introduced me to the books of Nanny Smith).

Other people whose discussions on motherhood have helped are Hilly Janes, Christine Anstice and Rachel Alexander (who guided my reading). On fatherhood, my thanks to Richard Groves, Thierry Brigodiot and Simon Crompton.

Most importantly, I would like to acknowledge the contribution of my clients. On many occasions, it seems I learn more from them than they do from me.

Index

Absentee parent 84–5, 87

accept the feelings but challenge the thoughts 117, 275

'Acknowledge and Name' technique 107

expecting your children to regulate you and 260

red-carpet kids and 239, 240, 247, 248, 253

toddlers and 107

understanding your own feelings and 274

Adapting: fifteenth to twenty-fourth year of relationship 42–4

affairs:

examples of 18, 20, 20–1, 118–19

vulnerability to 20–1

age brings benefits, ensure that 244–5

'Age of Competence' 119

apologies 131, 142

encouraging your child to apologize 117

the power of a fulsome apology 88–9, 142, 169, 196

to your child 88–9, 117

Appreciative Enquiry 193–4

arguments:

defending your position and 172–4

hidden subjects and 127

identity and 71

in front of the children 123, 135–6, 270

importance of 38–9

leading questions and 277

nesting and 37, 38–9

niggles and 167–8

'should' and 163–5

'what' rather than 'why' 165–6

assertiveness:

being assertive 52–4

passive-aggressive behaviour and 144

pleasure in partner's downfall and 145

recruiting others and 177

remember to be assertive 276

rights 54–5

skills 144

Ten Golden Rules and 289

training 55

babies 100–5

birth and *see* birth